CHINA OR BUST
...a Rookie's Guide to Living and Surviving in China as an ESL Teacher

老外之中国游记

柯兰 著　Lana Kerr

邱益鸿　译

Copyright © Lana Kerr 2012

All rights reserved. No part of this book may be reproduced, stored in a retrieval system or transmitted in any form or by any means, without the prior written permission of the author, except in the case of brief quotations as part of critical articles or reviews and appropriately referenced.

First published in 2012

China or Bust! A rookie's guide to travelling and living in China as an ESL teacher

ISBN-13: 978-1475266528

ISBN-10: 1475266529

Email:englishstoriesforfun@gmail.com

Website:http://www.englishstoriesforfun.com

Disclaimer

The author assures the reader that every effort has been made to ensure the accuracy of the information herein. All information and opinions expressed in this book are my own personal opinions and in no way are meant to defame or injure anyone mentioned. I expressly convey to you that were I to defame or injure a reader, it is entirely unintentional.

The intention of the author is to give accurate general information about working and living in China. While every precaution has been taken by the author to provide accurate, correct and useful information at the time of writing, this book is sold without warranty, either express or implied. The author will not be held liable for any damages caused either directly or indirectly by the information contained in this book. The author cannot be held responsible for any changes that have occurred since the time of writing.

It is the responsibility of the reader to verify current facts for themselves.

TESTIMONIALS

So many Australians head overseas to experience life in a "foreign country", or as we can say "get paid to travel" as an English teacher. Living and working in China is an extraordinary experience. Lana's account of her experiences in China reminds me of my tour of duty in the Middle Kingdom. Let's hope that "China or Bust", along with the very helpful information contained therein, encourages others to move out of their own comfort zone and experience China.

Lana has written her stories on her introduction to China telling it how it is, or how it was for her. China is an ever changing place—and full of adventures for us Westerners who visit—so much to see, so much to do, and so much to laugh about—mainly at ourselves!

… Di Hill. M.A. Author. Biographer. Former ESL teacher

Lana, your book is an absolute delight!!!! I could not put it down. It's witty, clever and full of insight. Thanks for letting me read it.

… Perry Sein, M.A., Education, Azusa Pacific University, California USA English Teacher: Suzhou University, Suzhou, China

Hold onto your hat! We are off on an adventure of China at it's very best. Lana and her husband, staid and bored, decide to take the plunge and head off to China to work as ESL teachers.

This book will guide you through the process of going to China to live. She covers subjects such as how to get a job, decide where to go, find accommodation, use the buses and trains, and the whole gastronomic process from the plate to the low Asian loos.

Written in a fast-paced hilarious style this book is a laugh a minute as we follow the author's experiences and challenges; both with day-to-day life and in the classroom. This book will help get you off your couch, out of your rut, and into an exciting life as an ESL teacher in China.

… Ricky Hunter. Author. Educator. Workshop Facilitator. www.rickyhunter.org

content 目录

INTRODUCTION ·· 4
　引言 ·· 5

TAKING A TAXI IN XIAMEN AIRPORT ··· 12
　厦门机场打的记 ·· 13

AN EVENTFUL FIRST DAY ·· 22
　波折的第一天 ·· 23

PERSONAL SAFETY IN CHINA ·· 32
　在华人身安全 ·· 33

CHINESE MONEY ·· 36
　中国货币 ·· 37

BEING A FIRST TIME TEACHER ··· 40
　初为人师 ·· 41

THE CHINESE LANGUAGE ··· 50
　感悟中文 ·· 51

ARE THERE TABOO SUBJECTS TEACHERS DON'T TALK ABOUT IN THE
CLASSROOM? ·· 54
　有教师不能在课堂上谈及的禁忌话题吗? ·································· 55

BOWELS ··· 58
　如厕 ·· 59

THE REALITY ··· 64
　遭遇现实 ·· 65

DENEICE AND EMERSON ·· 80
　戴妮丝和爱默生 ·· 81

THE STUDENTS ·· 98
　中国学生 ·· 99

TWILIGHT ··· 110
　特莱特 ·· 111

SUNNY AND MICKEY	116
米奇和姗妮	117
SHARK	122
沙克	123
HOLIDAYS AND TYPHOONS	126
假日与台风	127
CHINESE CUISINE, CANTEEN–ESE STYLE	140
食堂就餐记	141
A BOIL UP TO END ALL BOIL-UPS	148
吃火锅	149
CURL UP AND DYE IN CHINA	154
美发记	155
CHEAP TAIWANESE JUNK	162
便宜货	163
WHEN THE CHIPS ARE DOWN	168
兼职记	169
A STITCH IN TIME	176
做衣服	177
EVER BEEN FRAMED?	182
买相框	183
OUR FIRST WEEK IN CHINA	188
在华第一周的日子	189
THE CITY OF LONGYAN	194
小城龙岩	195
LONGYAN?—NO LONG RAIN!	200
多雨的龙岩	201
WHO'S BEEN MUCKING ABOUT WITH THE SUN?	208
是谁对太阳暗动了手脚?	209
POLLY WANNA CRACKER?	214
放鞭炮	215

WALKING ON WATER	218
购票奇事	219
MY DAILY BUS RIDE HOME FROM SCHOOL	226
下班乘车记	227
BOOKING TRAIN TICKETS IN ADVANCE	230
购票记	231
GUT WRENCHING GOODBYES	242
伤离别	243
LONGYAN REVISITED	248
重访龙岩	249
MY TOP TEN TIPS FOR LIVING IN CHINA	256
居华十条建议	257
THINGS WE LEARNED ABOUT LIVING ACCOMMODATION ON OR OFF CAMPUS	258
校内、校外住宿须知	259
DRIVING YOURSELF IN CHINA	272
在华自驾	273
SHOPPING	274
在华购物	275
TRAVELLING — BUSES, TRAINS AND HOTELS IN CHINA	280
在华旅游——巴士、火车和酒店	281
STAYING IN HOTELS IN CHINA	294
入住酒店须知	295
HEALTH CARE, DOCTORS AND HOSPITALS	300
中国的医保、医生和医院	301
ABOUT THE AUTHOR	312
作者小传	313
APPENDIX: TRAINING AND CONTRACTS	314
附录：培训与签约	315

老外之中国游记
A Rookies' Guide to Living and Surviving in China as an ESL Teacher

INTRODUCTION

China, a land of contrasts, where the old Hutongs sit cheek by jowl with magnificent skyscrapers: China, whose name means "The Middle Kingdom", the third largest country in the world in area, housing one fifth of the world's population: China, a nation proud of its long history, but forging ahead in modernity, where the world depends on its burgeoning economy. China, a land of mystery, mountains, and perceptions of old men with goatee beards fishing with bamboo poles.

Have you ever been to China, or had a hankering to visit? Many of us might dismiss the thought as a result of erroneous notions or viewpoints based on a lack of knowledge. Has a biased Western upbringing influenced your thinking?

Many people have a distorted view of China, perhaps due to the fact that it was a closed society for so many years. But its move into the 20th and 21st Century is nothing less than astounding, progressing from the feudal systems of old to today's communist based society, but one with an eye to becoming accepted as a contemporary nation, dependant on trade from the West. With its strong economic base it is ready and able to play its part in international affairs.

It is also a nation struggling to retain its old heritage, while at the same time being influenced by its close neighbours such as Russia, Japan and Korea. More importantly, it is trying to balance the former cultural lifestyle with the very powerful influences permeating from the West.

引言

中国是个融合古今、特色鲜明的国度，在这里，古老沧桑的胡同和宏伟高大的摩天大楼比肩而立。中国，顾名思义，乃"中央王国"之意，她坐拥世界第三大面积的国土，养育世界五分之一的人口。中国，虽历史悠久，却能在现代化进程中锐意进取，她蓬勃发展的经济助推着整个世界经济前进的脚步。中国是个神秘的国度。这里，青山连绵，群山起伏；这里，古时的长须老者曾手执竹竿、溪边垂钓，他们的见识隽永智慧，历久弥新。

您可曾到过中国，又可曾想去中国看看？也许，很多人因为对她了解不够，心存误解，打了退堂鼓。是不是生长在西方，让您对这个国度有了偏见？

或许是因为她一度闭关锁国，不少人看不到她的真面目。但是，20世纪和21世纪的中国，她的发展速度着实令世界震撼：她从过去的封建制度进步为现在的社会主义社会，并立足将自己打造为一个被世界认可的现代国家，与西方贸易往来密切频繁。中国，凭借自己强大的经济实力，将来一定能在国际事务中大展拳脚。

如今的中国一方面正竭力保留自己历史悠久的文化遗产，另一方面却又深受近邻俄罗斯、日本和韩国的影响。值得一提的是，她正尽力在传统的文化和生活方式，与西方国家强劲文化渗透之间，找到平衡。

毋庸置疑，中国是一个令人赞叹的国家。这里，世界一流的建筑水平，令百层玻

In reality, this is a most amazing country, where state-of-the-art architecture produces one hundred story glass towers. A land where The Great Wall perilously rides the backs of remote mountain ranges, reminding us that even ancient China had men of great vision. A country of such diversity, that every day life is exciting. A place I consider my second home.

My name is Lana Kerr and my husband Peter and I, an unworldly-wise couple in our late fifties, decided to rejuvenate our boring life and do something completely different. We went to China to teach English. It became one of Dr Phil's "life changing experiences".

I write this book with two goals in mind. Firstly, to entertain you, to recount stories of our first year in China, about the people and places, our experiences, hilarious and otherwise, our travels and teaching work. To also dispel some of the old myths that everyone lives in shanty towns or that it is a place that hasn't caught up with the times yet.

Secondly, if you decide to go there to work for a time as a teacher or in some other occupation, this book gives you much of the information you need to get a job, settle in, use the extensive transport systems, access health care and all the day to day matters you will face in a country where you can't read or speak the language and most of the people you'll meet can't speak English. It's a challenge like no other, but you'll have the time of your life.

So what led us to even consider such a move? To leave our comfort zone, our family and friends and head off into the unknown?

It was an information evening we had just attended about TESOL (Teaching English as a Second Language). The speaker, Lesley, was from one of the accredited organizations that would train us. Once we gained our TESOL qualifications, we could apply for vacancies.

Lesley was a very interesting woman, about 60 years old with a petite figure, red curly hair, dressed in a snazzy denim pants suit covered in an eye catching rhinestone pattern. She was a psychologist who'd worked in Asia and got into teaching English because of the poor English levels of her local staff. She progressed into the teaching area and was now in charge of training in Australia and New Zealand. She sat on the corner

INTRODUCTION 引言

璃幕墙摩天大楼矗立云间；这里，万里长城盘踞于绵延群山之间，提醒我们，古时候的中国人民便已这般具有远见。中国，是如此丰富多彩，这里的每一天都令人振奋；这里，便是我心中的第二故乡。

我叫柯兰，澳大利亚人，和丈夫彼得两个老顽童，在年近六十的时候，不甘寂寞，决定再年轻一回，走出枯燥的生活，换一种全新的活法。我们来到中国教授英语。此行成了美国名嘴菲尔博士所说的"改变人生的经历"。

我写此书有两个目的：一是为愉悦读者。本书既记录了我们夫妻俩来华第一年的遭遇，又有我们在华生活期间发生的趣闻轶事，还有我们的旅游见闻和教学故事；同时也为消除人们对中国的偏见，因为直至今日，仍有人误以为中国百姓大都生活在穷乡僻壤，把她看成一个跟不上时代潮流的落后国家。

二是为有意去中国工作的老外提供生活指南，告诉他们如何在语言不通且人生地不熟的中国求职安家、出行旅游以及求医问诊。

中国之行绝对是一大挑战，但你的人生也将因此而别样精彩。

那么是什么原因让我俩想到离开温暖的家园，告别亲朋好友，漂洋过海到陌生的中国？

那就要追溯到我俩参加的一场TESOL（对外英语教学）介绍会了。那天的主讲人叫莱丝丽，是一家有资格认证的正规机构的主管，她将负责培训我们。只要我们取得TESOL资格证，就可以申请国外教职。

莱丝丽是个很有趣的女士，大约六十来岁，长得小巧玲珑，一头红色卷发，身穿一套时尚的粗棉套装，服装上的水晶石图案格外引人注目。她是个心理学家，曾在亚洲工作过，因当地员工的英语水平太差而走上英语教学之路。她在教学圈内渐渐有了名气，如今负责澳大利亚和新西兰两国的培训工作。莱丝丽坐在桌角一侧，双腿不停晃动，声音低沉沙哑，兴致勃勃地给我俩讲述在国外教书的趣事。

"小事一桩，"她说，"只要你会讲英语，就教得来。就是现在不会，等学完我们的课程也就会了。工作机会多得要命。你们呢，既可以赚点钱，又可以大开眼界。"

of the table, legs swinging, her gravelly voice enthusiastically giving us fascinating information about teaching English overseas.

"It's a piece of cake," she said. "If you can speak English you can teach it, or you'll be able to once you've done our course. There are thousands of jobs available. You can make some money and have the experience of a lifetime."

Peter came with me to make sure that this information evening wasn't a scam. "Let's face it, there are plenty of people out there willing to take any ready cash you've got, or any cash you haven't got for that matter,' he said to me. "Let's just check it out. It sounds a bit suspicious to me."

I didn't mind. After all, if it turned out to be worthwhile, we could both do this, so I wanted him to come along and see for himself.

It seemed legitimate and so exciting. For me, it meant an escape from a life in a ten-foot-rut. I would take the bull by the horns and bloody well go, come hell or high water.

If you are in your "middle age years" you may be like me. My childhood and teen years were typical of a child in the fifties and sixties. The second twenty years were spent getting married, having five fabulous children, doing everything for them, and working part time. The third twenty years were spent in and out of boredom and mild depression. By the time I was in my fifties the family was old enough for us to leave New Zealand and head to Australia without them, to do something different. The thing is, that they followed us. That wasn't such a bad thing, because we were still all together, and then at short notice we inherited my elderly mother to care for, but we hadn't done anything "exciting and different".

Before I left New Zealand I worked full time in a large Government office and loved my work as Personal Assistant to a wonderful man. I had full control of the office, and it ran like clockwork. In Australia, again I worked in a Government Department. But this was different. This was a well-oiled machine, and I was the bottom cog. This position was exceedingly stressful, dealing with queues of customers all day. Everything was regimented. There was ten minutes for your break, not more and not less. The girls in the office were lovely, but I felt smothered. There was no room for putting your own stamp on the job; and I was used to being a bit of a leader and not a follower at the very rear.

INTRODUCTION 引言

彼得跟着我过来，就是想弄清楚介绍会是不是骗人的。他对我说："那些人不就是想骗你的口袋里的钱吗，可别钱没挣到，反而赔了本。咱们去摸摸底，我总觉得这事儿有点玄乎。"

我没把他的话放在心上。要是介绍会真管用，我俩不是都可以试试嘛，所以我拉上彼得，让他自己瞧瞧究竟。

似乎是正规组织，听介绍很让人兴奋。我呢，可以借此机会逃离一成不变的生活。管它前面是刀山还是火海，我都决定义无反顾了。

要是你和我年纪相仿，已经过了中年，可能经历与我大抵相同。童年和青少年时期的我跟20世纪五六十年代的小孩差不多。第二个二十年，又忙着结婚，拉扯五个孩子，为他们忙前忙后，还要做兼职挣钱。第三个二十年乏善可陈，日子过得无聊而沉闷。等我到了五十多岁的时候，孩子们已经长大了，我们老两口总算可以不管他们，离开新西兰去澳大利亚过不一样的生活。没想到，孩子们一个接着一个地尾随而来。这倒也不算什么坏事，因为一家人又团聚了。紧接着，又轮到我那年迈的母亲需要我照顾，所以一直无缘过上那种令人激动的"不一样的生活"。

我在新西兰时，在一个政府大机关工作，是一个很有作为的官员的私人助理，我很喜欢这份工作，管理整个办公室得心应手，事事顺利。后来在澳大利亚，我也是在一个政府部门工作，但情况却大不一样。比方说吧，我工作的部门是一台上好油的机器，我就是机器上最末尾的齿轮。这个职位压力真的超大，每天要和一长排一长排的客户打交道。所有事情都有严格的时间规定。休息十分钟就十分钟。我们部门的姑娘们倒是很不错，可我总觉得心里不舒服。在那里我压根儿没有说话的份儿，而我以前大小是个官儿，没当过最底层受人指挥的小角色。

所以，我换了份工作，不过是才出虎口又进了狼窝。新老板的脾气倒还凑合，不算太坏，麻烦的是他老婆也在里面工作。这个愚蠢的金发女郎，大部分时间不是在忙家务，就是上美容院去了，剩下的时间才会坐在办公桌前记记账，就这么点小事每天都要出状况，偶尔也会跑跑市场。

So I changed jobs and went from the frying pan into the fire. When my new boss was not being horribly bad tempered he was passable. His wife, also a full-time employee, was a total ditzy blonde who spent most of her time running around after her family, or at the beauticians. When she had the time she would be at her desk doing the accounts, which she messed up on a daily basis, and on occasion attended to the marketing.

She also spent an enormous amount of time recruiting staff. Either the staff left soon after starting because they couldn't stand the place, or she sacked them because they were never up to her capricious standards. It's not an easy thing for a boss to sack his wife, even if she was causing mayhem in the office, especially if she didn't want to go!

The wife was highly displeased to find out I was looking for jobs in China and sacked me one morning before the boss arrived. I took them to court and won my case and a few thousand dollars. Here was my chance. China was calling loud and clear. If going to China to teach English wasn't different, then nothing was!

还有，她花了好多时间招聘员工。要么是员工受不了这个地方，没来几天就走人，要么就是他们跟不上她朝令夕改的标准，被她炒了鱿鱼。可是，即使公司被老婆大人整得乱七八糟，可做老板的要想炒老婆的鱿鱼，肯定相当难办。倘若这个女人死赖着不走，情况还会更加棘手！

这位夫人发现我正在应聘中国的教职，满心不悦。一天早上趁老板上班之前解聘了我。我把他俩告上了法庭，我打赢了官司，获得了几千澳元的赔偿。如今机会来了，中国在呼唤我们。要是去中国教书都算不得人生的一个大变化，那么敢问世间，何事可为？！

TAKING A TAXI IN XIAMEN AIRPORT

The fruition of all our planning was nigh. We left Brisbane on the night of the 18th, landing in Xiamen (said Shar-min) on the morning of the 19th August 2006. Coming in to land we gaped at the scenes unfolding below us.

"Everything in China is high rise," we'd been told. Like thousands of stacks of cards, buildings reached for the sky, some modern, some old, many squished together with little room between.

Xiamen is an island and the road and rail bridges connecting it to the mainland were clearly visible. We flew over a large port and into the airport on the northern fringe of the island. We went through customs where we showed our lovely new visas and collected our baggage.

We had taken our maximum luggage allowance. One large heavy bag each, one full, heavy, carry-on bag each, I had my hand bag and a shoulder bag, and Peter carried another bag. Close to the exit was a café.

"Let's have a coffee before we do anything else. It's eleven, and I'm starving!" I said. "Oh, English," I grinned, looking at the menu. "This is good. They have club sandwiches. Let's have one each and a coffee. That okay with you?"

Peter nodded and ordered. The girl didn't speak English but by pointing, nodding and smiling she got the message just fine. A few minutes later our order was delivered.

"Good grief, what's this?" My eyes boggled.

"Not your normal club sandwich," Peter said, taking the layers apart. "Looks like

厦门机场打的记

辛辛苦苦计划了这么久，享受成果的时候终于降临了。2006年8月18日晚，我们离开澳大利亚的布里斯班机场，于8月19日早上抵达厦门。飞机快降落的时候，地面的景色让我俩目瞪口呆。

曾有人告诉我们："在中国，到处都是高楼大厦。"这里的楼房，仿佛由成千上万张纸牌堆就而成，直插云霄，有新有旧，许多高楼之间挨挨挤挤着一些小房屋。

厦门是座岛屿，连接岛外的道路、桥梁清晰可见。飞机飞过一个大港口，进入位于岛屿最北的机场。我们拿出漂亮的新签证顺利通过海关检查，然后取回行李。

我们的行李已达最高规定重量。我俩一人一个沉甸甸的大箱子和一个塞得满满的旅行包，彼得另外还提了一个包。机场的出口处有一家咖啡吧。

"咱们先喝杯咖啡再做打算吧，都11点了，我可饿坏了！"我提议道。"哇，英语呢。"我看着菜单，一脸笑容。"挺好的，有俱乐部三明治，咱们各要一个和一杯咖啡，怎样？"

彼得点点头，然后准备点餐。女侍者不会说英语，但靠比划、点头和微笑，她也能对付。几分钟后，我们要的食物就送上来了。

"天啊，这是什么东西？"我大吃一惊。

"反正不是你平日里吃的俱乐部三明治，看着像吐司、蛋和某种肉。"彼得边说边

toast, egg and some kind of meat."

"You got any butter on yours?"

"Nope, just egg, toast, and I don't know what this meat is, maybe dyed ham or something. Well I'm starving, I'm eating it," he mumbled as the first mouthful went in.

"That coffee could grow hairs on the chest of a rock," I gasped as the mud-like sugarless coffee hit my taste buds. "Boy, that's strong stuff!" I couldn't manage the meat, but I got the dry toast and egg down.

My personal motto is "Think ahead, be prepared." This trip took a great deal of thinking and preparation. We'd booked a room for three nights at a four star hotel, planning to acclimatise a little. Expecting little English to be spoken I had printed off all the details of our hotel, and with this in hand we headed for the main exit. There were lines of taxis constantly coming and going. We knew they were taxis; they had those long lights on top.

"Bit ramshackled," Peter commented as we viewed the cars surging in empty and flowing out full. "Rejects from the wrecker's yard."

We gazed in wonder at vehicles that would certainly not get a Roadworthy Certificate at home.

These cars were not what we were used to. They were a bit smelly, and pretty grubby. The front seat wobbled precariously and slid up and down as we got in. Some taxis were going down the road like drunken crabs. Some panels were tacked together with bits of tape, and rust bordered cavities gaped toothlessly at us. The suspension worked intermittently depending on how big the bumps were. More fumes came in the car than went down the exhaust pipe. The paint work was a grotty green or bleached grape skin colour. (You'll be pleased to know that new fleets of modern cars now ply the streets of China.)

"Well organized though. Here's the queue, have to get right up the end," Peter said, pushing our huge pile of luggage.

We joined the ever lengthening queue, which moved very quickly. At the top was a smart looking uniformed man ushering people into the cars. He motioned for us to get into the first car in line. Peter heaved the biggest bags into the boot, and the driver helped to pile the rest into the back seat beside Peter. I sat in the front with my instructions, showing them to the driver. He read the page then shook his head violently, saying

把三明治一层层取下来。

"你的里面有黄油吗?"

"没有,就只有蛋、吐司,我不知道这是什么肉,可能是风干火腿吧。管它呢,我饿了,我要开吃了。"彼得嘟囔着咬了一口。

当黏糊糊的无糖咖啡碰到我的味蕾时,我倒吸了一口凉气:"这咖啡死人喝了都能活过来,好浓呀!"肉我是吃不下了,但我还是把吐司和蛋吞进了肚里。

我的个人格言是:"未雨绸缪,有备无患。"为这次旅程,我动了不少脑子,做了许多准备工作。我们在一家四星级酒店订了一间客房,住三个晚上,准备先适应一下环境。考虑到可能会说英语的人不多,我们早已把酒店的详细资料打印好了备用。我们把资料拿在手上,走向出口。外面排了一长溜的士,有进有出,好不热闹。我们知道那些车辆是的士,因为车顶安装了长灯。

我们看着空车进来又载客离开,这时,彼得说:"有点破呢,拿去当清障车都没人要吧。"

我们惊奇地看着眼前的的士,要是在澳大利亚,这些车肯定是拿不到行驶证的。这里的的士跟我们平时乘坐的车子不大一样。车里有点儿味道,挺脏的。前排座位没固定好,我们上车时会前后挪动。有些的士行驶在路上,像极了醉酒的螃蟹。有的仪表盘上粘着胶带,锈迹斑斑的小缺口张着没牙的嘴巴,傻呵呵地盯着我们。而且,车一颠簸悬挂装置便不好使,钻进车里的烟比排放出去的还多。车身颜色不是丑兮兮的绿色就是漂白过的葡萄紫。(好消息:现在街面上的的士全都换新了。)

"不过,还挺有序的。在那儿排队,得走到队伍尾巴那边。"彼得边说边推着堆满我俩"货物"的行李车。

我们加入了永不见短的长龙,但队伍前行的速度很快。一个身穿制服的帅哥在最前方引导。他示意我们上第一辆车。彼得哼哧哼哧地把大箱子放进后备箱,司机帮助彼得把剩下的行李放入后座。我拿着指南坐在前面。我把地址指给司机看,司机瞅了一会儿,用力摇了摇头,语气严肃地用中文说着什么。

something serious in Chinese.

Obviously he didn't know this place.

"He wants us to get out again," Peter said.

"Why?" I asked the driver. He chattered away in Chinese. "I can't speak Chinese. Please take us here." I jabbed at the paper, my voice going up an octave.

The driver jabbered away, shook his head, got out, opened our doors and took all our luggage out, leaving us stranded with our bags all over the place. Someone else nipped into that taxi and he took off with a hiss and a roar. The uniformed man looked at us and called up another car.

Again, Peter heaved the heaviest bags into the boot as the uniformed man helped to pile our stuff into the second car. I gave the driver my printed page.

"We want to go here," I said in a very slow clear voice so he would understand. I showed him the address in Chinese. "Peony Wanpeng Hotel," I said, although I found out later my pronunciation was completely wrong. He looked at me, then at the paper and shook his head. I was getting angry by now.

"Surely they aren't all illiterate," I yelled at Peter. "He can't read his own language! How stupid is that!" I jabbed at the paper, "Here, just take us here!" But the taxi driver gabbled on, shook his head, got out, unloaded all our bags and left us stranded a second time.

I was trying to control my fury. I was tired, I was very hot, and I was not happy. The uniformed man took my piece of paper and read it. He piled all our bags back onto a trolley and beckoned for us to follow him inside to the information counter, where one of the women could speak a little English. I tried to explain our predicament. Ah, at last, someone understood me. She opened a map of Xiamen and drew a circle where we needed to go.

"Give to driver. Give to driver," she said.

"Thank you so much." I breathed a sigh of relief, as we aimed for the end of the queue again. A few minutes later we were facing the uniformed man again.

"Boy, I hope this works, or I'm going to scream," I muttered as Peter again loaded the big bags into the boot and everything else into the rear seat. I showed the map to the driver, he nodded and drove off. We both collapsed in our seats, thankful we had at last

显然他不知道那个地方。

"他要我们下车。"彼得说。

"为什么?"我问司机。他又说了一长串中文。"我不会说中文,麻烦你送我们过去吧。"我指了指手中的纸张,声音抬高了八度。

司机叽里呱啦了一番,然后摇摇头下车,打开车门取出我们的行李,把我俩丢在行李堆里。有人乘机钻进了车,车子"嘶嘶"两声便轰地夺路而逃。制服帅哥看了看我们,又替我们叫了辆车。

彼得又哼哧哼哧地把大行李箱放进后备箱,这回是制服帅哥帮忙我们把其他东西放入车里。我把打印好的地址拿给司机看。

"我们要去这个地方。"我一字一顿地告诉他,希望他能听懂。我把中文地址指给他看。"牡丹万鹏酒店。"我说,但后来我才知道我的发音根本不准。他看看了我,又看看纸张,然后摇摇头。这下子我火了。

"他们不会全都是文盲吧。"我冲着彼得大吼道,"这个人看不懂自己国家的文字!有那么蠢的人吗?!"我戳了戳纸张,说:"这里,送我们去这里!"司机叽里呱啦说了一通话,摇了摇头,卸下我们的行李,我们又被人撂下了。

我强按下满腔怒火,又累又热又生气。制服帅哥拿过我的纸张看了看。他把我们的东西重新装进推车,示意我俩跟他到问询处,那儿有个女工作人员懂一些英语。我把自己的遭遇说了一遍。好了,终于有人听得懂我的话了。她打开厦门地图,把我们要去的地方圈了出来。

"拿给司机,拿给司机。"她说。

"万分感谢。"我们再一次去队伍尾巴排队,但我心里舒坦了不少。几分钟后我们又遇见了制服帅哥。

"老天,希望这次能行,不然我会尖叫的。"我嘟囔道。彼得又把大件行李放进后备箱,再把其余的塞进后座。我把地图拿给司机看,他点点头即刻出发。我俩瘫倒在座位上,满心感谢,终于找到一个识字的司机了。

found a driver who could read.

We were just exiting the airport drive when he stopped at a large intersection and asked something in Chinese.

"Wonder what he wants?" I asked Peter. He was no wiser than me, so I just nodded. I found out later he had asked us if we wanted to take the scenic route. I'd said yes. Of course, it was twice as long, and twice the fare. The driver turned left, and we ogled out the windows taking in this new scenery.

"Some of these trucks came out of the ark, maybe were obsolete even before the ark," Peter commented as we passed old, dark blue trucks puffing out stinking black fumes. The taxi followed a nice beach, went over bridges, through little settlements, and into the city proper, then drew up in front of our hotel. I recognized it from the internet photos.

"Yes, this is it," I nodded to the driver. "Good. Thank you."

"It seems that not all Chinese people can read," I said to Peter. "Need to remember that for next time."

The larger four and five star hotels in China give excellent personal service. A young man dressed in formal hotel livery came to the car, opened the doors, brought out a trolley and loaded all our bags, making sure the driver was paid. He beckoned us to follow through the large shiny gold and glass entrance, past a line of uniformed young ladies who all said something to us in Chinese as we entered the foyer.

This was a rather grand place, polished corn coloured marble floors with shiny black and gold patterned inlay, with matching polished marble columns. There were large leather lounge suites, well-polished glass tables, a huge crystal chandelier and a beautiful circular marble staircase leading up to the other floors. We were led to a modern front desk.

"We have a booking," Peter said, giving our name. "An online booking. It's all paid for."

The young lady giggled, and looked at another couple of girls there. They giggled too. Peter repeated himself. They looked at us and we looked at them.

"Fair go! No English here either?" I groaned. "This is worse than I thought."

Someone said something in Chinese and walked away, returning after a few minutes with a lady who walked up to us, hand outstretched.

车子快离开机场车道时,司机在一个大十字路口停下,用中文向我们询问什么。

"他想问我们什么呀?"我问彼得。彼得跟我一样糊涂,我只好点点头。后来我才明白,他是问我们要不要走观光路线。我当时的意思是"要"。当然,这条路线双倍路程,结果是双倍路费。司机左转而去,我们眉开眼笑地看着窗外全新的景色。

的士经过几辆深蓝色的旧货车,货车的屁股后面拖着一溜刺鼻的黑烟。"有些货车好像是很久以前的老爷车呢,可能以前的老爷车也没有这么烂吧。"彼得说。的士驶离一片美丽的海滨,上了大桥,经过几片小住宅区,进入市中心,接着在一家酒店前面停住。我一眼就看到了网站上的照片。

"没错,就是这个地方,太好了,谢谢你。"我对司机点了点头。

"好像不是所有的中国人都是文盲,下次我们得吸取教训。"我对彼得说。

在中国,四星级以上的大酒店服务都特别好。一个身穿酒店制服的小伙子走到车边,替我们打开车门,取来行李车,把我们所有的行李搬到车上,等我们付钱给司机。之后,他示意我们跟随他穿过亮闪闪的金色玻璃大门,经过一排身穿制服的年轻女子,我们走进大堂的时候,她们齐声用中文对我们说了些什么。

这家酒店相当气派,玉米色的大理石地板锃亮锃亮的,点缀着黑黄两色嵌板,配着同样锃亮的大理石柱子。酒店里摆放着大大的皮沙发、纤尘不染的玻璃桌子、巨大的水晶吊灯和通向其他楼层的漂亮的环形大理石楼梯。我们被带到设计现代的前台。

"我们有预订,网上订的,已经付了钱。"彼得说完报上我俩的名字。

年轻的前台小姐嘻嘻笑着,接着看了看其他几个姑娘,她们也都笑嘻嘻的。彼得又重复了一遍刚才的话。姑娘们看着我们,我们看着姑娘们。

"见鬼了!这里的人也不懂英语?"我痛苦地说道,"真没料到情况会这么糟糕。"

有人冲我们说了几句中文,然后走开了,几分钟后领回一个女士。女士边走边向我们伸出了手。

"早上好,我是琳达,这里的经理。"她操一口相当漂亮的英语。我俩长舒一口气。

"Good morning, I am Linda," she said in quite good English. "I'm the manager." Oh the relief!

Linda checked us in, came up with us in the lift to the fourth floor and opened the door for us, giving us our key card and her business card.

"Call me if you need anything at all. Not many staff here can speak English. Can you speak Chinese?" she asked. We both shook our heads. "I'm here all the time, so please, call me if you need anything. Our Western restaurant is on the ground floor, breakfast is included in the price. Lunch is on soon."

The large hotel room was delightful, with a huge bed, solid wooden furniture, air conditioning and a well-appointed bathroom. Our luggage had been delivered. I sat on the bed, then raised my eyes in horror to Peter.

"It's like a cricket bat!" I squeaked. "It's as hard as the hobs of Hades! I'll never be able to sleep on this."

He sat, tested the bed, grinned at me and said, "Welcome to China, we came for an experience, we're going to get it."

We giggled like school kids just let loose for the holidays. "Come on, let's see what they've got for lunch," he said. "Hope it's better than the club sandwich."

Going down to the restaurant we found an extensive menu in Chinglish, (Chinese English) but it was understandable. Linda came up and talked to us while we waited for our food.

"Everything alright?" she asked.

"Yes, just fine, thanks," I replied. "Oh, one thing though." I pulled out my printed page with the hotel's name I'd shown the taxi drivers. "We're very surprised that some of the taxi drivers can't read."

Linda looked at it for a moment, then looked at us puzzled.

"We showed this to several drivers and they couldn't read it," I said.

Linda explained the problem.

Peter and I roared with laughter. Everyone in the restaurant looked at these crazy foreigners. I wiped the tears from my eyes, as I gradually calmed down.

"Japanese!" I snortled to Peter. "No wonder they couldn't read it. So much for all my careful planning, I printed the instructions in Japanese. Oh boy, what an idiot!"

琳达替我们办理好入住手续,陪我们进电梯到四楼,打开我们的客房门,接着将房卡和她的名片递给我们。

"有什么需要给我打电话。这里会说英语的员工不多,你会说中文吗?"她问。我俩一起摇了摇头。"我都在这里上班,有事儿请打电话给我。酒店的西餐厅在一楼,早餐费用已经算在你们的住宿费里了。午餐时间就快到了。"

我们的大客房很舒服,有一张大床、一套实木家具、一台空调和一个陈设齐备的浴室。行李已经送上来了。我坐在床上,惶恐地抬头看着彼得。

"好像板球棒哪!"我尖叫道,"硬得跟大炉盘一样!这样的床我可睡不来。"

彼得坐到床上试了试,冲我大笑道:"欢迎来到中国,我们是来体验生活的。体验之旅马上就要开始咯。"

我们像小孩一样吃吃笑开了。别计较了,就算是来度假好了。"快点,咱们去看看这里的午餐怎么样,希望比俱乐部三明治好些。"彼得说。

我们来到餐厅,看见一大本中式英语菜谱,好在我们看得懂。我们在等上菜的时候琳达走过来与我们聊了两句。

"一切都好吗?"她问。

"好,谢谢了。"我回答,"噢,有一件事儿。"我取出拿给司机看的那张印着酒店名字的打印纸,说:"真奇怪,有的司机不识字呢。"

琳达瞅了片刻,然后一脸疑惑地看着我们。

"我们把这个拿给好几个司机看,他们都看不懂。"我说。

琳达说出了原委。

我和彼得忍不住大笑起来。餐厅里所有的人都看着我们这对疯老外。我慢慢平静下来,用手擦去眼角的泪花。

"是日语!"我对彼得苦笑说,"难怪人家看不懂。这就是我仔细计划的结果,打印的居然是日语指南。噢,老天,我真是个大蠢蛋!"

AN EVENTFUL FIRST DAY

We were going to explore Xiamen. Breakfast was pretty good, Heinz Baked Beans, bread, strawberry jam from Austria, lots of dumplings, fried eggs, real bacon, fried potatoes, and all sorts of food new to us. There was black jelly, muffin type things, unusual breads, several kinds of watery looking rice porridge, several teas, and very strong coffee. Peter was a bit adventurous trying new food, but I stuck to what I knew. They did have New Zealand Anchor butter which was a great find.

We then went to the front desk to get directions.

"We want to go to the shops," I said. This drew a blank. I tried again, very slowly. No one understood.

"Sorry. Sorry," they repeated chattering and giggling. Then they fetched another girl.

"Can I help you?" she said hesitantly. "My name is Michelle."

"Oh, you can speak English? That's good."

"Only a little," which is the standard reply even if they can speak quite well.

"We want to go to the shops," I repeated.

She spoke in Chinese and they pulled out another map of the island. I'd left mine upstairs.

"Which shops?" she asked.

We soon learned that shops in China are not like your shops in the West. They just go on and on, in fact the ground floor of almost all the buildings are shops and all the

波折的第一天

我们打算在厦门好好走走。酒店的早餐相当不错，有亨氏烘豆、面包、澳大利亚草莓酱、水饺、煎蛋、真正的培根、炸土豆，以及许多我们以前从未见过的食物。比如，黑色果酱、一些稠乎乎的食物、奇怪的面包、清白粥、好几种茶和超浓的咖啡。彼得比较胆大，试吃了一些新食物，但我只敢挑一些熟悉的东西吃。餐厅竟然还有新西兰的安佳牛油，我俩心中窃喜。

早饭后我们到前台问路。

我说："我们想逛商店。"没反应。我又重复了一遍，这回放慢了语速。没人听得懂我的话。

"对不对，对不起。"姑娘们笑嘻嘻地一个劲儿地重复这句话，然后叫了另一个姑娘过来。

"我能帮您什么忙吗？"她想了一下才说，"我叫米歇尔。"

"噢，你会说英语，太好了。"

"只会说一点点儿。"这是标准回答，就是英语很好的中国人也会这么说。

"我们想到商店看看。"我又说了一遍。

她说了几句中文，伙伴们又取出一张地图，我把自己的地图忘在楼上房间里了。

"哪家商店？"

upper floors are apartments. That's very sensible when you think about it. Every couple of blocks you have a mini self-sufficient community.

"Maybe Zhongshan Lu," she said, making a mark on the map. "Take this with you. Show the taxi driver when you want to come back."

She handed me a card with the name of the hotel in Chinese, a little map and phone numbers. I have since found that most hotels have these, and as long as you keep one in your purse you can always get back to your hotel.

Zhongshan Lu, (said Jong shan loo) is one of the main shopping areas of Xiamen. It's a real mixture, with some high end department stores interspersed with old narrow lanes leading off, and further down some dark narrower alleys, looking crammed, dingy and a bit scary. Many of the shops are tiny, but even so may have two or three staff ready to serve you.

Many tourists visit this area and I oohed and aahed over some of the beautiful silk and jade. I drooled over a couple of beautiful bags. There were shoes and clothes, jewellery of every description, and the prices were so cheap!

One of the most amazing things we saw that morning was the bamboo scaffolding.

If you're in the construction industry you'll be flabbergasted at the scaffolding there. It's the most amazing thing you'll ever see.

They use great long lengths of bamboo, very thick poles about ten centimetres in diameter, and maybe six to eight meters long. The amount of construction under way in China is amazing, and many of these building sites are surrounded by this bamboo scaffolding. You know the twisty ties we use for rubbish bags? The fine metal strips, fine wire surrounded by paper? That is what they used to tie the bamboo together, the same thing but bigger.

The advantages of using bamboo are obvious. It is much lighter in weight than steel, it is easy to buy, obviously cheap, and biodegradable. It also seems to be very strong when tied together.

This is not scaffolding around a one or two floor building. We counted one building of thirteen floors clad this way, with both men and women working on different levels.

Getting around on the upper levels was easy. There were long woven mats of fine bamboo that they laid across to make walking areas and platforms to sit on with their

我们很快就发现了，中国的商场与西方国家的不大一样。这儿到处都是商店。事实上，几乎每座大楼的底层都是店铺，楼上才是公寓。仔细想想，这样的格局挺合理的。每两三个楼区，都有一个一应俱全的小社区。

"可以去中山路看看。"米歇尔边说边在地图上做了一个标记，"把这个带上，回来的时候拿给的士司机看。"

她递给我一张名片，上面有酒店中文地址、小地图和电话号码。后来我发现几乎所有的酒店都印制了这样的名片，客人只要放一张在钱包里，回酒店便不成问题。

中山路是厦门的主要商业区，大百货楼中间夹杂着许多老巷子，老巷子又通往一些更窄的黑乎乎的小巷。小巷非常拥挤，脏兮兮的，有点吓人。许多商店都很小，但是一般都有两到三个店员看店，招呼客人。

中山路上游客如织。精美的丝绸和玉石总令我啧啧惊叹。我兴奋地看着手中拎着的几个漂亮袋子。街上有鞋店、衣服店和各类首饰店，价格竟那么便宜！

那天早上，我们看到的最为神奇的东西就是竹脚手架。

要是你在建筑行业干过，看到这里的竹脚手架，肯定惊讶得眼珠子都要掉下来。它是你今生今世目睹到的最神奇的东西。

他们选用的是极长的竹竿，约10厘米厚，6至8米长。在中国，在建筑工程多得令人咋舌，许多建筑工地都围着这种竹脚手架。你们知道我们用来扎垃圾袋的东西吗？就是那种细金属条，外层是纸张的金属丝绳？他们就是用这个东西捆绑竹竿的，只是比金属丝绳略粗些而已。

使用竹竿的好处显而易见。它不仅重量比钢材轻，采购方便，而且价格显然便宜许多，还是可降解材料，把几根竹子绑在一起似乎也很结实。

这种脚手架可不是只用于建造单层或两层的小楼，我们数过，一幢十三层的大楼外面都围着这个东西，工人们（有男有女）在不同楼层忙碌。

脚手架的架子其实很容易搭建，只要把细竹子编织的长垫铺到竹竿上，就可供人走路、休息和搁放工具或油漆桶。我们好奇地看着一群女工给大楼刷浅黄色的油

tools or paint pots. We watched a group of women painting this building a pale yellow colour, even in the rain. We stood watching for ages until the cricks in our necks forced us to move on. What an amazing sight!

We enjoyed a fabulous morning wandering up and down, in and out, making a mental note of the KFC, and planned to go there for lunch. There was a shop full of crocodile skin products. Peter was browsing when a couple of men wandered in with their umbrellas. It had been raining, and somehow they got all tangled up with Peter.

"Where's my wallet?" Peter asked half an hour later, as we descended the steps in KFC for lunch. He went green, then white, then green again as his hand came out empty.

"Must be there," I said.

"Gone! It's gone," he said startled.

He patted his pockets, then emptied them all.

"Nothing! It's gone!"

"What, pinched?" I asked surprised. "How?"

"I don't know," he said going to a table and re checking everything.

"Not in your bag?" he asked me.

"No, I haven't got it. You put it back in your pocket when you bought that Tee shirt."

Realization hit. We haven't been in the country a day and his wallet's been stolen.

He sat down feeling sick, put his head in his hands and groaned.

"How much money did you have in it?" I asked, knowing we didn't have that much Chinese money with us.

"Not much, thank goodness. It must have happened in the crocodile shop, a couple of guys got all tangled up with me. I bet they took it then. Well they were pro's," he said. "They'll be long gone now."

"I guess we stand out like sore thumbs, there are no other foreigners around," I said. "What do we do now?"

We went back to the Crocodile shop trying to nonchalantly look in the rubbish bins in case they'd taken the money and thrown out the wallet.

"It's not so much the money, but my credit cards and other stuff. That's what I'm thinking of," Peter said. "I'm so mad that I let it happen. I should have been more careful. We'd better get back to the hotel and let the bank know."

AN EVENTFUL FIRST DAY
波折的第一天

漆。我俩站在楼前，仰头看了好久，后来脖子发酸了才恋恋不舍地离开了。这样的景观我们真是难得一见！

我们花了一早上，在街上逛荡，在店铺中进进出出，心里却默记着肯德基的位置，因为我们打算上那儿吃午饭。在一家鳄鱼皮具店里，彼得正在看货，这时进来几个手拿雨伞的男子。刚才下了一阵雨。不知怎的，这些男子都往彼得身边凑。

"我的钱包呢？"过了半小时，我们下楼到肯德基吃午饭时，彼得问我。他手中空无一物，急得脸色从青到白又从白到青。

"肯定在。"我安慰道。

"不见了！钱包不见了！"他又惊又急。

他拍拍口袋，然后把所有口袋里的东西都掏了出来。

"到处都没有！不见了！"

"什么！被偷了？"我吃惊地问，"怎么可能？"

"我也不知道。"他说着走到一张桌子边，又检查了一遍。

"会不会在你的包里？"他问我。

"不会，我没拿。买完那件T恤后你放回口袋了呀。"

我们到这个国家还不到一天，彼得的钱包就被偷了。我俩感觉当头一棒。

彼得难过地坐在那儿，双手捂着脑袋，叹息着。

"钱包里有多少钱？"我问，我知道我们身上没带多钱人民币。

"谢天谢地，带的不多。肯定是在鳄鱼皮具店被偷的，那几天个小伙子挤在我身边，我敢肯定是他们偷的。他们是老手，现在肯定逃之夭夭了。"他说。

"可能我俩太显眼了，因为周围没别的外国人。"我说，"现在咱们该怎么办呢？"

我们回到那间皮具店，装着没事儿一样看了看那里的垃圾桶，希望他们取走钱后把钱包扔在那里。

"钱倒不多，只是里面有我的信用卡等其他东西。我着急的是那些东西。"彼得说，"怎么让人偷了都不知道，真窝囊。我应该小心点嘛。咱们最好回酒店，通知银

This was when the fun started. Linda was busy. The girls at the hotel's front desk had no idea at all what we were talking about. I started writing things down.

"Sorry. Sorry", they said, interspersed with giggles.

"Collect phone call," I wrote.

Blank stares were what I got. I pointed to the phone and mimed making a phone call. Ah! They understood and took me into the business centre.

"No! I need to make a collect call."

Peter mimed having his wallet stolen. They understood that this was serious so went and told Linda who came straight down.

"We need to go to the Police Station at once," she said.

"I also need to contact our bank," Peter insisted. "Maybe I'll come with you and Lana can call the bank."

Ah well, even the simplest of jobs can be mighty complicated when everything conspires against you. Have you checked your credit card lately? Yes, there is an emergency number to call, but often the numbers are unreadable due to your name being pressed on the other side. Anyway, the hotel staff didn't know how to call Australia. The phones had IDD bars on them.

I was getting desperate by this time, then one smart thinking girl called the Bank of China in Xiamen. She talked to them in Chinese. They put her through to the Bank of China somewhere in Sydney, who put me through to the National Bank of Australia in Brisbane, where I explained the problem. Ah, but not so quick! You know about the Privacy Act? Safeguards us from crooks? Well, the card was in Peter's name, not mine, so they wouldn't talk to me.

"But he's gone to the Police Station," I said exasperated. "No one here speaks English."

"You should call the number on your card, there is an emergency number on your card," was the reply.

"Peter's card's been stolen! And the number on my one is unreadable! You can"t make reverse charge calls from here!" I yelled at her. "It costs a fortune to call you from here, nothing works like at home! Anyway I can't read all the numbers on the card!" explaining why. "What else can I do?"

行。"

真正的闹剧马上就要开演了。琳达很忙,前台的姑娘们又听不懂我的话。我只好把需求写下来。

"对不起,对不起。"她们边说边吃吃地笑。

"对方付费电话。"我写道。

回答我的是迷茫的眼神。我指着电话,然后做打电话的样子。成功了!她们明白了我的意思,带我们到商务中心。

"不对!我要打的是对方付费电话。"

彼得比划着把钱包被偷的情况表演出来。她们知道我们遇到大麻烦了,赶紧告诉琳达,琳达马上赶了过来。

"我们得立刻去公安局报案。"她说。

"但我们还得跟银行联系。"彼得坚持说,"这样吧,我跟你去公安局,柯兰去给银行打电话。"

人若时运不济,最简单的事儿都会变得复杂异常。最近您看过信用卡吗?对,上面有银行的紧急电话号码,只是因为背面印了您的名字,所以不大清晰。总之,酒店员工不知怎么打电话到澳大利亚。他们的电话不能打国际长途。

此时我已经抓狂了。这时,一个聪明的女孩想起给中国银行厦门分行打电话。她用中文通话。银行替她把电话转到悉尼某地的中国银行,然后这家银行又替我接通布里斯班的澳大利亚国家银行。我说明了情况。可是,没这么简单!你知道保密法吗?就是防止客户被骗的保护手段?糟糕的是,卡是用彼得的名字申办的,不是用我的名字,所以他们不能告诉我。

"可他去公安局了,而这里的人又不会说英语。"我急坏了。

"你应该打卡上的电话,你的卡上有紧急电话的。"对方应道。

"彼得的卡被偷了!而我卡上的号码又看不清楚。这儿不能打收话方付费电话。"我冲她大吼道,"从这里给你们打电话贵死了,跟我们国内完全不一样。总之,卡上

"Get your husband to fax us. Use this number and mark it urgent, we will see to it at once."

I could see a fax machine, took down the number in Australia, grabbed a piece of blank paper, wrote the bank a note and signed it with both our names. If they wanted to assume it was Peter, so be it. I sent it and they replied to say they'd cancelled the card. What a mission!

Meanwhile, downtown Peter was having his own troubles. The manager was wonderful.

"This is the oldest street in Xiamen," she explained to him in the taxi. "It is about 800 years old. We'll go in here."

Peter followed Linda through a maze of alleys to a large Police Station. Linda explained the situation to the policeman.

After waiting for about thirty minutes a policeman came and spoke to Linda.

"We need to go to a different station," she said. "They can't help us here."

At the second station Linda repeated the story. Peter was given some forms to sign twice, the manager signed twice and Peter had to apply his thumbprint three times and the manager twice.

"I'm just exhausted," I moaned when he got back. "I can't believe this has happened on our first day here."

"Linda said this particular street is sometimes targeted by pick-pockets, as many foreigners frequent this area," Peter explained. "There are a few crooks around who can pick out easy targets like us. One good thing though, she said crime against the person is rare, they never hurt us, but sometimes they are expert pick pockets. We need to be more careful."

Linda arranged for us to have international access on our phone, and we sorted out the rest of our cards, slowly calming down. What a day.

Suddenly Peter jumped up and said to me, "I haven't got any paperwork. I can claim all this on our travel insurance, but I need all the paper work, I didn't get anything from the Police station. I'll never find it again. It's down a maze of alleys!"

Hurrah for Linda. It took six months, several emails and two trips to Xiamen but finally the paper work came through.

的号码有些我看不清楚!"我再次说明原因,"你说,我能怎么办?"

"叫你丈夫给我们发传真,发这个号码,写上'加急',我们就会马上处理。"

我看见一台传真机,写下澳大利亚的号码,又抓起一张纸,给银行写了一封短信,签上我和彼得两人的名字。要是他们以为是彼得写的,就当是他写的好了。传真发过去了,对方回了一张传真,说卡已经销了。什么事儿啊!

期间,在市中心的彼得同样糟糕不顺。但是琳达真的是个大好人。

"这是厦门最古老的街道,"她坐在的士中对彼得说,"有八百多年的历史,我们要穿过这条街。"

彼得跟着琳达穿过迷宫式的小巷,来到了一座公安局大楼。琳达对警察说明了情况。

等了约半个钟头,一个警察过来对琳达说了几句话。

"我们得去另一家公安局,我们的案子不属于他们管。"她说。

到了第二家公安局,琳达又说了一遍情况。有人递了几张表格叫他们签名。彼得签了两次名,琳达签了两次,彼得还摁了三次指印,琳达摁了两次。

"我彻底累垮了,"彼得回来时我对他抱怨,"万万没想到第一天就出这种状况。"

"琳达说了,那条街是小偷经常出没的地方,因为老外们常去。"彼得对我解释,"还有一些骗子,专门骗我们这类人,不过琳达还说了,伤人案件极少发生。他们不会伤害我们,但有些小偷的手脚真的很快,以后我们得加倍小心了。"

琳达替我们开通国际电话。我们整理了一下其他的银行卡,心里慢慢平静了下来。这一天真是一波三折呀。

突然,彼得跳了起来对我说:"我什么证明都没拿到,我有旅游保险,可以索赔的呀,可我需要那些证明文件,我怎么就两手空空从公安局回来了呢。去那个地方,要穿过迷宫式的小巷,我肯定会迷路的。"

谢天谢地有琳达在。总共花了整整半年时间、好几封邮件和往返厦门两次,彼得最终才拿到了证明文件。

PERSONAL SAFETY IN CHINA

Having read this, if you are considering going to China to teach, you might think that this is a dangerous place to live, but in fact foreigners almost always feel safe in China. Many female teachers live alone and travel alone safely. As in every country poverty exists, so pickpocketing and theft can be a problem. So what can you do to keep yourself safe?

Use your common sense, keep your money and credit cards in zipped up handbags. It's rare for there to be crime against the person, the Chinese people are not violent, and if they plan to do a bit of pickpocketing on you, you won't know till after the event.

Here is an example of two teachers who went shopping at a Walmart department store in what is considered a fairly small city. They went their separate ways to browse. After a while the wife called the husband to see where he was so they could meet at the checkout. His phone number was in her mobile phone. The phone number for the police was also in her phone. Both numbers were side by side in the contacts list. By accident she called the phone number for the police. Someone in Chinese answered, and she soon realised her mistake. They were talking to her urgently in Chinese but she had no idea what they were saying. She apologised and hung up.

About ten seconds later she received a phone call from the police. They accessed the record of her in-call, and the person she spoke to immediately forwarded the number onto someone who spoke good English.

Her phone rang.

在华人身安全

要是你有意来华教书，读到这个标题，可能会以为中国的治安很不好。这你就错了，事实上外国人通常觉得中国这个国家相当安全。许多外国女子只身一人住在中国，到处游玩，安全得很。不过，跟所有国家一样，只要贫困存在，就有小偷存在。那么，该如何确保个人安全呢？

平时小心行事。譬如，把信用卡、金钱等贵重物品放入手袋中，拉上拉链。在中国极少发生伤人事件。中国人不暴力，但若是你被小偷盯上了，一般事后才会发觉。

曾经有两个外籍老师到一个小城市的沃尔玛购物，夫妻俩分开走，各看各的。过了一会儿，妻子给丈夫打电话问他在哪里，告诉他去收银台会合。她的手机里存了丈夫的手机号，也存了公安局的号码。两个号码紧挨着。她不小心拨出了公安局的号码。有人用中文应答她，她随即意识到自己打错了电话。对方口气急切，但她一个字也听不懂。她道了声歉，就挂断了手机。

紧接着她的手机响了。

"早上好，这里是公安局，您是不是给我们打过电话？遇到什么麻烦了吗？需要什么帮助？"一位女士操着一口流利的英语问道。

"对不起，我不需要帮助，我按错了号码。"

"您确信不需要我们的帮助？"

"Good morning, this is the police. You made a call to us? Are you in trouble? Do you need some help?" a lady asked in good English.

"No, I'm sorry, I don't need help. I pressed your number by mistake."

"You are certain you don't need any help?"

She explained what happened and they both laughed at her mistake.

However, she was very impressed with the speed of their reply, and knew that if she was really in trouble, help would have arrived very quickly.

The police presence on the street is good. There are often police or security people around. Every large building has a security office at the gate and your school will too.

Because China has such a dense population there are always lots of people around. You will have no qualms about walking alone at night.

You will have quite a few dealings with police stations on visa matters; residency papers need filling out every time you move apartments and every time you return to China after going out of the country. Your school will help you. Generally, experiences with the police are good.

In China they have different emergency phone numbers for fire, police and ambulance. Put them into your phone in case of emergency.

Police:110

Ambulance: 120

Fire:119

她向对方说明了情况,俩人哈哈大笑。

但公安局的反应如此迅速,让她印象深刻。她知道,如果自己真的遇到麻烦,能很快获得帮助。

街上的警力是充分的。不时有警察或保安巡逻。每幢大楼门口都有保安值岗,学校也一样。

因为中国人口众多,所以人来人往是常态。你不必担心,夜晚的街上就只有你一人形单影只。

为了签证,你可能要经常跟警察打交道。像每次搬家,每次出境返回中国,都要填写居住信息表。这个学校会帮你。总的来说,跟中国警察打交道,还是很愉快的。

报警号码: 110

急救中心号码: 120

火警: 119

CHINESE MONEY

Our experiences that day highlighted some of the complications involved when we were dealing with large businesses like the local Police or banks when we couldn't speak the language. For any dealings with the local Police, you will have a translator to help you. But learning your way around the Chinese money system will take you a little while.

There are three terms used for Chinese money. RMB, the Renminbi, is the official name for their currency. It is also called Yuan (said You-en). The slang term is kuai (said kw-eye) and normally used when shopping.

The RMB comes in many denominations. The highest note is 100RMB, so if you want to pay several thousand for a purchase you carry lots of notes with you. One RMB is divided into ten Jiao and each Jiao is divided into ten Fen.

For other money matters, here are a few tips:

1. Make sure you only carry what money you need with you for the day.
2. Keep a good record of emergency numbers for your credit cards.
3. Use zipped up handbags.
4. Be sensible with valuables.
5. Have good travel insurance.
6. Before you leave home check with your local bank about changing any RMB you may take home. The rules vary from country to country. It may be wiser to change your money while still in China.
7. Remember that 0800 and 1800 numbers in your home country cannot be called

中国货币

第一天的波折经历说明一个事实：如果你不会说英语，又要跟像公安局或银行这样的机构打交道，处理要事，事情会多么麻烦。跟当地公安局打交道，会有翻译从旁协助你。但是，要想了解清楚中国货币体系，就要费一些时日了。

中国货币有三种说法。RMB，即人民币，是该货币的正式说法。也可称为"元"，但当地人叫"块"，买东西时，店家大都说"块"。

人民币有许多币种。最大面值是100元，如果你要买几千元的商品，就得带一大沓人民币在身边。一元可分为十角，一角又可分成十分。

涉及与金钱有关的事项，以下几条建议可供您参考：

1. 身上只要带足一天的花销即可。
2. 保存好信用卡的紧急号码。
3. 随身携带有拉链的包。
4. 小心保管贵重物品。
5. 办理一份保障全面的旅游险种。
6. 离家之前向本国银行打听清楚，如何将可能带回的人民币兑换为本国货币。最好是在中国境内兑换。
7. 国内的0800和1800号码国外无法打通。

from another country.

8. Put someone you trust in charge of your accounts and statements at home, and get the phone number, fax number, and branch manager's name, mobile and after hour's number of your branch. Take that with you.

9. When you call emergency numbers at home you get a central call centre and not your local branch. The call centre probably will not know about arrangements you have made at your local branch.

10. If you call your bank to have a card cancelled, double, triple and quadruple check the details with the person at the bank. Twice, Australian banks have cancelled the wrong card leaving me with no access to money.

11. Keep a certain amount of Chinese money with you at home for emergencies. You'll be surprised how often you may need it.

12. With Skype you can call landlines and mobiles that do not have Skype, including banks. This is the cheapest way to make a phone call. You can buy credit and use it even if the other party does not have Skype.

13. Sometimes a bank will ask for your phone number and say they will call you back. Once they have hung up they may realize they are not allowed to make international calls, so you never hear back.

14. Due to privacy issues a bank will never give anyone else information about your accounts.

15. You should be able to use your home country credit cards and ATM cards in China. You will probably have to use the ATM machines at the Bank of China rather than any other bank. ATM cards are widely used in China.

16. Generally Chinese ATM cards will work in your home country. You need to use the ATM of your national bank, e.g. Bank of America, Bank of England, National Bank of Australia, etc.

17. Your school will open a bank account for you in China and your money will be put straight into that each month. They have quite an advanced banking system, but you do need someone with good Chinese to go with you. Some schools may pay you cash each month.

18. If you want to change Australian, New Zealand, American dollars etc, there are many banks now that can exchange the currency. You must take your passport with you.

8. 将国内的账户和账单交给某个你信任的人保管，并记下其电话号码、传真号码、分行经理的名字、手机号以及客服号码。将这些信息带至国外。

9. 打国内紧急电话时接通的是总部而不是当地分行，而总部通常不知道你在分行的情况。

10. 如果是打电话取消银行卡，须再三与银行工作人员确认个人信息。澳大利亚银行曾两次销错了我的卡，害得我无法取钱。

11. 带些人民币回国应急。需要使用人民币的情况多得令你惊讶。

12. 安装了Skype软件，可以给没有Skype的座机和手机通话，包括银行在内。利用Skype打电话费用最便宜。无论对方是否装有Skype，只要购买了充值卡即可使用。

13. 有时银行会要求你留下电话号码，承诺会给你回电话。一旦对方挂断电话，就可能是意识到自己无权打国际长途，因此不可能回电。

14. 因为保密限制，银行绝对不会将你的个人账号泄漏给他人。

15. 在中国，国内信用卡和ATM卡应该能够使用，但仅限于中国银行的ATM机。ATM卡在中国使用相当广泛。

16. 通常情况，中国的ATM卡可在你本国使用，但须到本国国家银行的ATM机上交易，比如美国银行、英格兰银行、澳大利亚国家银行，等等。

17. 校方会替你开立一个中国账户，工资每月直接打入该账户。虽然中国的银行系统非常先进，但若要到银行办事，仍需请一个熟悉中文的人同去协助你。也有的学校按月付现金给你。

18. 如想兑换澳元、新西兰元或美元等等，现在许多银行都能办理外币兑换业务，但须出示护照。

BEING A FIRST TIME TEACHER

Peter was a little apprehensive about the teaching.

"What will we teach them?" he asked a few times. "There's a whole year to fill in, and I don't think I have enough information."

"It'll be a breeze. We both have public speaking experience. Our careers entailed staff training. Our general knowledge is extensive and we're both well read. Remember too, we've got extensive resources from our TESOL training," I reassured him.

The training received through the TESOL College proved to be very useful. It soon became apparent that our life experience gave us invaluable wide general knowledge and our English was very good. The extra modules studied came with more manuals, so we had enough material to keep a whole school going. It was just a matter of deciding what to teach and in what order.

On investigating our apartment we found a pile of textbooks that had been left by the previous teacher for us to use in the coming year.

"Oh, this is great!" Peter said heaving a huge sigh of relief. "This is excellent material. There are textbooks on writing, reading, and several books on oral teaching. Now I've got some concrete lessons to work from I feel so much better."

During the next couple of days at the University, we had several meetings with Professor Gao, who was in charge of the Foreign Teachers Department. He and Paul were our main contact people, and whenever we needed a translator Paul would go with us. Professor Gao gave us carte blanche with our teaching. We could use the textbooks

初为人师

彼得对当老师一事还是有点儿忐忑的。

他问了我好几次:"我们要教学生什么呢? 一整年呢,恐怕我没有那么多东西可教呢?"

我安慰他:"没啥大不了的。咱俩都有上台演讲的经验,在以前的工作中常给员工上培训课,而且我们的知识面比较广,又读了不少书。再说,不是还有很多 TESOL 课程的材料吗,想起来了吗?"

事实证明,TESOL 培训对我们的教学大有帮助。显然,丰富的生活经历赋予了我俩极有价值的、宽广的通用知识,加之我俩的英语字正腔圆;另外我们还学习了一些课程,每门课程又提供了不少材料,因此教一学年课程的材料是绰绰有余的。应该考虑的是选哪些材料作为授课内容,顺序如何安排。

我们检查新住所的时候,发现前一个老师留下了一大堆教材,这些教材我们用得着。

"噢,太棒了!"彼得如释重负地叹了口气,"有写作、阅读教材,还有口语教材。知道具体要教些什么,现在我感觉好多了。"

到大学后的几天里,我们和外语系的负责人高教授见了几次面,我们主要是与他和保罗联系,只要我们需要翻译,保罗就会陪在我们身边。高教授将教学一事全权

but also had the freedom to write our own lesson plans.

"The main thing is that you give them lots of speaking practice," Professor Gau said. "Our students don't get enough practice in the classroom and having you here as foreign experts will give them a great boost."

We asked Professor Gao about exams. "Yes, you must give them exams and grade them," he told us. "But you can compile your own exam papers and give us the grades. That will be very satisfactory."

It all sounded pretty fair. In fact, we decided to do ongoing assessments during the year, and a final speaking test, which took away the "big final exam" feeling for the students.

We both allowed plenty of time for lesson preparation, making sure there was sufficient material and that we were thoroughly conversant with it. I believe that is still the most fundamental part of teaching.

One of the best aspects of lesson preparation was the fact that we both took eight different classes a week, each class twice, making up our sixteen teaching periods. But the same lesson was repeated in eight classes meaning we only had to prepare two lessons a week.

My classes were oral classes with sophomores, (second year students), except for one writing class and one freshman class. Peter's classes were all freshmen oral classes, except for two sophomore classes where he taught writing. This gave us a good variety. I found the freshmen harder to work with than the sophomores. The second year students had a better command of English.

A couple of times the lessons just went nowhere. They were like flat, lifeless lumps of gunk on the floor and no matter how hard I tried to resurrect them, they just didn't work. I gave up and did something different. Not every subject was riveting.

One of the main problems in China was that they had an excellent understanding of English grammar, but the students had very little speaking practice. So the freshmen had a good theoretical knowledge of English but their vocabulary was limited, or their accents were so heavy it was hard to understand them.

They were also terminally shy. To start with, the freshmen would rather die than speak and get it wrong. So they started out being a very quiet class. In my freshmen

交给我们自己安排。我们可以根据教材上课，也可以自己制订授课计划。

"关键是要给学生提供大量的口语练习，"高教授说，"我们的学生在课堂上口语练习量不够多，但你们这些外国专家来了，他们肯定会有很大的进步。"

我们又问了高教授关于考试的要求。他回答说："没错，考试和评分是必须的，不过你们可以自己出卷，把成绩提交给我们就行了。"

言之有理。其实我们决定采取持续性评价标准，结合期末口语测试成绩，综合评价学生的学习情况，这样期末考试就不会让学生们"如临大敌"了。

我俩都花了很多时间备课，确保材料充分，能让我们应对自如。如今我依然认为，备课是教学最基本的环节之一。

我们一周要上8个不同的班级，每个班两次课，共16节课。但是每次备的课程可在八个班级重复使用，因此一周只要准备两次课就行了。所以把课备好，便可高枕无忧，何乐不为？

我主要是给二年级学生上口语课，外加一个班级的写作课和一个一年级班级的口语课。彼得主要是给一年级学生上口语课，另外给两个二年级班级上写作课。这样的安排能让我们接触到不同的学生。我发现一年级学生比二年级学生更难教，因为二年级学生的英语程度更好些。

记得有两三次课我都快上不下去了。学生们死气沉沉的，如同粘在地板上的牛皮糖，我费了九牛二虎之力想清除它，结果都无功而返。我只好作罢，改用别的形式。毕竟，不是每个话题都是有趣的。

中国学生学习英语存在一个大问题：他们精通英语语法，但锻炼口语能力的机会却少之又少。所以，一年级学生懂得不少理论上的东西，但因为词汇量有限，或口音很重，说出的英语我们往往听不大懂。

还有，他们非常害羞。刚开始，要新生开口说英语、当众犯错，简直就像要他们的命，所以课堂上一开始总是静悄悄的。我第一天给新生上课时，注意到了一个躲在教室最后排的女孩，她低着脑袋，长发遮住大半边脸，不敢看我，不敢发言，如同

class, on the first day, I noticed this shy girl hidden away in the back, long hair hiding her bowed face, no eye contact, no speaking, looking for all the world like a little frightened sparrow.

At the end of the term I gave her an award for being the most improved student. She stood up the front of the class, shoulders back, head high, smiling as she gave a well prepared confident speech. These were the times Peter and I sat in our apartment completely overcome with the beneficial effect our teaching was having. We could see our work bearing fruit and it was a wonderful feeling.

I must digress here, and tell you a little story. One lunchtime we were in in the canteen with about 500 students all eating and talking and dexterously chop-sticking their rice at once. The noise was deafening.

"She's over there," I said to Peter.

"Who?"

"The girl that gave such a good speech."

"Which one?"

"Over there," I pointed. "Polly. She's the one that I gave the award for being the most improved."

Peter looked at me dumbstruck.

"Over there, Polly," I yelled in his ear. "The girl in my freshman class who I gave the award for most improved!"

"Most improved?" he repeated. Then he burst out laughing. "I thought you were trying to tell me she was the one who smoked and poohed."

Anyway back to the teaching. The students on the whole led a very cocooned existence. They saw little television, read very few newspapers, and those who had computers in their dormitories played games rather than read the world news. One of our aims was to expand their horizons a little. Bird Flu was rearing its ugly head all around the world with some human deaths reported in Turkey and South East Asia. This was a hot issue close to home so seemed an effective media example to use.

Often I would give them what I called, "Research and Report' assignments. I gave each student a different topic which they then presented to the class as a two minute speech. The student would learn from the research and the class would learn a little from

一只受了惊的麻雀。

但在学期末时，她却获得了我这门课的"进步奖"。她胸有成竹地站在教室前面，演讲时昂首挺胸，面带微笑，充满自信。我和彼得在家中，每次想起自己的努力带给学生的好处时，心里都美滋滋的。看见平日的辛勤付出终于结出累累硕果，自然喜不自胜。

容我跑题一下，告诉你们一个小插曲。一天中午，我和彼得在食堂用餐。食堂里大约有500多个学生，全都在拨动筷子，边吃饭边聊天，嘈杂得很。

"她在那里。"我告诉彼得。

"谁？"

"就是那个演讲很棒的女孩呀。"

"哪一个？"

"在那儿，波丽，我把进步奖给了她。"我用手指了指。

彼得愣愣地看着我。

我凑近他的耳朵大声说："在那儿，波丽。就是那个拿走进步奖的新生。"

"进步奖？"彼得重复了一遍，接着哈哈大笑起来，"我还以为你说的是那个会抽烟的小懒虫呢。"

现在，我们还是重新回到教学这个话题吧。这里的学生总体视野偏窄。他们几乎不看电视、不读报纸，有电脑的学生宁愿在宿舍玩游戏也不关注国际新闻。因此，我们的一大目标就是要拓宽一点儿他们的知识面。当时，世界各地爆发禽流感，在土耳其和东南亚已有几起禽流感致死案报道。这是个热门话题，关注度极高，拿来作教学素材，效果想来不错。

我经常给学生布置"调查报告"作业。我给每个学生不同话题，要求他们完成两分钟的口头陈述报告。学生可以从调查中收获知识，同班同学又可以从他们的报告中有所收获。我们涉及的领域有人文、地理、各国的领导人物、国际新闻如艾滋病，以及一些一般话题。在西方国家，20多岁的年轻人对这些话题大都略知一二，但中国

listening. We covered people, places, world leaders, world news AIDS, and other general topics the average twenty year old would know about in the West, but Chinese students never learned about.

Once we'd gained their confidence the students blossomed. Peter would come home after a morning's teaching all fired up. We were both enjoying everything about living and teaching in China. He was building up a wonderful rapport with his students, and delighting in their progress.

Based on the textbook subjects, we prepared many lesson plans using games, word lists, hangman, and translation exercises that they loved. We also used charades and songs along with all sorts of stuff to get them to improve their speaking. The Dean and Professor Gao sat in on our classes after a couple of weeks.

"The students love your classes! We're very happy with your teaching," they told us. "You'll have no interference from us. Just keep up the good work."

We were thrilled with the feedback and never looked back.

I could write a book just on the teaching, but if we can do it, anyone can. You should give it a go. It could be a real turning point in your life. The only piece of advice I would give is this; if you are a very self-sufficient person, consider going alone. If not, go with someone else. If I'd come on my own, I doubt that I would have survived the whole year. Even with normal, sane, Deneice, (an American teacher who also taught there) I don't think I would have lasted the first year, but after than it was easy. If you are a really gregarious person make sure you'll have company at your school. The TESOL College that you graduate from can often arrange schools for you to go to as a group. China is so very different, communication home can sometimes be difficult and taking the Chinese language problems into account as well, it can be a very isolating experience. So do it, but maybe do it with a friend.

One of the funniest aspects of our students in the first weeks was giving them English names. These students were English majors, they would use their English after graduation, and many have since gone into business or joined international trading companies. Many of them had suitable English names, but some were just not acceptable in a business setting.

In our eight different classes, we saw close to 240 different students each week.

学生却似乎闻所未闻。

一旦我们帮助学生们找到了自信，他们的表现自然个个出彩。彼得常常上完一早上的课，回到家里，满心欢喜。我俩都非常喜欢在这里生活和教书。彼得已经跟学生们打成了一片，他们的进步总让他心花怒放。

根据课本的话题，我们写了很多教案，包括深受学生喜爱的游戏环节、生词讲解、猜词活动和翻译练习。我们还会教唱英文歌曲，玩"看手势猜字"游戏等等，通过各种形式提高他们的口语能力。过了几周，系主任和高教授过来听课。

"学生们都很喜欢你们的课，你俩的教学，我们十分满意。我们不会干涉你们的，请再接再厉吧。"他们说。

听了他俩的反馈，我俩受宠若惊，从此不敢稍事懈怠。

单单谈教学我就可以写一本书了。不过我们能写，别人也就能写。你应该放手试试，说不定这会是你人生的一个真正转折点呢。我只有这么一条建议：如果你很独立，可以考虑单飞；但如果不够独立，就得结伴而行。我要是独自一人来华，恐怕这一年我呆不下来。即使有理智而健康的戴妮丝作伴（与我在同一所大学教书的美国老师），恐怕我还是挨不过这头一年，不过之后的日子就从容多了。如果你是个爱热闹的人，务必确保学校里还有其他外教。培训你的 TESOL 大学，经常能够安排几个老师一起到一所学校教书。中国真的是个很不一样的国家，就是中国人跟中国人交流，有时都困难重重。不懂中文，你会非常孤单寂寞。所以，中国可以去，但最好结伴同行。

第一周上课最有趣的事儿就是给学生取英文名字。他们是英语专业学生，毕业后经常要使用英语，许多学生会去经商或到大贸易公司上班。不少学生已经有了合适的名字，但有些名字是不适合商务活动的。

我们要给八个班级授课，一周要见到将近 240 名学生，刚开始，根本分不清谁是谁。在我们眼里，所有学生都是一个模样。更糟糕的是，在每个班级都有学生名字相同，因此每个班级都有女生名叫荷芙、莉莉、丝凯和曼蒂什么的。她们不仅长相

At first it was impossible to tell them apart. To us, they all looked just the same. To make matters worse, every class would have students with the same English name. So in several classes there were girls named Hope, Lily, Skye, Mandy etc. So not only did they look the same, but their names were the same. Getting to know the students individually became quite a challenge.

In some cases their names had been given them by Chinese teachers in the past, and the students were reluctant to change them. But they'd been given words as names rather than personal names, for example, there were students called Orange, Duck, Stone, Chair, Rabbit, Hello and Crazy.

You can see why these would not be suitable to use in a business setting. One student, the best in the school, who was always used to Emcee school concerts was called Seacow. He was a lovely young man, clever and well spoken. He had researched the name Seacow at some length and refused to change it. He thought they were beautiful animals and it was going to be his name. In the end a compromise was reached, and he chose the name Clark as in Clark Kent for his business name, but kept Seacow among his friends. We found it impossible to learn their Chinese names, so we only allowed English names in the classroom.

相同，而且名字也相同。要想分清他们，实在是难上加难啊。

有些学生的名字是以前的中国老师给取的，他们不愿意改名。但其中一些真的不像人名，比如橘子、小鸭、石头、椅子、小兔、你好甚至狂人，好生古怪。

这下你知道为什么有些名字不适合商务活动了吧。我有一个学生，他是全校最优秀的学生，经常担任学校晚会主持人，却取了英文名字叫"海牛"。这个小伙子聪明活泼，能说会道。他查了一些关于"海牛"的资料，一直不肯更名。他认为海牛很漂亮，以此为名挺好的。最后，他总算妥协了，改叫超人在地球上使用的名字"克拉克"，工作时用这个名字，在朋友圈中仍叫海牛。我们发现，我们没办法记住学生们的中文名字，所以课堂上只允许使用英文名。

THE CHINESE LANGUAGE

Over time, we did get to know some of them by their Chinese names because slowly but surely we picked up some of the language. However, there is no fudging the fact that Chinese is a difficult language to learn. The characters have no similarity to English. The sounds do not match the phonetic look of the words. The tones can be exasperating, and not only do they speak the language they also speak their punctuation.

Even if you can't speak a word of Chinese when you arrive, after a while you will be able to shop, use buses and taxis and make yourself understood in Chinese. However, some never get past "hello" and "thankyou" and manage very well.

There are many ways of getting around this problem. You could take lessons before you leave home, but if you do this make sure you get lessons from an authentic Mandarin speaker so you learn the tones and pronunciation correctly, otherwise it will be a waste of time and money.

Many schools offer basic lessons once you arrive. Quite a few "Chinese Language" Schools or universities run classes for foreigners. Students will be willing to teach you, but often the students don't know how to teach the language, and you need someone who can answer you every time you ask "why is it like this?" Also, students will want to use English as much as they can to practice their English.

It takes quite some time to realise that with the Chinese language each character is similar to a syllable. Some words are made up of several characters and each character can be made into a huge variety of words. But it's the same in English. Take the syllable

感悟中文

过了一段时间，我们的确记住了一些学生的中文名字，因为我们慢慢学会了几个中文字词。但是，说中文难学绝对不假。汉字跟英语没有丝毫相同之处。发音和字形没有一点儿联系，而且声调极其不好掌握，既指读音，还指调号。

不过，即使你刚来中国时一点中文都不懂，用不了多久，你也能上街购物、乘车打的，说点儿中文了。虽然，有些老外只会说"你好"和"谢谢"，但他们一样生活得好好的。

克服语言问题，有许多良方。可以在出国之前上中文培训课，不过上课之前务必确认，老师讲的是纯正的普通话，这样你学到的才是正确的发音和语调，否则就是浪费时间和金钱。

一到中国你就会发现，许多学校都开了汉语入门课程。相当多的"汉语"学校或大学开设了课程，教外国人学汉语。学生们也乐意教你，只是他们不大会教，你需要一个人，时时回答你"为什么会这样？"再说，学生们都想尽可能多地说英语，练习自己的口语能力。

过了一段时间我才恍然大悟，原来一个汉字就像英语中的一个音节。有些词语是由几个汉字构成，而每个汉字都能组成若干个不同词语。不过，英语也是这样。就拿"able"这个音节为例吧。它可以单独做一个单词，又可以是其他单词的一部分，比如enable（能够的），disable（使失去能力），understandable（可理解的）和 manageable（易

"able"…a stand-alone word, but also part of the word enable, or disable, understandable, or manageable, all these words having different meanings. Chinese is a pictorial language and you will start to see some patterns which help in learning.

If you are keen, learn a few basics before you go if you can, then arrange lessons once you get there. It's quite possible to live your whole time there with little Chinese. But you'll be amazed at how much you'll pick up without really trying.

处理的），这些词的意思各不相同。汉语是象形文字，你会从中看出一些图形，这些图形对你的学习大有帮助。

　　要是你对学习中文有热情，那么尽可能在出国前学点汉语入门知识，到中国后再上汉语课。不懂汉语在中国生活不成问题，不过，即使没去上正儿八经的汉语课，平时东鳞西爪地学，也能掌握不少，这一点会让你喜出望外吧。

ARE THERE TABOO SUBJECTS TEACHERS DON'T TALK ABOUT IN THE CLASSROOM?

Well, yes and no. It is usually the policy of an ESL teacher not to talk about religion and politics in the classroom and to be selective in whom else you chat to about these subjects privately.

When you sign a contract with a school it will probably have a clause to the effect that you will not spread religion or do anything that could be construed as being against the government. Anytime we visit another country we don't want to be seen as causing political problems, not only in China.

Many contentious subjects are talked about freely amongst the Chinese. They are becoming more and more informed about what is happening in the world. Nevertheless as foreign guests on their soil, we need to act sensibly. It may be that you would talk about these things privately, but not in a public situation like a classroom, where it might be seen as a way to influence students politically.

Some teachers have had instances of adult students giving opinions that made the teachers hair stand on end! When that happens just say, "These are not things we talk about in the classroom, our lessons are not on these topics", and steer the conversation away.

Often students, and especially adult students will ask quite pointed questions about politics, our views, how things are done in the West etc. You can't avoid these subjects, they are part of our life and Chinese people are often very inquisitive about how we live

ARE THERE TABOO SUBJECTS TEACHERS DON'T TALK ABOUT IN THE CLASSROOM?
有教师不能在课堂上谈及的禁忌话题吗？

有教师不能在课堂上谈及的禁忌话题吗？

关于这个问题，可以说有，也可以说没有。我们一般遵循这条原则：外教在课堂上不谈论宗教和政治，即使是私下谈论，也要谨慎择人。

你和学校签订合同时，合同上大都会写：禁止传教，或禁止任何反动言论。其实，我们到任何一个国家，都不想惹上什么政治问题，到中国也不例外。

许多颇具争议的话题中国人是可以自由争论的。对世界上发生的事情他们也越来越了解了。但是我们外教作为人家的客人，应该明智行事。你可以在私底下谈论这些话题，但是在公众场合，比如课堂上，还是少说为妙，因为可能会有人认为，你的言语会影响学生的政治觉悟。

有的老师可能会遇到这种情形：有的大学生会说出一些匪夷所思的观点！若是你遇上了，只要说："这些东西我们不方便在课堂上讨论，课上我们不讨论这些。"将话题引开便是了。

学生们，尤其是大学生们，会提一些政治方面的尖锐问题，比如我们怎么看，西方国家会怎么做等等。你不好避而不答，因为这些话题是我们生活的一部分，而中国人又很好奇，总想知道我们的生活情况和我们的生活与他们的有什么不同之处。不过这跟老师主动提及又不一样。如果有人问起你对宗教、政治等话题的看法时，一般回答是："我们本来不谈这个，但我想我可以……"然后泛泛说上两句敷衍话便可以

our lives and how our lives are different. This is not the same as teachers bringing up such subjects. If you are asked about religion/politics/whatever, a general response is, "I am not here to talk to you about religion/politics/whatever, but I guess I could say…" and then go on to talk to them about those subjects in a general way.

Some of the school text books talk about Bible stories, and Christmas and Easter are becoming widely celebrated. And when it's appropriate general discussions on democracy are very open, after all most of the world works on that basis.

One last thought on "taboo" subjects. Have you been into an airport lately? Have you seen the signs by the check-in desks? If you mention the word "bomb", boy, you are in trouble. Even in jest, we are told we should not use any words that may suggest a bomb or similar. Every country has its own "taboos".

And one thing is certain, once you have lived there for a while, you get to know that whether you like their methods or not, the government is doing its best to keep its people fed and employed, and that's more than some countries are doing these days.

ARE THERE TABOO SUBJECTS TEACHERS DON'T TALK ABOUT IN THE CLASSROOM?
有教师不能在课堂上谈及的禁忌话题吗?

抽身了。

有些教材中选用了圣经故事,过圣诞节和复活节的人也很多。在恰当的场合下谈论民主这个话题,大家还是可以各持己见的,毕竟民主是世界上大部分国家政治体系的根基。

最后再说说"禁忌"这个话题。你最近去过机场没有? 有没有看见登记处上的标识? 如果你说了"轰炸"这个词儿,你就惹上大麻烦了。曾有人告诉过我们,就是开玩笑也别说类似"轰炸"这样的词儿。的确,每个国家都有各自的"禁忌"。

只要在中国生活了一段时间,就会发现,不管你喜不喜欢中国政府的举措,他们都一直在寻找途径,让百姓衣食无忧,有工作可做;况且,与其他一些国家相比,他们这些年的努力更有成效,这一点毋庸置疑。

BOWELS

All my family knows about my bowels, so you might as well too. When I was fourteen years old I was seriously ill with Peritonitis. The doctors played chess with my insides, and had a great time chopping bits out and sewing them up again. After five weeks in hospital and nearly turning up my toes, I left hospital very thin and still very sick. I came right, but one of the aftermaths, was my "tummy".

I don't think I ended up with irritable bowel syndrome; it just played up from time to time. It was on these occasions that I learned the location of every public toilet in every town I have ever lived. Generally it was no big deal as I'd get a bit of warning. I also call it my shopping tummy, as most of my friends know, show me a shop then find me a toilet. It's just one of those minor irritations I have to live with.

When we considered going to China, I gave serious thought to my bowels. For me this was a serious matter because my hip and knee joints weren't so supple and I didn't know how I would get on with the low Chinese toilets. I studied the photo of the university we were going to. It was a huge building, but one building only. It was new. We knew our apartment was on the sixth floor, and, importantly for me, had a Western toilet. From the photo it was easy to see that the building only had six floors.

So my mind went this way: The classrooms were on the lower floors, but all my classes wouldn't be on level one, so, often I would be on other levels. There may be a bit of a distance to walk sometimes, but all was under one roof and so the weather wouldn't be a problem. If I needed a loo in a hurry, I could get home, if necessary, during a class

如厕

我的肠胃问题在我家中已经是个公开的秘密，所以告诉你们也无妨。14岁那年，我得了腹膜炎，大病了一场。医生把我的内脏彻底检查了一遍，又费了不少工夫，切除了一点东西，再把伤口缝好。我在医院躺了整整五个星期，差一点儿就作别了人世，出院时瘦得只剩皮包骨，仍然病歪歪的。后来腹膜炎是好了，却落下了爱拉肚子的毛病。

我觉得自己得的不是过敏性结肠炎，只是肠胃爱闹毛病罢了。就因为这个老毛病，我对自己居住过的所有地方的所有公厕，全都了如指掌。一般情况，因为身体会提前预警，所以不会给我造成多大麻烦。我还戏称自己的肚子为"商场肚"呢。朋友们大都知道，遇到尴尬之时，只要带我进商场找间厕所，问题就搞定了。我必须对付的只是些过敏性小问题罢了。

打算去中国的时候，我认真考虑过了在华如厕的问题。对我而言，这是个大事儿，因为我的臀部和膝关节不大好使，对自己是否能够使用中国卫生间里的蹲式便池，心中没谱。我仔细打量过那张我们即将任教的大学图片。图片上的楼房十分高大，但只是一幢楼。大楼很新。我们知道自己的公寓在六楼，里面有西式卫生间，这一点对我十分重要。图片上的大楼刚好只有六楼。

于是我一厢情愿地这么认为：教室都在低楼层，但我的班级不会在一楼，所以一

or break. It seemed to me to be quite workable. I asked Paul about this during one of our emails, but looking back later, I understood why he forgot to answer that question.

That was before we realized that we were not at the round building at all. No, we were at the old campus, which was nothing like the new one. When we arrived I asked Paul where the classrooms were, and he just said. "Oh, just over there," and pointed to a largish building. I found out a few days later that "just over there" was a girls dormitory. The classrooms were much further away. How far away? Well, 300 steps far away, plus some walking.

Going down to the classrooms was not such a hassle. We could leave our apartment and be in the classroom in five minutes without running. There were 104 steps from our front door to the ground, then you walked a little bit, then you went down about 100 more steps, then you walked along a road for about fifty meters then you went down another eighty or so steps, then depending which floor your classroom was on, you might climb one, two, three or four flights of stairs up to the classroom. Nothing to it!

But, the snag was, getting back again in a hurry. You see, there were no Western toilets anywhere else on the campus except in the apartments used by the foreign teachers. And with the change in diet, my insides were in a bit of turmoil. There were of course toilets in the blocks of classrooms, little Asian loos, squatty potties with no privacy at all, several in a room, and no hot water to wash your hands, no soap and no toilet paper, not to mention the pong, the used toilet tissues piled up in the corners and used sanitary pads scattered all around! (Over there you get used to taking your own packs of tissues everywhere. They make the cutest convenient pocket sized packs). The toilets also weren't clean. I refused to use them except in cases of dire emergency, of which there were a couple.

This then raised the problem. What could I do when the need arose urgently? Well what would you do? Same as me. Rush up 300 steps, interspersed with three short walks, to get to the toilet. With practice I could do this in ten minutes, but oh boy! It was no fun. Sometimes I could manage it in the twenty minute break between classes, sometimes I had to rush during the ten minute break between periods, and sometimes I'd just have to leave the class, telling them I'd forgotten something at home and head for the hills. I did have the help of dear Deneice who lived only one major flight of steps up, one long walk

般情况下我都是在其他楼层。虽然走路往返有点儿距离，好在住宿、教学都在同一座楼里，而且不用考虑天气问题。要是我在课上或课间突然着急上厕所，必要之时可以回家解决。我自以为这是个可行的好办法。之前，我在一封邮件里向保罗打听过这件事儿，不过回想起来，我才明白他为什么会忘了给我答复。

我们并不知道，照片上的圆形大楼并非我们的授课地点。没错，我们是在旧校区，而旧校区的情况与新校区有云泥之别。刚到龙岩时，我问保罗我们在哪里上课，他只说了句："噢，就在那边。"然后指了指一幢大楼。几天后我才发现，"就在那边"的是一栋女生宿舍。教学楼远着呢。究竟多远？ 这么说吧，300级台阶加一段平路。

去教室上课倒难不着我。出家门到班级从容步行五分钟就能到达。从我家前门下到地面总共104个台阶，再走一小段路，接着再下一百来个台阶，然后再走五十米左右的路程，再下80多个台阶，然后就要看你的教室在几楼了，是爬一层、二层、三层还是四层楼，看你的造化了。没事儿，小事一桩！

可是，需要往家赶时麻烦就大了。因为偌大一个校园里，除了外教公寓楼之外，再也找不到一间西式厕所。由于水土不服，我的肚子正捣腾得厉害。教学楼自然是有厕所的，但都是亚式便池，又小又矮，没遮没挡，没热水洗手，没肥皂、没手纸，臭气熏天，用过的纸张堆满角落，卫生棉到处都是！（到了中国，你会习惯去哪儿都随身携带纸巾的。这里有便携式的小包装，不占地儿。）厕所也不干净，除非紧急状况，否则我是坚决不上学校的厕所，可我还真遇到了两三次极其狼狈的时候。

后来，我开始认真考虑这个问题了。要是突然急着要上厕所，我该如何是好？换了你，你会怎么办？ 跟我一样。跑300级台阶和三小段路，直奔家里的卫生间。通过多次训练，我可以在10分钟内解决问题。老天，这可不是什么好玩的事儿！ 有时，我可以利用大课间的20分钟，但遇到10分钟的课间，我就得赶紧了；有时在课上突然内急，我只能告诉学生我把东西忘在家里了，然后朝山上狂奔。我的确得到亲爱的戴妮丝的鼎力相助，她住的地方只要爬完最长的台阶，走一长段路，再上三层楼就行了。万般无奈之下，我可以向她拿钥匙，冲往她家。但上趟厕所如此辛苦，我

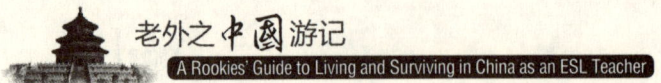

and three more flights of stairs. I could get her key and rush to her place when necessary. But it wasn't how I expected. It was not what the photo showed.

This was also a concern when I went shopping. We found one excellent restaurant with lovely clean Western toilets, but that was the only one. Even McDonalds and KFC didn't have them! I got used to using the low ones, but it was an inconvenient way of attending to this necessity of life.

> Tip: Western toilets are much more widespread now. If your hip and knee joints work well you won't have a problem using the low Chinese style toilets. If you have stiffer knee or hip joints, check this out when talking to your school.

始料未及，因为我们看到的学校图片压根不是这副尊容。

  如厕也成了我上街购物的一大难题。我们找到了一家极好的西餐厅，里面有既干净又漂亮的西式卫生间，但仅此一家。就连麦当劳和肯德基都没有！我慢慢适应了蹲式厕所，但面对人生之必需，毕竟还是很不方便。

  温馨贴士：如今，西式厕所越来越普遍了。要是你的臀部和膝关节没有问题，中式的矮便池就不会给你造成任何困难。但如果你的膝盖和髋关节不够灵活，就得向校方问明情况，再做打算。

THE REALITY

We spent ten hours in the air, two hours at Singapore airport and landed in Xiamen, Fujian Province on the 19th August 2005. Our adventure had started! After our few days in Xiamen, Paul came from Longyan to pick us up and take us to our new home for the next year.

Most schools have their own buses, minivans and drivers. Longyan is no exception, and we were met by a party of three.

Paul was a young man. It's so hard to tell their age as all Chinese look like they are about sixteen years old, but he was a teacher so obviously at least in his twenties. We found out later he was thirty-two years old. The men loaded all our baggage into the mini bus, and Peter and I squeezed in the back, our legs concertinaed up like a fold away table.

"We'll stop for lunch now," announced Paul.

"But we've only just started," Peter said. "We haven't left Xiamen yet!"

"It's lunch time now, time to eat, its twelve o'clock. Our trip will take more than two hours," he explained.

We soon found out that nothing interfered with eating. Meal times are strictly adhered to, and postponing meals is a rare occurrence.

This was our first foray into a real Chinese restaurant. Walking into the shop there was a long curved counter on the right filled with a huge variety of food to choose from. On the left was seating for about sixty people at little tables or booths. Customers made

遭遇现实

我俩飞了10个小时抵达新加坡机场,在机场呆了两小时,于2006年8月19日抵达福建省的厦门。冒险生涯真的开始了! 我们在厦门小住了几日之后,保罗从龙岩到厦门接我们去新家,我们要在那里住上一年。

多数学校都有自己的校车、小巴士和司机,龙岩学校也不例外,前来迎接我们的是一行三人。

保罗很年轻。我们不懂得如何分辨中国人的年龄,因为他们全都长得像16岁左右的小年轻,但保罗是老师,至少应该20多岁了吧。后来我们才知道,人家已经32岁了。三个男子把我们的行李全部搬进小车,我和彼得挤在后排,像折叠的桌子那样蜷着双腿。

"现在我们停车去吃午饭。"保罗招呼道。

"我们才刚上车不久呢,连厦门都没离开!"彼得不解地说。

"这会儿已经是午饭时间了,该吃饭了,都12点了。我们这一路上要开两个多小时呢。"他解释说。

没过多久我们就知道了,在中国吃饭是头等大事,任何事情都不得干扰。一日三餐的时间须严格遵守,推迟吃饭时间的情况鲜少发生。

这是我俩平生第一次上真正的中餐馆吃饭。一进饭店,右侧是一溜弧形长柜台,

their choices and little plates were plonked onto trays, and small bowls of soup were added. Everyone was given a small empty glass and a waitress constantly roamed the shop filling up the glasses with very tasty red tea.

"Choose what you want," Paul said. "The school will pay for this meal. You can have anything at all."

"Well there's plenty of it, but what is it all? I don't know what half of it is. They look like mushrooms, that is rice, and maybe that's chicken, but it's full of bones. I think that might be pork," I said to Peter pointing to a large dish. We chose what looked like pork and a large bowl of rice to share.

"Some of this looks like it should go straight into the bin, not via our digestive tracts," Peter muttered under his breath.

Paul saw our dishes and was horrified. "Is that all you are going to eat?" He asked. "That's not much."

"It's plenty for us thanks," we replied. Paul shook his head in disbelief and went to a nearby table to sit with the other two.

The three Chinese lads ate like horses. The table was full of bowls that they shared amongst themselves.

This was our first meal with real live Chinese people from this area. They ate, gobbled, slurped, put the bowls up to their mouths and shovelled, and then all the odd bits, bones and skin etc. were spat onto the table. By the time they had finished they were full, the table was a mess and little piles of rejects resided all over the table.

"Wow," I whispered to Peter. "That's different." We shared some looks that said, "I wonder if that is normal?" It didn't take long to realize that it was. Chinese eating is not to be confused with fine dining.

Getting back into the van, the driver got us settled and we started off for Longyan. It was boiling hot as we crossed a long high bridge and headed inland. Everywhere there was a misty look in the air. We started getting higher and higher, into remote mountainous territory, through tunnels, one after the other, climbing higher, getting hotter and hotter, and it was still misty. We thought we'd never see civilization again. After about 90 minutes we made a toilet stop. Peter went in, and came out shaking his head at me.

"Better hold on," he said to me, "not a pleasant sight." I'd read about the Asian

摆放着各种菜品供人挑选。左侧的小桌子或小摊位边坐了六十来个客人。客人点完菜后，一碟碟小菜就被放进了托盘，又加了几小碗汤。每个人都给了一个空玻璃杯，一个女服务员来回走动给空杯倒一种很可口的红茶。

"想吃什么就选什么，饭钱由学校付，吃什么都行。"保罗说。

"哇，真多呀。这些是什么东西？我连一半儿都认识不到。那个有点儿像蘑菇，这个是米饭，也许那是鸡肉，可是都是骨头。我想这个可能是猪肉。"我指着一大盘菜对彼得说。我俩选了那盘貌似猪肉的菜和一大碗米饭，分着吃。

"有些东西好像应该直接当垃圾扔了，干嘛要多此一举通过我们的食道。"彼得小声嘟囔道。

保罗看到我们的菜，大吃一惊："你们就吃这个？这怎么够呢？"

我俩回答："够了，谢谢。"保罗难以置信地摇了摇头，走到隔壁桌跟其他两人一起坐。

这三个中国小伙子简直像马一样能吃。桌上摆满了一碟一碟的菜，他们不分彼此一块儿享用。

我们第一次跟真正的本地中国人一起吃饭。只见他们把碗端到嘴边，扒拉一大口饭，再夹起一把菜塞进嘴里，大口嚼着，吃得啧啧作响，然后将一些奇怪的东西，比如骨头呀、肉皮呀，吐到桌上。等他们吃饱时，桌子上已经一片狼藉，到处都是一小堆一小堆不能吃的东西。

我小声对彼得说："哇，大不一样呢。"我俩面面相觑。我又说："不知道这是不是普遍现象？"不用多久我就知道了答案，是普遍现象。中国人的就餐模样绝对称不上文雅二字。

回到小车里，司机等我们各就各位后，驱车直奔龙岩而去。这天，天气炎热异常，小车穿过一条长长的高架桥，朝内陆驶去。空中到处都是灰蒙蒙的。车子越爬越高，进入偏远的山区，穿过一个又一个隧道，地势越来越高，天气也越来越热，只是天空依旧灰蒙蒙的。我们以为再也看不到人类文明的痕迹了。汽车大约行驶了一个

toilets, but was not prepared for there being no Western loos around at all. My head was pounding from being cramped up in the back of this boiling hot minivan.

We arrived at Longyan, a small city of about 350,000 people. All the buildings were high rise. Driving through the university gates and up a hill we looked in anticipation for the round university in the picture they sent us.

"Where is the round building?" Peter asked suspiciously. "This doesn't look like the photo."

"Oh," said Paul with an innocent look on his face. "I'm sure I told you that there were two campuses? Yes I'm sure I did. I'm sure I told you that the English department was still in the old campus."

"No you didn't." Peter said, "You sent us pictures of a round building, that's where we have come to teach."

"Oh, yes of course, that's the new campus. The English department will be moving into the new campus soon," he said.

Liar, liar, your pants will catch fire. We did visit the nice new round building, but never got to teach there.

The van pulled up outside a tall largish building.

"You have one of the best apartments on the whole campus," Paul announced as everyone unfolded themselves from the van outside a rather old building.

"Not by the look of this place," we thought.

Paul called some students who hauled our luggage up six flights of stairs. They got an old rag mop, cleaned the floors and brought us some water.

"Welcome to Longyan University. We hope you enjoy your stay with us."

Peter and I sat on the bed in horror.

"We don't have to stay. Haven't signed anything yet," I whispered to Peter.

He hesitated. "We're here for an adventure. It's only a year. We'll be fine," he reassured me. He was right.

One of the biggest hassles we had in our new abode was with computer access. You know the saying, Romeo, Romeo, Wherefore Art Thou Romeo? Shakespeare obviously knew about our trip to China when he wrote those words. They have been misquoted right down to our day. I have found the original manuscript and it reads this way:

半小时停下,让我们去厕所方便。彼得进去了,出来的时候冲我拼命摇头。

他对我说:"最好忍忍,实在太糟了。"我在书上看过亚式卫生间的模样,但没料到里面一个西式马桶都没有。挤在滚热的小车后座,我的脑袋开始嗡嗡作响。

终于到达了龙岩,一个人口约35万人的小城市。这个地方到处都是高楼大厦。当汽车进入学院大门朝山上驶去时,我们满怀期待地寻找那栋圆形大楼。他们寄了一张图片给我们,上面是一栋圆形大楼。

"那栋圆形大楼在哪儿呢?"彼得充满疑虑地问,"这里怎么跟图片上的不大一样啊?"

保罗一脸无辜地说:"噢,我肯定告诉过你们,学校有两个校区?没错,我肯定说了。我肯定告诉过你们,英语系仍在旧校区来着。"

"噢,你没有,你给我们寄了张圆形大楼的图片,说那儿就是我们教书的地方。"彼得回应他。

"没错啊,那是我们的新校区,英语系很快就会搬过去的。"他说。

骗子,大骗子,你会遭到惩罚的!我们的确参观了漂亮的新校区,但从未在那里上过一节课。

汽车停在一幢大楼前。

"你们住的是全校最好的公寓。"保罗大声说。大家纷纷起身,走到车外的一幢相当沧桑的楼房跟前。

"看这外观,不可能吧。"我们心想。

保罗叫来几个学生帮我们把行李搬到了六楼。他们拿来一把旧拖把,拖干净地板,然后端了两杯水给我们。

"欢迎来到龙岩学院,希望你们在这儿生活愉快。"

彼得和我坐在床上,惴惴不安。

他犹豫了一下安慰我道:"我们来这儿就是为了冒险,只一年时间,没事儿的。"他的话在理。

"Internet Internet, wherefore art thou Internet?"

And the resounding reply comes back.

"Error on page, your domain could not be found, please try again later."

This was the story of our lives in China with communication problems, and became the most frustrating and difficult part of life that first year.

The computer and internet was our only inexpensive lifeline to the outside world and our family. Sometimes the internet could be down for a week at a time for no apparent reason and no one could fix it. Sometimes in tears I would haul down my suitcases and tell Peter, "Get hold of Paul now, and tell him that if it's not fixed by tea-time I'm going home today. I'm packing my bags!"

This bag-packing happened a couple of times, but the frustration was a regular thing. The internet was down as much as it was going, and often I was exasperated beyond endurance. This was especially so when I'd arranged to talk to the family or made other dates online and I couldn't keep them. After a while we told our family that this happened all the time and if they didn't hear from us for a week or so, we had probably not been murdered in our beds but the flaming internet was down again.

Using telephones there was also a lesson in futility. There was no telephone book for Longyan. Most people looked at me in complete blankness when I asked such a stupid question. They'd never heard of such a thing. Yellow pages? What are they? Telephone book? Why want one of those? Paul said you just phoned some particular directory type number and asked for the phone number you wanted. Easy if you could speak Chinese.

Trying to find information in this place was horrific. I wanted to research the possibility of getting Peter 2 some assistance with creative writing. The university could offer no extra courses so I hoped to access something local. But how do you look up the information in Chinese when you don't even know what they call it here? I tried all sorts of things on the Internet and in the end gave up.

I did find that a kind of Yellow Pages did exist. One of the teachers, who ruled the roost with an iron rod, was called "The Queen". I found out after about four months that there was one in her office and that you could buy them from the post office. But the whole thing was in Chinese so hopeless from our point of view.

We both bought cell phones so we could communicate with one another when we

入住新家后，令我俩最头疼的就是电脑无法上网。你知道那句话吧，"罗密欧，罗密欧，你到底在哪儿呀罗密欧？"莎翁写句话的时候，肯定已经知道了我们的中国之行。流传至今的台词是被别人篡改过的，我找到了最初的手稿，上面明明写的是：

"英特网，英特网，你究竟在哪儿呀英特网？"

回答我的是一声巨响。

"网页错误，找不到该网址，请重新尝试。"

这就是我们在华遭遇网络不通的情景。通信问题是我们头一年在华生活最大的烦恼。

电脑和英特网是我们与外界和家人联系唯一的比较划算的途径。有时候，无缘无故就上不了网，而且一坏就一星期，还没人修得好。有时候我会哭哭啼啼地取下行李箱，对彼得说："快联系保罗，告诉他要是到午茶时间还没修好，我们就马上走人，我已经在整理行李了！"

有几次，我已经绝望到准备打包离开的地步，小状况已成家常便饭。网络时断时续，令我忍无可忍。尤其是在我打算和家人通话，或在线安排下次联系的时间时突然掉线，而我又无法连上的时候，更是令我火冒三丈。后来，我们告诉家人，这种情况经常发生，如果他们一整个星期都没有我们的消息，不用担心我们被害于床上，这种可能性微乎其微，是网络又坏了。

打电话也是件很头疼的事儿。没有龙岩市电话号码簿。好多人一眼茫然地看着我，我怎么会问这么傻的问题。他们从未听说过这东西。黄页呢？那是什么？电话号码簿？要那东西干嘛用？保罗说，只要拨通一个问询台的号码，问问不就知道了。是很简单，前提是你要会说中文。

想在这个地方打听消息真的很困难。我想给小彼得打探点消息，帮他提高写作水平。因为学校不会再开相关课程，所以我想看看本地有没有什么机会。可是你中文大字不识一个，怎么查找信息？我在网上查过各种资料，最终只能半途而废。

不过，我的确发现一种类似黄页的东西。有一个老师，以严厉出名，人称"女

were apart, in different classes or up town etc. We soon got tired of running up six flights of steps to see if the other one was home to find the nest was empty. Somehow even texting Australia was only spasmodically successful.

Phoning overseas was a terribly complicated business using long-winded phone cards from our landline, so that was kept for emergencies.

Hence the internet and email was of massive importance to us, and often it was not working. We had so many complications that we were always nagging Paul to get the problems sorted out. He spent hours at our apartment trying to fix it, along with many "experts" he sent, the "experts" being 3rd or 4th year students who knew more than he did. Each expert said the problem was something different from the expert before, so the computer got a thorough going over but it was never rectified properly. Not only that but the memory was wiped clean, or all the favourites disappeared, or the address book vanished. I'm not kidding, this was not funny.

I need to emphasise that I am not talking internet in English here. Every program on the computer was in Chinese. So in Microsoft Word, although I could key in English, the entire drop down boxes and menus were in Chinese. Fortunately the drop down menus had the C for copy, so with a great deal of guessing I could use most basic Word features for simple documents. It was the same with all the Hotmail instructions, all logging in was done in Chinese and we had no idea what the buttons meant. We just kept clicking buttons willy-nilly till we got things opened or closed, but it was anyone's guess in the end.

By the end of the first semester, Paul had exhausted all local means of repair so got someone from town to service the computer and install English versions of everything. What a difference! We now knew what the machine was saying to us, and what we were agreeing, or disagreeing to. We were thrilled.

However our accessibility to the internet did not improve, it could be down for days on end. The most perplexing question was why did our computer not access Hotmail, Yahoo or Gmail? It could access anything else on the web, I could access Google but I could not open my normal email programs. This was just the last straw. The most thought provoking part was this, Deneice could get Hotmail and I could access my Hotmail through her computer. I was starting to get paranoid about Big Brother. Had someone

王"者，四个月后我在她的办公室看到一本黄页，邮局有卖。可是所有的内容都是用中文写的，我用不上。

我和彼得各买了一部手机，这样我俩分开的时候就可以联系对方，比如给不同班级上课或进城的时候等等。很快，我们就厌倦了爬到六楼的家里，推门一看，里面空无一人，不如打电话来的方便。不知什么缘故，就连我们给澳大利亚发短信都是时而成功时而不成功。

用长途电话卡通过家中座机打国际长途，过程相当麻烦，不到万不得已，我们不用此法。

因此，网络和电子邮件对我俩来说十分重要，可网络又常常不给力。我们整天对保罗唠叨，要他想办法解决这个问题。他在我家呆了好几小时，捣鼓我家的电脑，结果可跟他叫来的"专家"一样无功而返，他叫的那些专家都是大三或大四的学生，不过他们的电脑技术要比他本人略高一筹。每个"专家"诊断的原因都跟前一个"专家"不同，可怜的电脑，里里外外都被拆了装、装了拆，还是一直不好用。糟糕的是，里面的记忆被格式了，收藏夹里的内容没了，通讯录也不见了。我没开玩笑，情况糟透了！

必须强调，我讲的不是英语网络，因为我的电脑里装的所有程序都是中文版的，微软的 Word 软件也一样，虽然我能输入英语，但所有的下拉列表框和菜单指令都是中文。好在下拉菜单是用字母 C 表示复制，通过无数次尝试，我学会使用基本的 Word 软件，完成简单的文档。Hotmail 指南也是中文版本的，登录指令都是中文，我们压根儿不知道那些按钮有什么功能，只能胡乱瞎点，直到打开或关闭目标文档为止。完全是瞎猫碰到死老鼠而已。

等到第一学期末之时，保罗已经把当地的维修人员全用过一遍，最后从市里请来一位技师，替我们安装了英文版本的软件。好大的变化呀！现在，我们知道机器说什么话了，我们要同意什么，不同意什么。这下可把我们乐坏了。

然而，网络连接依然故障频频，有时一坏就是好几天。我俩好生纠结，为什么

pushed a button that said I could not access these programs? It was just frustrating in the extreme.

Paul blamed Longyan and the old campus. "Longyan was an old city, a long way from anywhere and the internet connections were not good," was his catchphrase. After a while we put this in the liar, liar, your pants are on fire category. To be sure, this campus (not the new round one we were promised) was 50 years old, and when constructed the WWW had not been thought of, so all of these newfangled connections were done in a New Zealand Mickey Mouse way. (Not an Aussie Mickey Mouse way, in Australia, Mickey Mouse means really good. In New Zealand it means, jiggery pokery, jerry-built, or Taranaki gate method). But there were dozens of Internet Café's with thousands of kids wasting hours on internet games, and if they were subjected to the same frustrations we were, those places would be empty. So I think Paul's explanation was a sticky plaster on a festering wound, and not much help at all.

One day our desktop computer gasped its final breath and died. We were promised a new one. Well, not absolutely brand new. Paul let slip that a recycled one from Professor Gau's office was coming our way.

We came back from our Spring Festival holiday to find a brand spanking new one all set up in our apartment. A lovely black thing, very elegant looking, nice keyboard, very swish! We were really happy little campers. They'd installed new English versions too. Oh the bliss turning on a computer and having Hotmail appear every time, and with the bonus of a fast connection.

We emailed to our hearts delight, but after a day or so, I said to Peter something was radically wrong. On questioning Paul we found out that they'd used the same old pirated discs which were full of viruses! Oh yes, of course we had virus protection, but it seemed comparable to an electronic colander which let all the viruses in, kept them in, and refused to let them out again. We had a rootkit virus, there was no way we could get rid of it, and it mangled up the whole works.

I soon realised that half the programs were installed in English but the operating system was all Chinese. Somehow I got my Chinese version of Word back again. Fair go! Peter, who was totally computer illiterate and generally went purple with apoplexy when faced with a screen, became a very adept little fixer-upper. Mind you, he had no

电脑连不上 Hotmail，Yahoo 和 Gmail？可其他网站都打得开。我能打开 Google，却打不开平常使用的邮箱。该死的网络差点儿把我气疯了。诡异的是，戴妮丝可以打开她的 Hotmail，我在戴妮丝的电脑上也能打开我的 Hotmail。最后整得我开始疑神疑鬼起来。难不成是有人按了什么键，故意不让我使用这些程序？我简直快崩溃了。

保罗却把责任推给龙岩和旧校区，总是说："龙岩这个城市很老了，去哪儿都不方便，网络连接一直不好。"后来，我们认为他在说谎，说谎的人是会遭报应的。确切说来，这个校区（不是诱惑我们前来的新校区）有 50 年历史了，当年建校的时候，没有想到还有英特网这种东西，因此连接网络的玩意儿都是像新西兰的米老鼠。（不是澳大利亚的米老鼠，在澳大利亚，米老鼠是指好东西。但在新西兰，它就是"欺骗、豆腐工程或粗制滥造"的代名词）。可是，这里有十几家网吧，几千个小孩在里面玩游戏，要是网吧里的网络也是麻烦不断，肯定早已关门大吉了。由此可见，保罗的话好比给化脓的伤口贴膏药——不顶事。

一天，我们的台式机喘完最后一口气，彻底报废了。校方答应给我们一台新电脑，当然咯，绝对不可能是崭新的。保罗不留神说出了真相：他们准备把高教授办公室里的一台旧电脑拿去修一修，再送给我们用。

寒假过后我们回家一看，一台簇新的电脑神气地住进了我家公寓。是个可爱的黑家伙，很精致，键盘也很漂亮，很高级的样子。我俩很知足。电脑还安装了新版英文软件，我们特别高兴。这回上 Hotmail 次次成功，而且链接速度很快。

我们满心欢喜地发送邮件，可是才过了一天左右，我告诉彼得，电脑好像出了大问题。我们详细问了保罗才知道。他们用的居然仍是以前那张染上病毒的盗版光盘！对，没错，我们当然有杀毒软件，但这个软件就像一把电子漏勺，病毒一旦被放进来就不会走。我们的电脑染上了内核形蠕虫病毒，清除不了，可是我们所有的文件都中了毒。

不久我便意识到了，这台电脑里只有一半软件是英文版本，操作系统全部是中文版本。不知怎的，我的 Word 软件又变成中文版本的了。没事儿，否极泰来！彼得

idea what he was doing, but he played and puttered and downloaded and deleted to his heart's content. After hours of fiddling around he got rid of the rootkit virus, much to my joy.

Finally we owned a computer that worked perfectly most of the time. Peter spent ages reading the New Zealand and Aussie newspapers every morning on the internet before classes, swotting up on the sports results and sending smart little messages to our boys about the New Zealand and Australian teams.

There was always a bit of talk of foreigner's emails being monitored. I don't know how true that was, so sometimes I didn't feel so security safe with my emails. I guess anyone with a few clues can hack into anything, and I suppose Hotmail must be an easy target if you know what you are doing. So Peter and I opened another email account with a different provider for personal stuff, and kept Hotmail for day to day contact. If they want to read our emails, let them search for them I say.

Note: I have to say that in all my subsequent schools and apartments, internet connects were usually very good. However, I did learn that it is very unwise to swap flash discs from home computers to school networks. For some reason all school networks seem to be awash with viruses. I had to clean up my computer a number of times.

Another vital reality is "saving face". We all consider our self-respect and personal honour to be a sacrosanct matter, and preserve it with vigour. That's quite right and proper. Chinese people also intensely preserve their personal honour, but somehow it seems to work differently.

Most of us don't mind getting up in front of others and making a bit of a fool of ourselves. We might be happy to speak up in front of others, get things wrong, admit it, apologise if necessary and get on with life.

For Chinese people, making a mistake in public is a serious matter. To be seen in the wrong is generally considered bad form. And even if there is no intention to make them look bad, that is often how they see it. They may not say much, usually Chinese people dislike confrontation, and they may never say we have hurt their feelings, but they have a way of putting on an inscrutable face, closing up and withdrawing.

One example is getting information. In the West if we're asked something by a customer, and don't know the answer, we said we didn't know and tried to find out. In

是个电脑盲,通常一看到显示屏就头晕脑胀,糊涂发愣,这次竟然手脚变得灵活了起来。听我说,他其实心中无数,只管东点西点,下载删除,玩得不亦乐乎,过了几个小时,居然清除了蠕虫病毒,可把我乐坏了。

终于,我们拥有了一台大多数时候运转正常的电脑。每天早上课前,彼得都要在网上呆上一段时间,看新西兰和澳大利亚报纸,查阅赛事近况,再把自己对新西兰和澳大利亚队的高见发给儿子们。

总听人说,外国人的邮件是受到监控的。我不知道此话是否属实,但有时也会觉得自己的邮件不够安全。我想不管是谁,只要得到一些线索,都能闯入他想进入的地方。我觉得,一个人真想了解什么,最简单的莫过于进入 hotmail 了。所以,我和彼得在另一个网站注册了一个新邮箱,处理私人事务,不过我们每天都会检查一遍自己的 Hotmail。要是有人想看我们的邮件,尽管看呗。

注意事项:我得说清楚,在我后来任教的学校和生活的公寓,网络都很通畅。但是把自家电脑上的闪盘带到学校去用,是很不明智的,我自己就吃过这个亏。不知为何,每一所学校的系统好像都带有病毒。有好几次,我的电脑感染了严重病毒,只能彻底查杀系统。

我们遭遇的另一件事情是跟"面子"有关。我们大家都觉得,自尊和名誉神圣不可侵犯,因此全力以赴地加以维护。这么做是正确的,也是合理的。中国人也一样看重个人名誉,但维护的方式却不尽相同。

我们西方人大都不会介意站到人群面前,闹点笑话出点儿丑。有机会各抒己见,我们都很高兴,说错了话,认个错,必要的话道个歉,生活照样继续。

但中国人却不一样,在公众面前犯错可是件严重的大事儿。让人发现错误是很损个人形象的。即使你无意为之,他们还是会觉得自己脸上无光。或许,他们嘴上不会说什么,因为中国人通常不喜欢与人正面交锋,也许他们一辈子都不会说出口,我们令他们难堪了,但他们会摆出一副高深莫测的表情,禁闭心扉,不再接近你。

有一个例子很说明问题。在西方,要是客人向我们打听什么,如果我们不懂,会

China the shop attendant often will not say they don't know. They will refer you on to another sales assistant, and if they don't know, the referrals can go on for quite some time. You can be sent all over the shop and in a large department store to several floors until you give up in frustration and go home.

For this reason, there is a way of dealing with Chinese people that is a little different. Openly accusing them of doing wrong in front of others brings them personal shame. Making them look as if they are in the wrong in some way does the same.

That doesn't mean that we bow and scrape and always say they are right. But discussing things on a one to one basis rather than in front of others is often a better way to do things.

This point is worthy of consideration because in most teaching situations, our bosses are Chinese. They may have dealt with foreigners for some years and got to know our ways, but at the end of the day they are the bosses and they hold the power, and keeping an amicable working relationship is very important.

There are schools where this will not be a problem at all, and others where it will be. This is just something to be aware of, and good interpersonal skills are very useful here dealing with different individuals. For the Chinese, losing face is a big thing. It is deeply embedded and no matter what you do, you will not change it. Learning to work with it will make your life much easier all round.

直接告诉对方，再想办法弄懂。但在中国，店员通常不告诉你，而是叫你去问另一个店员，要是他们都不知道，还会找出一长串的人，叫你去打听，让你在商店里跑来跑去，碰上大百货商场，你还得楼上楼下忙乎，最后只能悻悻作罢，打道回府。

鉴于此，跟中国人交往，方式须有所不同。当着他人的面指出错误，会令他们颜面尽失。让他们感觉什么地方出了问题，一样叫他们难堪。这么说并非要求我们低眉顺眼地委屈自己，或一味附和。明智之举是选择没有他人在场的时候，与他们单独面谈。

这一点不可掉以轻心，因为在我们教书的地方，顶头上司多为中国人。也许他们跟外国人打过几年交道，知道我们的行事方式，但人家毕竟是领导，大权在握，跟他们处好关系是至关重要的。

在有些学校，这一点根本不成问题；但在另一些学校，可能就是大问题了。对此，我们要心中有数，在这里，我们要跟不同的人来往，掌握正确的人际交往技巧大有裨益。对中国人而言，丢脸是大事儿。这种伤痛会令他们刻骨铭心，无论你怎么补救，都无济于事。知道这方面的进退尺寸，会让你在中国的日子轻松许多。

DENEICE AND EMERSON

The value of having another foreign teacher at the same school soon became obvious to us. Deneice was from the deep south of USA. In her southern drawl she how'y'all'ed everyone.

She was in her mid-fifties, an experienced school teacher, with friends in a city close by, and this was her first teaching post in China. She also knew how to use taxis, buses and her mobile phone. On top of this, she was a wonderful person, so having her to show us the ropes was a huge advantage.

We met Deneice the day Paul took us to Longyan from Xiamen. Her apartment was in a different block, but we could see each other from our balconies.

Deneice got very involved with caring for some of the local children who were orphans. She had a heart of gold, and a big heart it was too.

Peter, Deneice and I became very good friends. Her nickname for Peter was TDH, (Tall, Dark and Handsome–in reality he was average, grey and average). We travelled together often, and spent much "out of class" time together. You could say we became a little family of three. This family slowly expanded to include other teachers and students, but the three of us were at the core.

Another American teacher who went to Longyan was Emerson. He was twenty-six-years-old, used to having his own condo and sports car. He was a teacher in Miami before going to China, but was not really prepared for the lifestyle. He also got a bit muddled between China and Japan, having gone to China to see the geisha girls.

戴妮丝和爱默生

跟另一个外国人同校为师的好处很快便尽显无遗。戴妮丝是美国南方人,带着浓重的南方口音,见谁都一一问好。

她大概五十五六岁的样子,是个经验丰富的老师,有几个好朋友在龙岩附近的城市教书,但她本人是初次来华任教。她知道如何打的士、乘公交和使用手机。最重要的是,她这个人非常好,我们初来乍到,有她从旁指点一二,好处不在话下。

保罗把我们从厦门接到龙岩的那一天,我们就见到了戴妮丝。她住在另一栋楼里,但我俩站在阳台上可以望见对方。

戴妮丝花了大量的时间和精力照顾几个当地孤儿。她有一颗金子般的心,仁爱而高尚。

我、彼得和戴妮丝成了莫逆之交,她叫彼得 TDH(即高黑帅之意,其实彼得不过是个中灰平,也就是中等个头、灰色头发、相貌平平)。我们三个人经常一块儿旅游,课后也常常呆在一起,差不多成了一个三口之家。后来,我们这个家庭渐渐地越变越大,加入了几个老师和学生,但核心成员依旧是我们仨人。

另一个来龙岩教书的美国人是爱默生。当时他 26 岁,之前住在自己的公寓里,开一辆跑车。来中国之前在迈阿密当老师,不过他准备不够充分,接受不了这里的生活方式。像我们一样,他也把日本和中国弄混了,还想来中国看日本艺伎来着。

Culture shock was a problem for Emerson. He hated the canteen food so asked me to go shopping with him to get the necessities so he could cook for himself. His first meal was a total disaster. I don't think he had ever cooked for himself before, and didn't know you needed to boil the rice before frying it. Have you ever tried to fry uncooked rice? You get little hard black bullets.

Emerson was of tall solid build, with long wavy hair pulled back in a ponytail. He was very handsome with a fabulous smile. I think he broke every girl's heart at the school, and every unmarried female teacher hoped to marry him. He made some friends among the students, and of course joined us a great deal, but he was lonely for friends his own age. We often passed him as we went home after dinner at one of the local restaurants. We'd be going home to bed, and he'd be going out to try and find the scarce nightlife in our small city.

Emerson took considerable care to learn Chinese and he soon became proficient. One day we decided to try a different restaurant close by, one we dubbed "the sweet and sour restaurant". The menu was all in Chinese.

"It's okay, I know enough to read this," he said picking up the menu.

He browsed through, reading out the dishes, asking us what we wanted to order. We all put in our requests as he called over a waitress.

"We'll have one of these, and these, and these," he said in Chinese, itemising our dishes. He continued chatting to the waitress and she went off to the kitchen. We were all starving hungry and the food was very slow in coming. It was also a Wednesday, so we had less than an hour to eat and walk back to school for English Corner.

The food started appearing one dish at a time. Conscious of the time, we all started on the first dish. We worked our way through the second and third dishes as they appeared. After about fifteen minutes and quite a few dishes we were full, but the food kept coming.

"How much did you order?" we asked Emerson with some consternation.

"I just ordered what we wanted," he said, confused.

"There's more and more coming!" We were getting really worried.

"We'll just have to leave," said Deneice, "English Corner starts soon. We can't wait any longer."

爱默生就遇到了文化冲击问题。他讨厌食堂伙食，叫我陪他上街采购必备的厨房用具，好在家里自己煮饭吃。他煮的第一顿饭以完败告终。我想，他以前肯定没亲自下过厨房，连要用煮熟的饭炒饭都不知道。你试过用生米炒饭吗？其结果就是炒出一锅小黑炭。

爱默生身材魁梧，长长的卷发在脑后扎了个马尾辫，笑容满面，英俊潇洒。我想全校女生都为他心醉，全校未婚女教师都巴望着他能成为自己的如意郎君。他在学生中交了几个朋友，自然也经常与我们呆在一起。但是因为缺少同龄朋友，他还是感觉非常寂寞。我们常在一家当地餐馆吃晚饭，回家时总能遇见他。我们回家睡觉，他却往校外赶，想在这座几乎没有夜生活的小城市，寻个好玩的去处。

爱默生在学中文，学得十分上心，因此没过多久他的中文水平就相当不错了。有一天，我们决定到附近另一家我们称之为"酸甜饭馆"的餐馆用餐，餐馆只有中文菜单。

"没事儿，我看得懂。"爱默生说着拿起菜单。

他浏览了一遍菜单，然后念出每道菜名，叫我们点菜。我们把各自看中的菜名告诉他，由他转告女侍者。

"我们要点这个，这个，还有这个。"他用中文报出菜名，又跟女侍者聊了好一会儿，然后女侍者去厨房下菜单了。那会儿，大家已经很饿了，却迟迟不见上菜。那天恰好是星期三，我们都得赶回学校，参加英语角活动，所以只有不到一小时的用餐时间。

总算开始上菜了，一次一道。由于时间紧张，我们便一起吃。之后是第二道、第三道菜。大约一刻钟之后，我们已经吃了好几盘东西，肚子已经饱了，可食物仍一盘盘端上桌。

"你点了多少东西啊？"我们惶恐地问爱默生。

"就点了我们想吃的那几道呀？"他也满头雾水。

"又端过来了，又端过来了！"我们着急坏了。

"I don't understand …" Emerson mumbled as another dish appeared.

Poor Emerson, none of us knew what he'd ordered but it kept coming. We gave him our share of the cost and rushed back to school leaving him to sort it out. He paid the asked price and was accosted by the waitress with another dish as he walked out the door.

We never went back there again. But we did learn that the most dangerous time with the Chinese language is when you think you know it all—but you don't.

Emerson got too homesick and returned home after one semester. However a year or so later he went back to China and stayed for some time, thoroughly enjoying his life there.

The value of having other foreign teachers came to the fore when travelling on weekends or during holidays.

Deneice suggested we do a train trip one weekend. We wanted to see as much of the country as we could and decided to go to another city not too far away. One of Deneice's students was from Changting. (Said Chung ting) It was three hours there by bus and about the same home by train.

The bus was chokka-block, not only with people but with all the goods they carried, e.g. baskets with chickens in them, sacks and bags full of clothes and food. There was very little leg room and our legs were much longer than the average Chinese person.

Emerson came too, and this was a test for his frame. He's solid and tall, and another skinny little Chinese man was sprawled over his own and Emerson's seat. This skinny little man was not going to move for anything. So Emerson sat sort of sideways, with his long legs poking out into the aisle. After a while he went and sat right up the back in the middle to have more room.

We assumed this bus driver was qualified, but unfortunately he couldn't have driven this bus before, because he couldn't find any of the gears. There we were, in the middle of the main street, stationary, holding up all the traffic while he's trying to find first gear to get us moving. This trip lasted close to four hours, and he never did master that gear lever.

We expected a slow trip through some very hilly country. The driver practiced his gear changing in the most unfortunate places, like going up a steep hill while trying to

"我们得走了,英语角马上就要开始了,不能再耽搁了。"戴妮丝说。

"怎么会这样……"爱默生看着刚刚端上桌的另一盘菜喃喃自语。

可怜的爱默生,我们谁也不知道他究竟点了什么东西,反正菜是一道一道地送过来。我们把该付的饭钱交给他,便匆忙赶回学校了,留下他一个人收拾残局。他照价买完单,离开的时候女侍者的手中还端了一盘菜,殷勤地招呼他。

此后,我们再也没进"酸甜饭馆"吃饭,但我们从中吸取了一个教训:当你自以为中文水平不错而事实不然的时候,危机已然降临。

爱默生因为太想家了,只教了一个学期书就回美国了。不过,大约一年后,他又回到中国,呆了一段时间,这一次他过得非常快乐。

周末或假期外出旅游的时候,有其他外国人同校为师的好处,立刻彰显了出来。

一个周末,戴妮丝建议说,我们坐火车出去玩一趟。我们也想多出去走走看看,于是决定结伴到附近的一个城市转转。戴妮丝有个学生是长汀人,坐汽车到长汀大约三小时的路程,再从那儿乘火车返回,差不多也是三小时。

汽车十分拥挤,被乘客和他们携带的各种货物,像关了小鸡的鸡笼子、大袋小袋的服装和食品挤得水泄不通,几乎连搁脚的地方都没有,而我们几个外国人的腿脚比普通中国人的又长。

爱默生也来了,对他这个块头的人来说,坐在车里真是一大考验。高大魁梧的他坐在一个瘦小的中国人旁边,这个"小瘦子"歪着身子占据了两个位置,丝毫没有挪动身体的意思,他只好侧身坐着,将两条长腿伸到过道上。过了一会儿,他离开原位,坐到最后一排的一个中间位置上,那里空间稍微大些。

我们原以为司机的驾驶技术肯定过关,但可以肯定这辆车他从未开过,只见折腾了好半天都不知如何挂档。这下好了,在大路中央,一辆汽车静止不动,堵着道,而司机却挂不着档,开不动车。这一趟路程用去了将近四个小时,而他至始至终用不顺那根变速杆。

我们本以为汽车会缓缓行驶于连绵山间,殊不知司机为了练习换挡,选择的时

pass an old traction engine truck full of sand, while another faster bus was also trying to overtake us. Imagine if you will, a two lane road, with three big vehicles all going round the corners, uphill, side by side.

There was however, one thing that made this all quite all right. There were some very strict road rules in this area. One of the road rules that was adhered to with super glue (we saw this one practiced all the time) was the "mind out I am behind you" rule. As a driver approached a vehicle from the rear, it was imperative that you let them know you were there by honking your horn. (Of course they knew this from their rear vision mirror, but just in case...) This was the number one rule. And of course, if there were two people in front of you, a cyclist and a car, you must honk twice, once for each person.

The same principle applied if there were ten different kinds of traffic somewhere in front of you, at least in your vision. You needed to honk for every one so they knew you were there. And if you honked the first time but you were some distance away, then of necessity, you must honk again once you are closer.

Not only that, but as you went around corners, it was necessary to honk louder and longer in case someone was coming the other way and was on your side of the road. After all, there was no guarantee that everyone was driving on their own side of the road, especially when passing or in a hurry. The other necessary action was to honk at someone coming towards you, even if on the other side of the road, because it was possible they hadn't seen you, so you must advise them of your presence.

This made for somewhat noisy driving. This rule didn't just apply to you, but to every vehicle on the road, so everyone constantly honked at everyone else. Some of these vehicles had very loud horns, including our bus. So every few seconds there was this ear splitting blast from the horn, some shorter some longer, depending on the urgency of the message the driver was trying to convey. We slowly but safely made our way along to Changting. As passengers we were at the driver's mercy so we just went with the flow.

The other fabulous subject I haven't covered yet is the spitting. I don't know what is special about Chinese men, but they all spit. I don't mean a delicate little "spit" I mean a deep throated, full bodied hoooiiiiikkkk, and then they just let fly wherever they are. Of course our bus driver was no exception, so every five minutes or so, he hauled up from the depths of his soul a great wad of "stuff" and hoicked it out the window. You wouldn't

机总是不对。譬如，他想在上坡的时候超越一辆装沙旧拖车，而另一辆巴士正以更快的速度赶超我们这辆车。试想一下，在一条两车道的路上，三辆大车在上坡的路段，排成一列，同时转弯，情况会何等凶险。

所幸此地交规严格，我们的人身安全才得以保障。其中一条用强力胶写的交规是（这条交规处处可见）："请注意身后车辆"。超车时司机须鸣笛提醒前方及后方车辆（当然在后视镜中可以知道路况，但这么做能够以防万一。）这条规则应当严格遵守。当然，如果前方同时出现一辆汽车和一辆自行车时，须鸣笛两次，一次提醒一个人。

以此类推，如果在你的视野内出现十种不同的交通工具，你必须为前方每个人鸣笛一次，以示提醒。如果第一次鸣笛时，距离前车较远，那么靠近该车时应该再次鸣笛。

不仅如此，车辆拐弯时，必须持续鸣笛，以防另一方向有车辆行驶在同一车道。毕竟，谁也不敢保证，人人都行驶在自己的车道上，尤其是在超车或赶路的时候，更难保证。另一个必要之举是，当见到前方有行人向你走来，即使这个行人在道路另一侧，也应鸣笛，因为他可能没有看到你的车辆，需要你的提醒。

这样一来，路上会比较喧闹。这条规则适用于来往车辆，因此大家都会鸣笛，相互提醒。有些车子的喇叭特别响亮，就像我们乘坐的这辆巴士。因此，每隔几秒钟，就会听见一个震耳欲聋的喇叭声，或长或短，依司机想要表达的紧急程度而定。我们安全而缓慢地走在去往长汀的路上。身为乘客，身家性命被司机捏在手上，也只能听天由命了。

另有一件奇事我尚未提及，那就是中国的吐痰现象。我不知道中国人有哪些不一样的地方，但我知道他们一个个都爱吐痰。我指的不是轻声地"咳"两下，而是指扯着喉咙使劲儿咳，接着毫无顾忌地将口中之物吐出，不管它落往何方。我们的司机也不例外，每过五六分钟，就要从胸腔挤出点什么"东西"，倏的吐往窗外。要是哪个骑摩托或滑板车的倒霉蛋刚好从车旁经过，正中司机的"飞镖"，那情形可就惨不忍

want to be the rather unfortunate person on a motor bike or scooter coming towards the bus just as the driver let fly. It would not be a pretty sight.

The country side we passed through was just beautiful. It was harvest time and large paddocks were full of stooks from the stalks left over, all neatly arranged in rows. From our vantage point on the train it was a wonderful sight. The rice was harvested by hand, threshed, then spread all over any hard surface to dry, even on flat house rooftops. It had to be turned frequently for three days, collected into baskets then stored in large sacks, all done by hand. These sacks were then carried on their backs to the storehouses. It was labour intensive, back breaking work and I tell you this, most Kiwi's and Aussie's are proper pansies in comparison!

Other crops, including vegetables, were grown in this area too. We arrived in Changting, a place of historical significance and beauty we were told, although in reality, it was dirty, dusty and not very beautiful at all. Alice the student was with us, and we found out en route that a friend of hers had a relative in Changting who had arranged accommodation for us at a friend's hotel. He also treated us to a special dinner, including a famous Changting chicken dish. Chinese hospitality was just wonderful, as they considered it an honour to care for their guests. He phoned Alice several times asking if we had any other requests. Wine? Alcohol? He said he was delighted to host these foreign teachers visiting his hometown.

Once off the bus we walked into the street, heading for our hotel which was close by. Alice said the last time she knew of foreigners being in Changting was about ten years ago. She wasn't kidding! We had to cross the road to get to the hotel. The traffic just came to a stop, all four lanes of it, as they just gawped at us. People everywhere looked, stared, pointed, shouted out to others to come and look, and made the town aware there were four aliens in town. And this is a big town, 400,000 give or take a few.

In China we didn't expect the same standard of accommodation that we had at home, but we did like a Western toilet. This hotel looked quite good, maybe three stars, with large rooms, although the toilets did pong a bit. After a short rest it was time to go for dinner, but for some reason there were no taxis. Instead we had to take bicycle rickshaws. One poor Chinese body, very thin, a bit old looking, with spindly looking little legs pumped away, taking Peter and I to the restaurant.

睹了。

　　沿途的乡村景色相当悦目。时值水稻收获季节，一大片一大片的水田里堆放着收割下来的稻草，一排一排，整整齐齐。坐在车里向外眺望，着实漂亮。水稻先由人工收割，接着打谷脱粒，再铺到结实的干燥地面甚至平屋顶上晾晒，需连续翻晒三天，才能装进箩筐，然后再装入大麻袋保存，前前后后所有工序全靠劳力。最后，农民肩扛背驮，将一袋袋稻谷送进谷仓，非常之辛苦，一天下来足以叫人腰酸背疼。要我说，新西兰和澳大利亚的农民跟他们相比，不知轻松多少倍！

　　这里也种植了其他农作物和各种蔬菜。终于我们到达了长汀县。据说，长汀是座历史名城，风光很美。可实际一看，到处脏兮兮的，尘土飞扬，半点儿美感都没有。戴妮丝的学生爱丽丝陪我们同行，在路上她告诉我们，她的一个朋友有一个亲戚住在长汀，已经替我们在他朋友的酒店里安排好了住宿，并安排了一顿特色晚餐，包括长汀名菜——长汀土鸡，替我们接风洗尘。中国人真的非常热情好客，对他们来说，能够招待客人，不胜荣幸。他给爱丽丝打了好几通电话，问我们还需要什么。要不要红酒？白酒？他说，能够招待我们几个来他家乡旅游的外国教师，万分高兴。

　　下了巴士，我们走进一条街道，准备前往街道附近的酒店。爱丽丝说她上次在长汀看到外国人的时候是十年之前。人家说的是真话！我们一行人得穿过大街到对面的酒店。这时候，所有的车辆都停下来了，总共四车道的车辆呢，就为了看我们几个老外。周围的行人，有的盯着我们傻看，有的朝我们指指点点，还有的在忙着叫其他人出来观看，一时间全市上下都知道，城里来了四个外星人。这座城市可不小，有40来万人呢。

　　我们不敢承望中国的住宿条件跟家里一样，但我们确实想要一个西式卫生间。酒店看上去不错，可能是家三星级酒店，客房很大，只是厕所有点儿气味。我们稍事休息，就到了吃晚饭的时间。不知什么缘故，这里竟然没有的士，我们只得坐三轮黄包车过去。可怜的中国车夫，瘦瘦的身躯，看着年纪挺大，细长的瘦腿吃力地踩着踏板，送我和彼得去餐馆。

When we first arrived in China we learned to ask what was in everything. You have no idea what the Chinese eat, and we were a tad fussy. This night, our host greeted us at the door. As is the custom for a host entertaining guests, there was enough food for an army. There was fish soup, made from little fishes. There followed an immediate intake of breath from all four foreign teachers, and we all knew no-one would eat the soup. We've seen where many of these little fishes come from, possibly the local rivers. So we asked all the time, "what's in this? What's in that?"

We all took copious helpings of boiled rice, then added bits of this and that. I loved their little dumplings but couldn't abide the very bitter greens they often ate. At the end they brought out a local specialty, a sort of fried pizza which was very tasty. They also provided several bottles of good red wine. Our host had gone to great lengths to make us welcome, and we really appreciated that.

I needed some batteries for my camera so went to the mall to get some. All the shoppers were staring, pointing at us, and showing their children where to look to see us. We smiled widely, said hi to everyone, shook their hands, talked to the children, shook the children's hands, tickled the babies under their little Chinese chins, and generally did the "royal wave" during our "walkabout". But our progress was very slow. Alice found some batteries and we made a grand exit, waved off by all. Outside it was now dark, so we were not so obvious.

The other thing we found in the mall was a man.

"Do you remember me?" he asked Peter. "I had lunch with you at Longyan?"

We'd eaten lunch with zillions of Chinese people in the canteen, but after a while Peter realized who he was.

"Yes, you are the government inspector. I remember you."

"I am so pleased to see you," he said. He found out we were staying the night, and escorted us for the rest of the trip, delighted he could practice his English.

We decided to visit the famous Great Wall. This was not to be confused with the real Great Wall, but was a significant wall on the edge of the Ting River, built about 1200 years ago. The local people call it "The Castle", and it's easy to see why, with its huge stone construction and battlements on top.

This wall measured about one kilometre long and probably surrounded the original

到中国不久，我们就养成了一个习惯，看到每一样菜，都要问问这里面是什么东西。因为我们不知道中国人吃的是什么东西，可又特别好奇。这天晚上，主人站在门口迎客，按照中国请客的惯例，准备了足够喂饱一只军队的丰盛菜肴。有一道菜是鱼汤，主料是一种小鱼。一看到这道菜，我们四个外教全都倒吸了一口凉气，大家知道，这汤我们几个只能敬而远之。因为我们曾亲眼见过这样的小鱼儿是从哪里捕捞来的，没准就是当地的小河鱼。正因为如此，我们才会老问："这里面是什么？那里面是什么？"

我们每个人都盛了一大碗饭，配着各种菜肴。我很喜欢吃这里的小水饺，本地人吃水饺时常沾青椒酱，但我不敢学他们的样。最后上的是一道当地特色菜，有点像比萨那样的煎饼，非常美味。他们还送来了几瓶上好的红酒。主人变着法子希望我们吃得开心，对此我们万分感激。

吃过晚饭，我想买相机用的电池，大家就一起去了当地一家商场。商场里，顾客们纷纷投来好奇的目光，用手指着我们，叫孩子们看。我们笑容满面，逢人便问好、握手、跟小孩说话、握握他们的小手、捏捏小婴孩的脸颊，边走边像"皇室成员"一样挥手致意，因此走得很慢。爱丽丝替我买到电池，我们隆而重之朝门口走去，一商场的人挥手送别。此时天色已晚，出了商场我们反倒不那么显眼了。

在商场的另一个奇遇是碰见了一个男子。

"你还记得我吗？我俩一起在龙岩吃过饭。"那人问彼得。

我们在食堂和无数人一起吃过饭，但过了一会儿彼得认出他了。

"对了，你是那个政府检查员，我想起来了。"

"很高兴见到你们。"他说。当他知道我们要在这里过夜，便决定接下来陪我们游玩。能趁机练习口语，他很开心。

我们决定去看看长汀的古城墙。可别弄混了，这不是真正的长城，只是汀江边上的一段具有历史意义的城墙，大约建于1200年前的唐朝。当地人称它为"城堡"，理由一望便知，因为城墙上有巨大的石头建筑和工事。

city. We walked to an area where the wall converged with a temple and gave us a good view over the city. There was another foreigner there filling in time before he caught a train. He was a journalist from Hong Kong and he was thrilled to have someone to talk to in English. After he left we walked the length of the city, getting back to the hotel very tired.

I have spoken before about the cricket bat beds, well this surpassed the others. It was like sleeping on rock. The movie Sister Act was on television in English, so we watched that till about midnight and dozed off with a couple of mammoth mozzies keeping us company.

During our evening walk our kind host rang to say he'd arranged a Western breakfast for us. With high anticipation for some good Western food we arrived at 8am at the address given. However, it was not what we expected at all.

Let me explain a little about breakfast for many Chinese. It's quite common for them to eat just bread, not bread as we know it, but white and very sweet. They might have this with milk, or just eat plain bread, or sweet buns. They don't know about muesli or cereals. The other thing they like is rice porridge, watery rice. For our "Western breakfast" we anticipated a plate of bacon and eggs, so we had a good laugh at our unrealistic expectations. However this shop did make fabulous coffee which we really enjoyed.

Our "government man" also came for breakfast and he accompanied us as we were shown around the local museum which was surrounded by a large 1200 year old courtyard with massive old trees.

We were taken past other city highlights, then to one of oldest streets in town. This was the real "old China", with narrow winding alleys and well stocked tiny shops that have been run by the same families for generations. Old men and women with tiny frames and wrinkled faces, often somewhat toothless, sat in the sun enjoying the local community atmosphere.

There were many wood carvers in this street, making hand carved images, as had been done for generations. No modern tools were used, just adzes and hammers. There was a noodle shop where they were making fresh noodles by hand. In a huge half barrel full of flour, a woman was adding eggs and water. Once the consistency was right, she

这段古城墙大约长一公里，很可能是环最早的古城而建。我们走到城墙和一个寺庙交集之处，在这里可以一览长汀城的风光。我们还邂逅了另一个外国人，他是利用等火车的空档上这里玩的。他是一名香港记者，能用英语与人聊天，把他高兴坏了。记者走后，我们把整个城区都逛了一遍，回到酒店已经精疲力竭了。

记得前面我提到过酒店的硬板床，怎么办呢，这里的床还要更硬，感觉就像睡在岩石上。电视上正在播放英文原版电影《修女也疯狂》，我俩守着电视一直到深更半夜，在两只巨蚊的陪伴下，打了一个盹儿。

晚上我们出去散步的时候，那位友善的东道主打来电话说，他替我们安排好了，明天的早餐是西餐。我们满怀期待，以为早餐肯定非常丰盛。第二天早上八点，我们来到指定地点，结果却大失所望。

请容我先介绍一下中国人的早餐吧。他们的早餐就只吃面包。这里的面包跟我们所知的不大一样，是白色的，非常甜。有的会配一杯牛奶，有的就光吃面包或甜馒头。他们不懂得什么是牛奶什锦和燕麦。此外，他们喜欢喝粥，就是稀饭。因为对方说的是"西餐"，我们还以为至少会有一盘培根鸡蛋，所以亲眼一看，不由得笑了，笑自己不切实际。不过，这家店的咖啡确实不错，我们很喜欢。

"公务员"也过来跟我们一起吃早饭，他陪我们参观了长汀县博物馆，博物馆四周是一个拥有一千两百多年历史的"汀州试院"，院子里的几棵古树郁郁葱葱、枝繁叶茂。

参观完城区的主要景点，我们来到一条长汀县最古老的巷子。这里才是真正的古镇，小巷狭长弯曲，两侧一溜迷你小商铺，商铺都是家族代代相传下来的。老头老太们大都身材瘦小、满脸皱纹，大都掉了好几颗牙齿，坐在阳光下，怡然自得地看着左邻右舍来来往往。

这条街上有许多木雕艺人，手工雕刻各种物件，这门手艺也是他们祖上传下来的。没有任何现代工具，只有手斧和锤子。街上还有一家面店，制作新鲜手工面条。我们看到一个大桶，里面装了半桶面粉，一个女子正往里面加蛋和水。等面和好了，

gave a large bowl full to her husband.

You may have seen the small pasta making machines many people have in their kitchens? In this shop was a huge ancient local version with a conveyor belt about six feet long being driven by a rattly old motor turning belts that then turned three large wheels about half a meter in diameter. Once the dough gained the right thickness it was finely sliced and wound into bundles for sale.

There was a barbers shop with a chair that must have been at least 100 years old. It was fashioned from wooden slats with metal plates holding it together. It had a swinging foot rest, a slatted back, shaped wooden arms and a wooden pedestal. They did however have two sets of electric clippers along with the normal combs, scissors etc.

Further along was an equally old dentists shop with a similar chair, and some mean looking pieces of equipment. We had a wonderful time wandering along this ancient street. And the best part? They seemed to be happy with their lot in life. They had a sense of identity and belonging. They had security, a close-knit community, with friends and family on hand. They were satisfied with their food, clothing and shelter, and best of all, their lives were safe. Westerners might look at them and think they lived in poor conditions. They would probably look at us horrified at our stress levels and crime rates.

We left this fascinating street, had a quick lunch and made for the train station. It was quite a distance to the train station so expected to pay the rickshaw riders more for the trip. In fact, we always gave them extra because their incomes are very low, and they used plenty of energy peddling us around.

We arrived at the train station in three separate rickshaws having our bags as well. The problem was, each rickshaw owner asked for different amounts for the trip, and as they realized that some of them received less than the others, there began a slanging match of magnificent proportions, of course in their best quality Chinese. They were yelling at one another, then at us, but we had no idea what they were talking about, although obviously it was something to do with us. It took a while for Alice to work out what was wrong, because they were yelling in their local dialect. Alice collected the three rickshaw riders together, paid them all exactly the same and left them to it, their voices still vibrating in the air as we entered the station.

Comparatively speaking, the cost of travel in China was very cheap. The bus ride

她便舀起一大碗递给丈夫。

不知你见过小型面食机没有？许多人家的厨房里都有。只是这家店铺的机器更大更原始，传送带大约一米八长，一台老掉牙的马达嘟嘟地响着，转动带子，再带动三个直径约半米的大轮子。只要面团厚度适宜，便将它均匀地切成细条，卷成一团，以备出售。

街边的一家理发店里放了一张椅子。这张椅子肯定用了不下一百年，是木板做的，用金属条扎牢，脚踏板可以晃动，木板椅背，扶手和椅子腿都是木制的。不过店里还有一些普通的剪刀、梳子和两把电动理发推子。

理发店前面有一家一样年代久远的牙科诊所，里面放了一张跟理发店一样的椅子和一些模样难看的器械。走在古街上，我们感觉十分惬意。可是，让我们感觉最舒服的东西是什么？好像是人们怡然自得的神情。这里的居民了解自己和自己的居住环境，知道自己生活有保障，邻里关系亲密友好，亲朋好友就在身边。他们对目前的吃、穿、住各方面条件均无怨言，对社会治安尤感满意。也许在西方人眼里，他们的生活条件差强人意，但是，要是他们知道了我们西方国家的犯罪率和高强度的生活压力，肯定会用惊悚的眼光看着我们。

离开这条充满惊奇的古街，我们随便吃了顿午餐，就赶往火车站了。因为火车站离我们很远，我们决定到时多付点儿钱给黄包车车夫。其实，我们一般都会加点儿钱给车夫们，因为他们的收入很低，而且载我们特别辛苦。

我们各自带上行李，分坐三辆黄包车到达火车站。可是问题来了，每个车夫开的价钱都不一样，因此有的车夫收费比别人低，于是三个车夫开始用流利的中文，计算自己的得失。他们先是冲同伙喊叫，接着便冲我们喊叫。虽然我们知道此事与我们有关，可是不明白他们究竟在喊什么。爱丽丝费了好一会儿工夫才弄清楚其中原委，原来他们说的是本地话。爱丽丝把三个车夫叫到一块儿，付给三个人同样的车费，便甩手离开了。直到我们进站之时，三个车夫的声音仍在空中回荡。

相较而言，在中国旅游非常便宜。巴士票每人34元，相当于三个半车程花5澳

cost 34 Yuan each, approximately, $5.00AU for three and a half hours. The train cost 9 Yuan, about $1.50AU for three and a half hours. Changting had a large modern station, and true to form, there were hundreds of passengers waiting to catch the same train. The railway system in this vast country moves millions of people daily. They have got it down to a fine art.

This was where the fun started. We were ushered into little queues where the train doors opened when the train stopped. It's not just people and suitcases getting on the trains, but all the extra stuff they take with them. Snacking is indulged in by most passengers too, so when they travelled they had little bags of fruit and snacks in their hot little hands.

We realized that this was not going to be easy, because as the train pulled into the station we could see the train was already packed with about another 500 to board somehow. First those on board had to disembark. They did by this by taking their life in their hands, shutting their eyes and sort of slithering out between all the bodies trying to get on. And get on they did. In the most undignified, squashing, cramming, crushing, hair pulling, body pulling, yelling, elbowing, me—first and get out of my way, GET OUT OF MY WAY I'M GETTING ON kind of way. We concluded that getting into that carriage was hopeless so went to the very end carriage and scrambled on. Not a spare seat was to be seen. It was a seething mass of black heads, bodies, legs, bags and sacks.

Being foreigners sometimes had its benefits, and being four aliens had distinct advantages that day. We wandered to the rear of the last carriage and the guards let all five of us sit in their curtained off compartment, giving us the best seats on the train. We could stand on a little verandah at the back and watch the world chugging by. I took lots of photos and when I felt tired could sit in comfort. It was the most unexpected turn of events giving us a fabulous trip home.

Having Alice with us, we could ask the guards lots of questions. There were about 120 tunnels on this piece of track. The longest was seven kilometres, and a couple of others not much shorter, so the trip often consisted of tunnels interspersed with a bit of blue sky. We got back to Longyan about 5pm, tired, grubby and covered in diesel fumes, but we'd had a fabulous weekend away. Travelling in China was exciting and educational, one of the best ways to spend a couple of days.

元。火车票9元，即三个半小时车程1.5澳元。长汀的火车站宽敞现代，跟往常一样，里面有几百个乘客等候同一列火车。在这个幅员辽阔的国度，火车每天载着成百上千亿的乘客南来北往。火车的功效被发挥得淋漓尽致。

真正的趣事即将上演。我们被引至一个地方，排到一条短短的队伍后面，那里就是火车停站时车门打开的地方。上火车的不仅是乘客和行李箱，还有他们携带的其他各种东西。多数乘客喜欢吃零食，所以外出时热乎乎的小手里总会提着好几小袋的水果和小吃。

我们意识到了，得经过一番厮杀才能上得了火车，因为火车到站的时候车厢里已经满满当当，而站台上还有五百多人。先得让火车上的乘客下车。之后，下面的乘客开始将家当抓在手中，闭着眼睛，不管不顾地，像泥鳅一样在人的躯体间钻来钻去，抢空当挤上车。功夫不负有心人，他们成功了。可是景象却那么狼狈：又是挤又是推，又是踩脚又是扯头发，还一边嚷嚷一边用胳膊肘顶，使上了浑身解数，为的就是我先上，你们让路。让路，我要上车。好一番肉搏。我们一看情形，想上这节车厢毫无希望，赶紧跑到最后一节车厢，跌跌跄跄地爬上火车。里面座无虚席，放眼望去，全都是黑色的脑袋、腿脚、身躯以及大袋小袋。

身为外国人在中国有时是有好处的，而四个外星人同时现身，好处自不待言。我们走到最后一节车厢的后面，乘务员让我们五个人坐进他们那个拉了布帘的包厢，这可是整列火车最好的座位。我们可以站在后面的走廊里，看着外面的世界在哐当哐当声中变化。我拍了很多张照片，累了就在座位上舒舒服服地休息。这意想不到的好运，送给我们一段幸福的回家旅程。

有爱丽丝在身边，我们向乘务员打听了很多事情。这一段路上大约有120个隧道，最长的隧道长达七公里，另外几个也短不了多少，所以一路上是在隧道和一小块蓝天之间交叉前行。下午五点左右到达龙岩，我们几个又脏又累，浑身汽油味儿，但都觉得这个周末无比美妙。在中国旅游既令人兴奋，又开眼界。有空时外出玩上三两天，那感觉再惬意不过了。

THE STUDENTS

Well how could I describe the students? In a word, marvellous. They were terrific students to teach, in their late teens or early twenties and became our surrogate children while we were away from home.

Our classes were with English Majors, mostly girls, with a small percentage of boys, perhaps four or six in a class of forty. They were old enough to be independent but cocooned enough to be children. They were respectful, obedient, avid learners. What more could a teacher ask? Once they got to know us they came out of their shells, spoke up and took part in any class activities. But they did have their own little quirks.

Privacy didn't exist with the Chinese students. Even a teacher's privacy didn't exist. If I was doing speaking tests and marking their work during the class, it was no problem for them to go to my papers behind my back, take them out and see their scores. We learned to lock away papers or carry them with us during the breaks between periods.

I took special care to respect the privacy of the students. At the end of the year I had a personal interview with every one of my 240 students, giving them feedback and their end of year marks. I soon realised I was wasting a huge amount of my time. As soon as each interview was over, they would rush into the classroom or to their friends and loudly announce their scores. To them, this wasn't private stuff at all.

They lived in small dormitories of eight students to a room. There were eight bunks with small desks underneath, and a small bathroom with an Asian toilet. These toilets are a bit of a shock on your first encounter. They are ground level ceramic encased

中国学生

我该怎样描述我的学生们呢？一个字，棒！这群二十来岁的年轻人都是一流的好学生，在我们这段远离家乡的日子里，他们就是我们的孩子。

我们教的是英语专业的学生，班上大多是女生，男生少得可怜，好像40人的班级里男生数只有四到六个。他们这个年纪早就该独立了，可内心依然像个孩子。学生们个个都很懂礼貌、听话、好学。弟子如此，师复何求？与我们相熟了之后，他们就会走出自己的小世界，大胆发言，参加班级的各种活动。不过，每个学生都有各自的小性格。

中国学生之间没有隐私可言，甚至对老师也无隐私一说。比如，我给他们随堂口试评分，但课间总有人偷偷取走成绩单看分数。后来我们学乖了，到了课间就把成绩报告锁起来，或者随身携带，省得成绩外泄。

我本人相当注意尊重学生的隐私。一年之末，我通常会找时间和240个学生一一面谈，告诉他们我的感受和他们本学年的成绩。不久我就发现了，我这是多此一举。面谈一结束，他们就冲进班级或朋友堆里，嚷嚷着说出自己的分数。在他们看来，成绩压根儿就算不得什么个人隐私。

他们都住在八人一间的小宿舍里。一人一个小床铺，床下放了一张小桌子。宿舍里有一个卫生间，卫生间里安装了一个蹲便池。初见那玩意儿，我着实吓了一跳。说

holes-in-the-ground, that you have to squat over. There was a cold shower, no hot water, no heating, and because room was at a premium, they hung all their clothes outside on hangers on long rods which went the entire length of every floor of every dormitory. The lights were turned off at 11pm and turned on again at 6 am. Your normal Australian student would have a hissy fit and go home in a huff. These Chinese students were grateful for being allowed this opportunity of having an extended education.

Due to this confined living they spent much of their time almost in one another's laps. I think the Chinese people are so used to overcrowding that it is a way of life and no one thinks anything of it. They're all very conscious of the overpopulation of the Chinese nation. I think they're very well informed about contraception, and the one-child policy is still alive and well. It's causing problems due to too many boys and not enough girls to go round the excess boys.

They all had their "close friends". These are friends they eat with, sleep with, sit with in class, and share their innermost thoughts and feelings with.

The other thing they did, which took us by surprise, is they held hands, cuddled, sat on one another's knees, wandered around with arms around one another, and had very close human contact. This is girls with girls and boys with boys. I don't think there was anything unseemly in their attitude it's just what they did. They were quite innocent in many ways. They knew about the birds and the bees, there was probably a little hanky panky going on in the dorms, but "my personal space" didn't exist for them.

During one of our lessons, both Peter and I talked to them about this. We just mentioned that it was surprising to us to see such close personal contact. "Why?" they asked all innocent looking. We just said that it wasn't the way teenagers acted in the West and left it at that.

Actually, I saw a great benefit in this sort of close contact. They felt loved, they got their "warm fuzzies" and "good strokes" from friends all the time. They didn't feel the need to rush into immature boy girl relationships just to get the love that so many Western teenagers feel is missing in their lives. They believe that marriage is to be entered into in their mid to late twenties. Why bother? They felt good about themselves from their friends. Depression did exist due to the high stress levels of having to achieve, but not on the level seen at home. However, because most of them lived on campus and have done

白了，就是在地上嵌了个陶瓷坑，你得蹲下去方便。宿舍里，没有热水，只能洗冷水澡。因为空间有限，大家只能把衣物用衣架挂到外面的长杆上晾晒。每座宿舍、每层楼都有这样长长的晾衣杆，跟楼宽一样长。每晚11点，宿舍准时熄灯，到次日早上6点才会开灯。要是在澳大利亚，学生们早就雷霆大怒，气愤愤地跑回家去了。而这些中国学生却不一样，能有机会上大学，他们就已经感激万分了。

基于这种亲密无间的居住环境，学生们大多数时候都是生活在他人的视线之下，我觉得中国人早已习惯了在人群中生活，这几乎成了他们的一种生活方式，没人对此感到不适。对人口过剩的现状，这里的人们都很清楚。我猜少生优育的观念早已深入人心，计划生育政策依旧行之有效。然而，由于中国男女比例失衡，男性人数多于女性，无妻可取的光棍们正成为社会的一大问题。

每个学生都有自己的"密友"。他们与"密友"同吃、同睡、同座，分享各自心里最隐秘的想法和情感。

但是，"密友"间的某些举动还是让我们颇为讶异：好朋友们常手牵手，搂搂抱抱，或坐在对方的腿上，还会勾肩搭背地走在外面，做出许多亲密的举动。上述举动可都是发生在女孩之间，或者男孩和男孩之间。我想他们的行为并无不妥之处，完全是发乎自然之举。这些学生相当纯洁，也知道男女之事，可能在宿舍里，也有人偷尝"禁果"，但"私人区域"对他们而言是不存在的。

我和彼特都曾在课上提到过这一现象，对他们说，看到他们同性之间这么亲密，我们很吃惊。"为什么呀？"他们一脸无辜地问道。我们说，在西方国家，年轻人一般不会这么做，并没有与他们深入探讨下去。

我发现其实这些亲密行为有一大益处：他们能从中感受到爱，感受到朋友的关怀和温情，因此不会像西方国家的年轻人那样，因生活中缺少爱而早恋。他们认为，应该到25岁以后再谈婚论嫁。他们觉得和朋友们朝夕相处非常开心，何必为情所苦？当然，繁重的学业的确让他们伤神苦恼，但在放假回家的日子里，他们是相当逍遥自在的。不过，多数学生是住校生，成天呆在学校，不能和家人团聚，难免有时

so for much of their school lives, they did miss the family contact, sometimes getting quite homesick.

We had one student by the name of Peter. As my husband was Peter, we called the student Peter 2. This boy was one that stood out, for many reasons. In his own words, he called himself a "special boy", and this he was. When he was eleven years old he lost his left hand in an accident. This caused him considerable inconvenience. I talked with him privately several times to see how he'd dealt with this tragedy. He was adamant that he'd come to terms with the loss and all was well in his life, but I was doubtful. Counselling for such things was unheard of, so he coped the best way he could.

This boy's ability in writing was outstanding. I taught him in oral classes and Peter taught him writing. Every time Peter 2 did a written assignment we sat down and read it all. He wrote long assignments, and they were full of life, full of anger and full of emotion. He bared his soul on paper.

He was also a good speaker, and did excellent pencil sketches. He might have only one hand, but boy, it worked overtime. I hoped to see him expand his creative writing, but it was just not possible at the time, their days were so busy. I have kept most of the assignments he wrote. He will never see his full potential, and that is very sad. He was such a nice person, although over compensated in some ways for what could be an inferiority complex.

During one of Peter's writing classes, he asked the students to write a book. They were horrified at first. Write a book! But Peter was adamant they had to write a book and if three chapters were all they could manage, then three chapters were enough. Of course this also entailed hours of grading. Some of the stories were middle of the road stuff, but some were just remarkable. Peter marked them all and then gave them back.

I got to see one of Peter 2's chapters, and asked him if I could see the rest of his story. After reading them I started typing them up. He called his story "Out of the Mists". It was a love story. It took me a long time to understand why it was so different. It was the point of view he used. He wrote the whole story as if he was the girl, using the girl's perspective, a very difficult way to write. The introduction went like this:

"He was the Sun in the thick mists in the early morning. That's the very impression he made on me at first sight. And now, he is still the same Sun. But before he rises into

会想家。

我教了一个学生，英文名字叫彼得，而我先生也叫彼得，所以我们管他叫小彼得。这个男孩与众不同，多才多艺，自嘲地称自个儿为"神奇小子"，倒也名副其实。小彼得在11岁那年，出了场意外，失去了左手，从此给他的生活造成诸多不便。我私底下找他聊了好几回，就是想知道他如何面对自己的伤残之身。小彼得始终坚持，他过得很好，因为他早已接受了事实，对此我却一直心存疑惑。不过，这种事情别人无法感同身受，好在他已经尽己所能走出了困境。

小彼得作文写得很漂亮。我教他口语，彼得教他写作。小彼得的每篇作文，都能让我俩沉心坐下，细细品味。他的文章写得很长，生活中的点点滴滴尽在笔端，愤懑之情溢于言表，饱含感情。他是真的用心在写作。

小彼得口才也很好，还能画一手好素描。虽说他只有一只手，不过可别小看他这只手，这是只能超负荷运转的手。我希望小彼得的写作水平能更上一层楼，但他实在腾不出时间，因为他们每天都很忙碌。我保留了他写的大部分文章。很遗憾，他这份无与伦比的潜能也许一辈子都得不到充分发挥。他是个如此优秀的孩子，不自卑，只是过分要强了。

有一回，彼得在写作课上，要求学生们一人写一本书。他们一听，全都吓坏了。写书，开什么玩笑！可彼得坚持己见：如果写不出一本书，至少也要交出三个章节的东西。显然，改这样的作文费时不少。有些故事非常粗糙，不知所云；但也有些故事相当精彩。彼得一一改完之后，将文章发回给学生。

我向小彼得要了其中一章来读，完了问他其他几章能否也给我看看。看完后，我把他的故事打印成稿。他给自己的作品起名为《走出迷雾》。这是个爱情故事，我费了好长时间才弄明白，什么他的故事如此不同寻常。原来他采用了一种与众不同的叙述视点，一种难度很大的写作手法——从女性视角叙述整个故事。故事开头是这样的：

"他仿佛清晨浓雾间的朝阳，这是我第一次见到他的感觉。如今，他还是那一轮

the blue sky, I cannot help revealing his veil by memory."

By the time we got half way through his story we realized there was a girl he was very fond of, and she was in this story. Her English name was Skye. Once when he was visiting us, we asked him about this. He was quite open about it, said he was very keen on this girl, but didn't have the courage to say anything.

I also had the advantage of sitting at the front of class every break, and watching the interaction between these two students. One day Peter 2 came up to our apartment.

"I have three pieces of news! One of them is very bad," he called out as he came through the door.

"Okay", I thought. "Love story flops big time".

"What's your news then?" I asked.

"Our team lost the football match."

I knew he was football crazy. "Oh that's a shame," I replied. "What's the second piece of news?"

"I've hurt my leg. Look!" He showed us his grazed leg.

"That looks painful, are you okay?"

"Yes, I'm fine", he said, always putting on a tough act.

"So then, what's the third bit of news?" I asked.

"I did it!" he said, his face lighting up. "I spoke to Skye. All is well. She likes me too. I'm so happy."

We applauded his courage in speaking up, and he trotted back down our six flights of stairs very happy with himself.

Once his story was completed I edited it a little and gave it to him on a disc as a gift when we left. He was delighted.

At the time of writing, Peter 2 has been working for an international company for two years and using his English every day.

One of the best parts for me was the students' perception of beauty. Some of their compliments would heal any wounds you may have had. They think Westerners are beautiful. Many times I was told how beautiful I was, how they loved the colour of my hair, praised my beautiful high nose, and generally thought I was pretty good to look at.

Well, I'm not the hunchback of Notre Dame, but I'm no Princess Diana either. I've

太阳，只是我等不及看它升入蓝天，就已经陷入了记忆，渴望掀开笼罩它的面纱。"

读到了一半，我们才恍然大悟，他有个心上人，正是故事中的"她"。女孩名叫丝凯。有一次，他上我家来玩，我们问起了他。他倒也大方，说自己很喜欢那女孩，只是没有勇气表白。

当老师有个好处，就是可以在课间时分坐在前面，观察那两个孩子的举动。一天，小彼得找上门来。一进门便嚷嚷道：

"我有三个消息！其中一个相当'杯具'。"

"好了，准备倾听他的爱情故事吧。"我心想。

"到底是什么消息呀？"我问道。

"我们的足球队输了。"

我知道，他是一个足球死忠，便说："唉，真令人难过。那么，第二个消息是什么？"

"我弄伤了脚。瞧瞧！"说着便让我们看他的腿伤。

"怎么样，很疼吧？"

"疼，不过没事儿。"一如既往地扮坚强样儿。

"那么，第三个消息呢？"我再问。

"我成功了！！"他一脸兴奋地说，"我跟丝凯表白了！顺利极了，她也喜欢我，我太开心了！"

我们狠夸了他一顿，说他很勇敢。接着他就乐呵呵地跑下六楼，自个儿美去了。

他把整个故事写完后，我替他稍微润色了一下，刻入光盘，离开时作为分别礼物送给了他，他非常高兴。

我写这篇文章的时候，小彼得已经在一家外贸公司上班两年了，天天与英语打交道。

学生们独特的审美观带给我许多美好时光。平心而论，有时褒扬的话语，能治愈所有的伤口。他们一致认为，西方人很漂亮，老夸我长得漂亮，特别喜欢我头发的

lived with my face for a long time and know that it's not the pinnacle of beauty. But their comments were very good for the inner-person. Soon after arriving in Longyan, I was talking to a student named Stone.

"Mrs K," he said, "I saw a foreigner up town. I was wondering if it was our other foreign teacher."

"I don't know, Stone," I said. "What did she look like?"

"She was very beautiful," he said.

"What do you mean by beautiful?"

She had a beautiful face, and lovely hair.

"What colour was her hair?"

"It was grey. I'm sure she must be our other foreign teacher. She's a very beautiful woman."

"Well that sounds like Deneice then," I replied, trying hard to keep a straight face.

Deneice laughed when I repeated this conversation later that day. She's our grey haired fifty-five-year old, with a few wrinkles from the USA.

I had one person compliment me on my nose.

"You have a very beautiful nose", he said to me one day.

"I do?" I asked somewhat bemused. My nose was just a nose to me.

"Yes," he said. "Your nose is beautiful. Just like a kangaroo's nose."

It sounded very funny, but he meant it as a sincere compliment, so I took it as such.

As time went by, we got to know some of the students very well. If some were struggling we gave them extra tuition after hours at our apartment. We never got paid any extra but we were happy to do this.

On a few occasions we had meals cooked for us in our apartment by the students. I was surprised to find that some of these girls were very competent in the kitchen. One girl in particular, Hope, cooked several lovely meals, was quick and efficient, and left the kitchen in spotless condition. I was very impressed.

The Chinese students just didn't understand our Western sense of humour. We tried elephant jokes, knock-knock jokes and riddles. By the time we had explained how the joke worked, it had taken half an hour and we gave up. They had their own Chinese jokes, but our sense of humour left them completely bamboozled.

颜色，我的鼻子也很好看，瞧着就是一个大美女。

当然，我不是《巴黎圣母院》中的丑八怪，但我绝对不是戴安娜王妃。我带着这张脸活了这么多年，自然知道自己不是什么大美人儿，但他们的夸赞让我心里很舒服。刚到龙岩的时候，有一次，我与一个名叫斯通的学生聊天。

"柯老师，我在市里看见过一个老外，她会不会也是我们学校的老师？"他问道。

"不知道呢，她长什么样？"我应道。

"很漂亮。"他回答。

"怎么个漂亮法儿？"

"她的脸很美，头发也很美。"

"那她的头发是什么颜色的呢？"

"灰色的。我敢肯定她也是我们学校的外教，非常漂亮。"

"听你这么说，倒也像是戴妮丝。"我一本正经地说，强忍住笑意。

过后，我把这件事儿告诉了戴妮丝，她听了不禁大笑。她已经是个头发花白、满脸皱纹的55岁美国老太太了。

曾听一个人夸过我的鼻子。

"你的鼻子真好看。"他说。

"真的？"我半信半疑地问道。我的鼻子不就是普普通通的鼻子嘛。

"真的，你的鼻子很好看，跟袋鼠的鼻子一样。"他回答。

我听了哭笑不得，但他是真心赞美我，不接受反倒矫情了。

过了一段日子，我们对一些学生的情况也比较了解了。我们会在家里给学习比较困难的学生免费补课，虽然没有报酬，我们却乐此不疲。

有几回，学生们到我的住所，煮东西犒劳我们。有几个女孩的厨艺相当不错。尤其是荷芙，手脚十分麻利，不一会儿就端出了好几道美食，厨房却仍旧干干净净、一尘不染，令我好生佩服。

西方的幽默常让中国学生摸不着头脑。我们试过大象笑话、敲门游戏和猜谜语。

One girl, Jolly, was very interested in our riddles, and each week we gave her a new one to work on. At the canteen at mealtimes, she gave us an update on her progress. The one "what goes 99 bonk, 99 bonk," took her a week, and she got the centipede bit, but the wooden leg had her stumped. (Excuse the pun). The "knock knock–who's there–Lydia–Lydia who? Lydia teapot," left them bewildered. I tried one lesson using jokes, but gave up after the first attempt.

We were quite taken aback at one of the books printed by a Professor. He found lots of the jokes on the internet, ones we all knew and then he explained them at great length. When English is our mother tongue we understand the "plays on words" the puns, the using a word in a slightly twisted way, but they can't follow that at all. Every student and teacher got his or her own private copy of the Professor's book. Ours is signed by the author. I doubt if the students understood much of the book at all.

有时单单解释游戏规则，就耗费了大半个钟头，只能放弃。他们有自己的笑话，只是理解不了我们的幽默。

有个叫朱莉的女生，特别喜欢猜谜语，我们每周都会出个谜语给她解。我们在餐厅吃午饭的时候，她会过来告诉我们解谜的最新进度。有这么条谜语：什么东西敲99次响99次？ 她想了整整一周时间才猜出谜底是"蜈蚣"。可是为什么蜈蚣有条假腿，让她百思不得其解(对不住了，这里用了一个双关语①)。再比如敲门游戏。敲敲门——是谁呀？——我是莉迪亚——哪个莉迪亚——小茶壶莉迪亚。这个游戏把他们整晕了，老半天不懂该怎么玩。有一节课，我想讲几则笑话给他们听，讲完一个笑话后便知难而退了。

我们看了一本奇书。作者是位教授。他从网站上搜集了许多笑话，这些笑话我们都很熟悉，他却花了长篇大论，解释个中原委。因为英语是我们的母语，所以笑话中的文字游戏呀、双关呀、谐音呀，都难不住我们，但中国学生却很费解。全系师生人手一册该教授的书。我俩的书上还有教授本人的亲笔题名。我很怀疑，书中内容学生能够完全读懂。

---

① 原文的"stump"有两层意思，即给短腿装义肢和让人不解之意。而按照西方人的传统说法，蜈蚣的100条腿中天生有条断腿。

TWILIGHT

Twilight was one of Peter's students. She was a freshman, a first year student, with a bright open face, of course the black eyes and straight black hair, and a very friendly manner. She made friends with us soon after we arrived and was always involved with anything that was happening on campus. She attended English corner every week, practiced as much as she could and was a little bit "in your face", but in a nice way.

She was a quick student, and by the end of the first term was top of the class. Her English wasn't fantastic, but she was not shy, she spoke up in class and gave anything a try.

After a while I thought I'd ask her to give me Chinese lessons. Unfortunately she wasn't a "teacher" of Chinese, so I learned words and phrases but not conversation or sentences which were what I needed for day to day life. The main problem was that I was a pretty hopeless student.

Learning the Chinese language is not something to do just for the fun of it. It's very hard because it doesn't sound anything like English. There are four tones which are imperative to know as the same word can mean four different things depending on the tone.

Even basic counting took ages to learn, which was awkward because we bought fruit and other bits and pieces most days, and the shop keepers just rattled off the prices as if they were rifles spitting out bullets. It was easy enough for them, they knew what they were talking about.

特莱特

特莱特是彼得的学生。她是一个大一新生,长着一张阳光开朗的脸,黑黝黝的眼睛,黑黝黝的直发,待人很是友好。我们到校不久,就和她交上了朋友。我们在学校的各种活动中,都能看到她的影子。她每周都会参加英语角,不放过任何说英语的机会,因此有点儿"张扬",不过这么张扬是好的。

她学东西很快,到了第一学期末,便一跃成为班级的佼佼者了。她的英语并不完美,但她不害羞,爱发言,任何事情都愿意尝试。

认识了一段时间后,我想请她教我们中文,可惜她不是真正的中文"老师",我认得了几个汉字,却没学会日常生活必备的句子和会话能力。主要问题出在我身上:因为我是个极其难教的学生。

学中文可不件好玩的事儿,因为汉语的发音完全不同于英文,学起来真的好难。汉语的四个声调非学会不可,因为同一发音声调不同,意义不同。

就连最基本的数字,我都是花了好长时间才学会的。我们每天都要买水果等零碎物品,而店主们报价的速度又像机关枪扫射一样,噼里啪啦一阵。因为他们心中有数,说起来当然不难了,可我听起来就费力了。

特莱特没有知难而退,我终于有了些许进步。不久,我能够读、写、说百来个字了。我们的手机每天都能收到天气预报,告诉我们明天的天气情况,该如何穿戴和

Twilight persevered and I slowly improved. After a while I could read, write and say about 100 words. The weather forecast was sent to our mobile phone every day. It outlined the weather for the next day, told you what to wear and what to eat, and I could understand much of this.

Different expressions were used to describe weather. At home we said heavy rain. There they said big rain. At home we said showers, there they said little rain. It has rained so much that I rarely saw the character for sun. It was rain, big rain, and rain. The word tomorrow is made up of, wait for it, the character for sun, the one for moon and the one for day. That makes sense, tomorrow is one moon one sun which makes one day.

Twilight was a local girl and knew all the shops down alleys and in corners that we didn't know existed. Nothing was too much bother, and she ran around after us as needed.

She was also a very kind girl. When it was her birthday, she came and saw us, and brought us a little piece of cake. I asked if it was part of a big cake.

"No," she said "I haven't told my roommates it's my birthday, many of them don't have much money and I don't want them to feel bad that they can't buy me a gift."

That was very thoughtful. One of the students made an unusual jigsaw, and was very proud of himself, so for a surprise she got it framed and gave it to him as a gift. That was her way.

We told her we would like to meet her parents before leaving Longyan. They were also keen to be introduced to us so Mr and Mrs Ma invited us to lunch one Sunday. They met us at a Western style pizza restaurant down town and we were their guests. The staff milled around, unused to having foreigners eating there. The manager could speak a few words of English, and he asked if the staff could have their photos taken with us.

Although the parents spoke no English the lunch progressed well. Twilight interpreted, and there weren't any deafening silences. We took our family photos and a couple of picture books of Australia to show them. Mr Ma visited Sydney on business a couple of years ago, so recognized some of those pictures.

The meal was excellent. These restaurants have the most fabulous fine bone china cups. Mr and Mrs Ma had never eaten pizza before. It was funny to watch first timers with this new type of food. Twilight and her father could use a knife and fork, but not her

饮食，我能看懂大部分内容。

中西方描述天气的词汇并不相同。在澳大利亚，我们说"heavy rain(重雨)，这里的人们却说"大雨"。我们说"shower(花洒)"，他们说"小雨"。这边时常下雨，我很难看到"晴"这个字。雨，大雨，雨。中文里明天的"明"字是由"日(太阳)"和"月(月亮)"两个字组成的。真的很有道理，日月交替，便是新一天的开始。

特莱特是本地人，大街小巷、几旮旯里的所有商店她都一清二楚。我们要找什么地方都很方便，必要时，她会鞍前马后地陪着我们。

她非常善良。记得她生日那天，拎了块小蛋糕来看我们。我问她，是不是大蛋糕中的一块。

她说："不是。我没告诉舍友今天是我的生日，大家都不富裕，不想让她们因为没买礼物给我而内疚。"

真是个善解人意的好女孩。有个男生做了幅很棒的拼图，十分得意。特莱特请人把男生的拼图装裱好，送给他当礼物，让男生倍感惊喜。这就是特莱特。

我们告诉特莱特，离开龙岩前想见见她的父母。她的父母也想认识我们，于是邀请我们周日共进午餐。他们请我们到市里的一家比萨店吃饭，我们欣然赴约。服务员很少看到有外国人在此用餐，好一阵忙碌。经理能说几句英文，问我们能否和员工们一起留影纪念。

虽然特莱特的父母不懂英文，但这顿午饭却吃得轻松愉快。特莱特是翻译，席间没有出现尴尬的沉默。我们随身带了家人照片和几本澳大利亚图册给他们翻看。特莱特的爸爸马先生几年前曾到澳大利亚出过差，能认出其中几幅图片。

午餐棒极了。餐厅的骨瓷杯小巧精致。特莱特的父母以前从未吃过比萨。看人家初次享用新美食，其实非常过瘾。特莱特和她爸爸会用刀叉，但她妈妈却用不惯。用餐期间，马先生打了通电话。特莱特说，是打给她爷爷的，告诉他老人家他很开心，正在和女儿的老师一起吃饭。看来，回澳大利亚后，我会很失落的。

中国人很在意孩子的名字，取名时特别用心。特莱特姓马名叫远征，意思是"为

mother. Part way through lunch, Mr Ma made a phone call. Twilight said he was talking to his father, telling him about being at lunch with us, and how happy he was to be with Twilight's teachers. Coming back to Aussie is going to be something of a letdown.

The Chinese give a great deal of serious thought when it comes to naming their children. Twilight's family name is Ma. This word means horse. Her first name means going a long way, being successful. The Chinese are inclined to use words as names, words with quite beautiful meanings. So her name meant "going a long way like a horse, and having a successful journey." It would be comparable to us calling our child "Happy Successful Kerr".

When Twilight started university her father also chose her English name. We asked why he chose Twilight. She said because it not only means the end of the day but also dawn, so this name could mean the beginning of a day, a new dawning in her life, with a long happy day in front of her. Lovely isn't it?

So that was Twilight, a bouncy happy friendly girl, one we will never forget.

成功而长征"。中国人爱用寓意美好的字眼为名，跟我们亲切地叫自己的孩子为"幸福成功的小柯"一样。

特莱特准备上大学的时候，她父亲替她选了这个英文名字。我问他为什么挑中了"特莱特"？她替父亲回答说，因为特莱特（twilight）既有"黄昏"之意，又可以指"黎明"，所以这个名字可以指一天的开始，她人生的新开端。很美好，不是吗?

这就是特莱特，一个快乐友善、充满活力的女孩，一个我们永远不会忘记的女孩。

SUNNY AND MICKEY

Mickey was a wonderful gentle girl, and like many of these students who lived at boarding schools for many years, craved affection. She regarded us as grandparents, and had a real soft spot for Peter.

In my class for her end of year speech, she stood at the front of the class and said,

"I am a blue girl. I am not a happy girl, so I call myself a blue girl. But when I talk to Mrs K I don't feel so blue …"

At the end of the year I gave her a card with this letter inside.

Dear Mickey,

We have enjoyed, so much, being with you all in Longyan. We have come to know some of the students very well, and saying goodbye is difficult.

You say you are a "blue girl." What we are on the outside is sometimes quite different to what we are on the inside. From time to time, when you are feeling "blue" inside, look at this photo. This is what the outside world sees when it looks at you. It sees a bright, beautiful, radiant, sunshine yellow person.

I hope the "sunshine yellow" penetrates to become the inner person too.

We will both think of you often with fondness.

Mrs K.

I enclosed a photo that had been taken earlier in the year with encouragement to

米奇和姗妮

米奇是个十分温柔的女生，跟其他常年住校的学生一样，特别渴望关爱。她把我俩当成自己的爷爷奶奶，对彼得更是亲近有加。

她在我课上的最后一次演讲中，面对全班说：

"我这个人平日里总是郁郁寡欢的。因为不是非常快乐，所以会说自己忧郁。但我和柯兰老师聊天的时候，却发现自己不再那么忧伤了……"

学期末，我送给米奇一张卡片，并写了封信给她。

亲爱的米奇：

我俩在龙岩生活的这段时光，能够有你们陪伴，真的很开心。如今，你们大都成了我的朋友，现在就要离开你们了，心中万分不舍。

你说自己是个"忧郁的女孩"。其实，外人的感觉常常有别于你的内心。从今往后，当你感到忧伤的时候，就看看这张照片，这就是外人眼中的你：一个美丽开朗、活力四射的阳光女孩。

希望内心的你也能成为那个"阳光女孩"。

我俩都会很想你的。

爱你的柯老师

stay positive.

Peter had a student named Sunny. We had lots of students in different classes named Sunny. It was a very popular name in China, having connotations of pretty, clever, smart, attractive, appealing etc. In this particular lesson he asked them to write a letter, but they were not allowed to write to him, it had to be to a friend or family member. She did her assignment but also wrote a note to Peter.

Dear Mr K.

You are so kind. You remind me of my granddad but my granddad died last year. Please do you mind if I call you granddad in my heart?

Your student,

Sunny.

He was very touched. Wouldn't you be too?

Just before we left, in our apartment, we had a special supper for some of the students. We cooked Australian food, gave them personalised gifts, and played English games. It was a fitting finale for these fabulous students.

There were some hilarious times in the classroom. At the beginning of each class we spent a few minutes getting the students relaxed and ready to work. One of the exercises was the "progressive story".

On the board I wrote the first sentence of a story. The students sat in pairs across the room and about six rows deep. The first pair in each row wrote my sentence on a piece of paper. In turn they handed this paper to the pair behind them who added another sentence. I collected the finished stories from the pair sitting at the back of the row.

The beginning of this story that I wrote on the board was, "There was a loud bang in the airplane". I thought this would give them scope to take a story in several directions, which it did.

Most of the groups wrote predictable stories where there was going to be a crash, but someone saved them at the last minute. I didn't read each story through first, which turned out to be a mistake. I read three of the stories to the class, and started on the fourth

我在信中夹了张她的照片，这张照片是今年年初我替她照的。当时我们在一旁使劲儿给她打气，叫她做一些乐观积极的表情。

彼得有个学生，名叫姗妮（Sunny）。我们教的每个班级都有学生名叫"姗妮"。这个名字在中国很抢手，可能是因为它蕴含着"美好、聪慧、美丽、迷人"等诸多含义的缘故。在一堂课上，彼得叫学生写封信，但是写信的对象不能是他，必须是家人或朋友。姗妮按照吩咐完成了作业，但附上了一张便条。

亲爱的柯先生：

您真的非常好，您让我想起了我的爷爷，可惜他去年过世了。我在心里悄悄叫您爷爷，您会介意吗？

学生，
姗妮

彼得非常感动。换了你，也会吧？

临行前，我们在住所准备了一顿特别的晚餐，招待几个学生。我们做了澳大利亚菜，给每人准备了一份礼物，还玩了英语游戏。唯有以这样的方式同这些卓尔不群的学生告别，我们的心里才会舒坦些。

课堂趣事

我的课堂常有趣事发生。每堂课前，我俩都会花上几分钟，让学生们轻松下来，准备上课。其中一个方法就是故事接龙。

我的班级都是两个学生同坐一张桌子，总共六排。我在黑板上写下故事的第一句话，然后让第一排的学生拿出一张纸抄下句子，另外补充一个句子再传给后一排的学生，以此类推。最后，我从第六排的学生手中收回故事。

这一次我在黑板上写下的故事开头是："突然飞机上传来一声巨响"。我认为这个

one.

I read the first line, which was written on the board, and then I started reading the students' sentences. I just cracked up. I was standing there, crying with laughter, unable to continue. By this time the whole class was giggling. Of course they didn't know what was on the paper, but I must have been quite a sight, bent over my desk, completely helpless with laughter.

Eventually I asked one of the girls to finish reading it for me. (I hope this doesn't turn out to be one of those situations where you have to be there for it to be funny). I think it was the unexpectedness of it that took me by surprise and once I started laughing, well that was that. Here is the story, it's only very short. I hope you get a laugh. I will number the different parts written by each pair.

1. There was a loud bang in the airplane. All the passengers were frightened. They all shouted, except an old man.
2. He stood up and said, "Calm down, please. It was just a fart."
3. Someone shouted, "Don't try to fool us at this critical situation!" Another roared angrily, "How can a fart be so loud?" The old man said, "Because there is a speaker under my buttocks!"
4. But nobody believed him, there were still a lot of people rushing to the exit.
5. The old man said "Please, please calm down, it's really a fart."
6. The passengers shouted to the old man "Why don't you control it?"

I dare you to stand in front of 40 students, read that and keep a straight face.

开头能给他们提供一个自由发挥的空间，结果证明果然如此。

多数小组的故事都是我们预想得到的，写的是坠机事故，在生死存亡的最后时刻有人挺身而出解除了危机。当时，我没有把所有的故事全都看过一遍，真是失策了。我读完三个故事后，准备读第四个故事。

我读完第一句话，就是我写在黑板上的那句话，接着读学生们的句子。我忍不住哈哈大笑起来，怎么也停不下来，没法往下读。看到我这样，学生们也傻呵呵地跟着我乐。当然，他们不知道纸张上的内容，但我的模样肯定非常滑稽，我趴在桌上，笑得话都说不出来。

后来，我请一个女生替我把故事念完。（希望你们没有亲历这样的囧事）。我想，我当时肯定是太意外了，完全没料到学生会写出这样的故事，所以失控了。故事其实很短，我写下来，希望博你一笑。我给不同小组写的句子标上了数字。

1. 突然飞机上传来一声巨响。所有乘客都陷入恐慌，吓得尖声大叫，只有一位老人例外。
2. 他站起身来说："冷静，请大家冷静，我只是放了一个屁。"
3. 有人大声质疑："都死到临头了，别糊弄我们！"另一名乘客也愤怒地咆哮道："胡说，屁怎么可能这么响。"老人说："因为我的屁股下面有个扬声器。"
4. 但是没人相信他，还是有许多人涌向出口。
5. 老人叫道："冷静，求求你们冷静一下，那真的只是我放的一个屁。"
6. 乘客们集体冲老人大吼："那你干嘛不忍住不放？！"

我敢打赌，要是你站在全班四十名同学面前读这个，肯定也会忍俊不止，狂笑不已。

SHARK

On Wednesday nights at 7pm we held English Corner. All students were welcome to come to a courtyard in front of the main teaching building. Our little group of English teachers spoke to several hundred students, sometimes becoming almost hoarse at the end of the two hours, trying to yell over the top of all the noise.

People from the city also knew that they could come, and often adults attended. Amongst these visitors were a doctor, other businessmen and two young men named Roger and Shark.

The first night they came we invited them up to our apartment for a visit. They were interesting to talk to, both having finished their university lives and were working. We were always interested in the English names of the students. I asked Shark what his name was. Due to the noise around me, I mistook what he said. I thought he said "Jacque". I said his name was French and asked who had given him this name. It was unusual to have a Chinese person with such a name, although I did have one rather flamboyant student named Francisco, that I nicknamed "The Fonz".

It was at this point that I realized that I had not heard correctly. His name was Shark. Oh, that was a bit different. He explained that he was given this name at university, because he wore a T-Shirt with a shark on the front.

He was a lovely boy, about twenty-four-years old with an open face, and when he smiled his whole face lit up.

Roger and Shark came for every English corner, and soon Shark was a regular visitor

沙克

我们学校每周三晚上7点都会在教学大楼前举办英语角活动,全校学生均可参加,我们几个外教要和几百个学生说话,周围闹哄哄的,只能尽可能抬高嗓门,两小时后声音常常都喊哑了。

市民们知道他们也可参加,因此常有一些成年人光顾,来者中有一个医生、几个生意人和两人年轻小伙子,他们中一个名叫罗杰,另一个名叫沙克。

他俩第一次上英语角,我们就邀请他们到自己的住处做客。与他们聊天很有意思,俩人都已经大学毕业了,在上班。我俩一向对学生的英文名字很感兴趣,于是问沙克叫什么名字。当时周围一片嘈杂,我没听清楚他的回答,以为他讲的是"雅克",便说这是个法国名字,谁给他取的。中国人不大叫这样的名字,不过,我的确教过一个爱赶时髦的学生,叫弗兰西斯科,我亲切地叫他"范兹(The Fonz)"。①

这时我才意识到自己听错了,他叫沙克(shark),意思是鲨鱼。哇,好不一般的名字。沙克解释说,这个名字是他上大学时别人给取的,因为他当时穿了件胸口印着鲨鱼的T恤。

---

① 范兹(The Fonz)是上世纪80年代初,电视连续剧《欢乐时光》(*Fonz and the Happy Days Gang*)的主角之一 Arthur Fonzarelli(即 The Fonz),这个人物后来被评为历史上最伟大的流行文化偶像之一。

during the week. He worked until 6pm, went home for dinner, then ran several laps round the university sports track. After that he came and visited us. In the hot summer he'd be dripping with perspiration, so he had a shower, then all cooled off spent a few hours with us.

He was a very quick thinker. The Chinese people are great card players. They have some rather intricate games, and Shark was a pro. He could remember all the cards played, and knew what was still to come. He won practically every game.

I taught him Scrabble, and because his English vocabulary was more limited, I won, but at cards he was always the champion.

We kept the freezer stocked with a delicious mango flavoured ice-cream on a stick. Shark loved these, and often asked to have one.

Two other students were also constant visitors, Hope and Jolly. There is a "thing" in China about which school you went to. When the girls found out that Shark attended the Hangzhou University of Technology, they swooned. "Such a famous university," they said. He must be a "great man". Of course, they giggled and went all shy when he was around, but the name, "The Great Man" sort of stuck. In reply, he just said he was a "Humble Man".

Towards the end of our year there, he became part of the family. He visited whenever he wanted, texting first to make sure it was okay. He took us to his home where his father cooked us a lovely meal, and we took photos with his family. His mother died during the time we were on holiday in Thailand. I knew she was not well, but didn't realize how sick she was, and I never did get to meet her. I regretted that.

He'd also been given another English name. When he first started work his boss said that Shark was not a suitable business name, so named him Alex. He used this name more as the year went on, so he became Alex to us rather than Shark.

If we were having other students around, Shark was there. At our farewell party, he was there. He became like a son to me. Leaving Longyan also meant leaving Shark. It was going to be very hard.

沙克很活泼，24岁左右，性格开朗，笑起来一脸灿烂。

罗杰和沙克每次英语角必参加，没过多久，沙克便成了我家的常客。他傍晚六点下班，回家吃晚饭，然后到大学操场跑上几圈，之后便上我家。夏天，因为跑完步一身大汗，所以会先回家冲个澡，然后再清清爽爽地来我家与我们呆上几小时。

沙克思维敏捷。中国人都是玩纸牌的高手，有些玩法相当复杂，但沙克都玩得很溜。他不但记得住出过的每张牌，还能算出哪些牌没出，因此他极少输牌。

我教他玩拼词游戏。因为他的英文词汇量有限，所以总是我赢，但玩起牌来常胜将军非他莫属。

我们的冰箱里常年放着一种美味的芒果雪糕，沙克可爱吃这东西了，常向我们要。

爱上我家玩的还有我的两个学生：朱莉和荷芙。在中国，上什么大学是件关乎"面子"的大事。当两个女生获知沙克上的是杭州理工大学时，惊呼道："名牌大学呀！"他肯定是个"牛人"。当然了，沙克在场的时候，她俩只懂咯咯傻笑，羞答答的，说些他很"牛"之类的话。沙克则回答说，他只是个"普通人"而已。

到我们聘期将满的那一年，沙克已经成了我们家中的一分子了。他想什么时候来我家都行，只需事先发个短信看看我们是否方便。他领我们去过他家，他父亲很会煮饭，我们还和他的家人一起合过影。我们去泰国旅行的时候，沙克的母亲去世了。我知道她身体不舒服，但没料到她病得这么厉害，我再也没机会见到她了，心里好生难过。

沙克以前还有一个英文名字。他刚入职上班时，老板觉得在商场上用这个名字不是太妥当，要他改名为亚历克斯。后来，他大都用这个名儿，所以他不再是我们的沙克，而是我们的亚历克斯。

只要我们家有学生来访，沙克就会现身。告别聚会时，沙克也在场。他几乎成了我们的儿子。离开龙岩意味着离开沙克。真的好舍不得呀。

HOLIDAYS AND TYPHOONS

For the last few weeks we had been looking forward to our week's holiday, Golden Week, National Day holiday during the first week in October. It's a big deal and almost everyone has this holiday.

Officially there is a five day break, but we had been given seven days, which was five days plus a weekend. After much discussion we decided on a few days in Xiamen.

"You realise you have to work the weekend after you get back? Saturday and Sunday?" came a text message from Paul.

"No!" Peter replied.

Paul phoned. "Yes. Everyone does, to make up the two extra days you are having off. You must work Saturday and Sunday of the next weekend."

"You are kidding, aren't you," Peter retorted.

"No! We all will work. There will be lessons that weekend."

We were flabbergasted. In the kindness of their hearts they give us two days off we didn't ask for, but we have to work a weekend to make up for it.

"Oh well, we'll just have to work the weekend then," said Peter resignedly.

"We also need to go to the bank," said Paul, "and get your money cards. The university has paid you two bonuses."

"Really?" Peter said. "That's marvellous. How much?"

"500RMB for Teachers Day, and 300RMB for National day. It's in your bank account now, but we need to arrange PIN numbers and cards for your withdrawals. Meet

假日与台风

最后几周我们一直盼望着国庆黄金周的来临，也就是十月份的第一周。这是举国同庆的日子，几乎全民放假。

其实，正式放假的天数是 5 天，但是加上周末两天，我们就有 7 天假。经过反复商量，我们决定到厦门度假。

"你可知道，回家之后周末是得上班哟？ 也就是周六、周日要补课？"保罗发来短信。

"不会吧！"彼得回了条短信。

保罗打来电话："这是真的，大家都一样，补多放的两天假的课。下周周六、周日必须上课。"

"你在开玩笑，对吧。"彼得抢白道。

"没的事！ 我们大家都得上班，下周末要上课的。"

我们大为惊愕。虽然我们没有要求，可他们却好心好意地给我们多放两天假，只是没想到下周末得补回来。

"行了，我们下周末会回来上班的。"彼得没有再为难他。

"我们还得去趟银行，取你们的银行卡。学校给你们发了两笔津贴。"保罗说。

"真的吗？ 太好了！ 多少钱？"彼得忙问。

me at the gate at 3pm. We'll go down together."

The university had opened bank accounts for us, and our first wages were due to go in plus these bonuses. After queuing at the bank, Paul finally reached the front of the queue and after much argy-bargy he was told we were at the wrong branch, right bank, just the wrong branch.

"Where's the other branch?" we asked Paul.

"Oh not far," Paul said. "Just up by the supermarket."

"We've been going ten minutes Paul, how much further?" we asked after walking quite some distance.

"Just up here," he said. We learned early on in our time in Longyan that a five minute walk to a Chinese person is in fact a half hour walk. We reached the bank. Paul filled in the paperwork, went to the counter and came back.

"Made a mistake. Have to do them again," he said. He's doing forms in Chinese for Peter and I, Deneice and Emerson. Two and a half hours later we have our cards and PIN's. There's no way to speed these things up, you just have to go with the flow. One good thing though, we were given our cards immediately, no waiting for them to come in the mail.

Then we knocked the teller off her perch by asking how to do international money transfers. She looked at us as if we had asked about Martian money. She'd never heard of it, so suggested we go to the Bank of China.

So with our new ATM cards and bonuses at the ready, we took a bus to Xiamen for a few days holiday. I had a list of things to do and see. The first job was to go to Walmart. We had heard so much about this fabulous shop we wanted to see it for ourselves. It was, in reality a six floor mall. We walked all six floors and couldn't for the life of us work out what the Walmart bit was. There seemed to be six floors of shops and little stalls.

"Maybe Walmart is just all these stalls?" I said to Peter. He was as confused as I was.

"Walmart? Where?" I asked someone in my bad Chinese.

A man took us to the door. "Out," he said, and then gestured to show we had to come back in the other door. We'd already done that twice but we did it again. Nothing had moved. It was still six floors of shops and stalls. Totally bamboozled we just stood there.

"教师节 500 元人民币，国庆节 300 元人民币，已经打入了你们的账户，但我们得去设密码，这样你们好取钱。下午三点钟在学校门口等我，我们一块儿过去。"

学校已经替我们在银行开好了账户，除了这两笔津贴外，工资也应该发了。我们在银行排了好一会儿队，终于轮到保罗了。他跟银行职员唇枪舌剑了一番，却被告知我们来错了地方。银行是对的，但不是这家分行。

"另一家分行在哪儿呢？"我们问保罗。

"噢，不远，就在超市那边。"保罗回答。

"我们已经走了十分钟路了，保罗，还要走多远？"走了好长一段路之后，我们忍不住问他。

"就在前面一点儿。"他回答。我们到龙岩不久就明白了，中国人说走五分钟路，其实得走上半小时。我们总算到了银行，保罗填好表格，走到柜台边，又回来了。

"出了个差错，得重填。"他说。他在用中文替我、彼得、戴妮丝和爱默生填表格。整整过了两个半小时，我们总算拿到了银行卡和密码。这种事情急不得，只能耐着性子等。好在银行卡是当下就给了我们，无需等邮件寄送。

接着，我们轮番问银行出纳外汇怎么兑换，差点儿把她烦死了。她看着我们，好像我们问询的是火星人使用的货币。她从未接触过外汇兑换业务，叫我们去中国银行打听。

带上新的 ATM 卡和卡中的津贴，我俩坐上巴士去厦门度假了。我把想要做的事儿和想去玩的地方都列了出来。首先是去沃尔玛。听说这家商场非常好，我们想眼见为实。事实上，这是一家六层楼的商场，我们从一楼走到六楼，愣是没搞清楚，沃尔玛是什么东西，似乎是六层楼的商店和小店面。

"莫非沃尔玛就是指这些小店面？"我对彼得说。他跟我一样一头雾水。

"沃尔玛？在哪里？"我用蹩脚的中文问一个人。

一个男子将我们领到大门口，说："出去。"接着做了个手势，叫我们从另一扇门进来。我们已经进进出出了两次，这已经是第三次了。没有什么变化呀，还是一样的

I asked someone else in my bad Chinese. They pointed to an escalator going down.

I looked at Peter in amazement and asked, "Why call a place "Walmart Superstore" and hide it in the basement?"

It was a massive department store. Peter got some shoes. He couldn't get anything in Longyan, his feet were size 44 or 46, and they go to a size 42 in Longyan. Let's face it, Chinese have tiny bodies and tiny feet, why should they stock large sized shoes for people like Peter?

Satisfied with our shopping day we had dinner at the hotel. Deneice phoned us to say there was a typhoon coming, and we should consider going home in the morning before it struck. The only snag was that I had a big day planned for tomorrow and I hadn't counted on a typhoon!

Early next morning the weather seemed settled enough so we set off with a long list of jobs to accomplish. I had a good map with all the places to visit marked out in Chinese and English.

"If we get off a number 21 bus at this stop we'll find the book shop we want," I told Peter showing him on the map. Of course Peter in his wisdom listens to the words of his wife. We got off the bus.

"Where's this shop then?" Peter asks.

"Opposite the Cultural museum," I replied looking around. "That might be a museum, it's hard to tell."

No one spoke English and all the signs were in Chinese so we might as well have been on the moon. We asked, we walked, we got lots of bewildered looks, but not a bookshop in view. By this time I was getting a tad tetchy.

On a large intersection Peter suggested we waited to see which way a number 21 bus went and we could walk that way.

"Sorry love, I'm not walking anywhere! I've had enough. Let's get a taxi."

We hailed a taxi, got in and showed him the map. Remember the taxi drivers cannot speak English. They have fabulous Chinese, but no English. (We have fabulous English but no Chinese). It's all pointing and nodding and stuff. The taxi driver dropped us off with long instructions in Chinese and much pointing. We nodded knowingly, got out, but we were still none the wiser.

六层楼的商店和小店面。我们疑惑地站在里面。我又用蹩脚的中文问了另一个人。他指了指下行的扶梯。

我诧异地看着彼得问："为什么堂堂一'沃尔玛大超市'藏身于负一楼？"

下面是一家很大的百货商场。彼得买了一双鞋。他在龙岩买不到鞋穿，他要穿44或46码的鞋子，而龙岩的鞋子最大只有42码。话又说回来，中国人身材小，脚也小，干嘛要进超大码的鞋子，只有彼得这样的人才会穿？

我们痛痛快快地购了一天物，回到酒店吃晚饭。戴妮丝打来电话，告诉我们台风快来了，我们应该乘它登路之前明天早上赶回龙岩。唯一的障碍是，明天的活动我已经安排满了。可是我失算了，没想到还有台风这档子事儿！

第二天一大早，看天色一时不会变，我们赶紧出去，完成清单上一长串任务。我怀揣了一张详细地图，主要景点都标着中英两种语言。

"坐21路公交车到这一站下车，就可以到我们想去的书店。"我指着地图对彼得说。当然，彼得有自知之明，对妻子言听计从，于是我俩登上了21路公交车。

"那家店在哪儿呀？"彼得问。

"文化宫对面，也可能是个博物馆。"我边说边四下张望。

没人说英语，所有的标识都是中文，我们跟在月亮上差不多。我俩一路走一路问，可是大家全都一脸茫然，而周围连书店的影子都没有。我开始有点恼火了。

到一个大十字路口，彼得提议我俩呆在原地，等21路公交车过来，看它往哪儿开，我们就往哪儿走。

"对不起，亲爱的，我不走了，实在走不动了，打的士吧。"

"我们招来一辆的士，坐进车中，把地图给司机看。还记得吧，的士司机是不懂英语的。他们的中文个个顶呱呱，英语却一窍不通。（而我俩是英语顶呱呱，中文一窍不通。）我们靠比划和点头交流了一会儿。司机开到一个地方停住叫我俩下车，他说了一长串中文，还连比带划，告诉我们怎么走。我们会意地点点头下车，而依旧不知身在何处。

"Get the map out Peter, maybe that'll tell us what this place is," I mumbled.

He patted his pockets, looked in my bag, hung his head and said, "I've left it in the taxi. I put it on the floor and forgot to pick it up. Sorry!"

So there we were, stranded with no map. Having the Chinese and English instructions on the map were imperative because we couldn't say where we wanted to go, but the taxi drivers could read the instructions. I accosted some poor boy who looked like a student. He spoke no English, so I phoned Mary, the Chinese teacher. We had a triangular conversation, with Mary talking to the student in Chinese then to me in English. We do this sometimes when we don't know what else to do.

"Walk to your left just a little way and you will see your shop," said Mary.

"Yes, I can see it," I told Mary after a minute or so. "Wonderful. Thanks so much."

It was only a little shop but we enjoyed browsing and buying what we wanted. By this time it was almost lunchtime and we had done one thing on our list, had lost our map so had no instructions for the afternoons visits, and the wind was getting up.

I'd taken a pamphlet from the hotel which advertised a travel agency with English speaking staff. We were desperate to find a local agency where someone, anyone, could speak English. We hailed another taxi and showed him the address. He shook his head and mumbled in Chinese.

"He doesn't know this place," Peter said.

"He should, the pamphlet is all in Chinese."

The driver sat mumbling and shaking his head, then made a phone call. Suddenly we were off like a rocket arriving at a small shop in a back lane behind the Marco Polo Hotel, a big five star establishment.

"Hello, can I help you?" a young Chinese girl asked in wonderful English as we entered.

"Oh, your English is excellent. Oh! We are so pleased to find someone who speaks such good English," I gushed.

She laughed. "I only employ good English speakers," she said. "We deal with many foreigners from all over the world. My name is Apple."

I cringed just a little bit at the name, we had an Orange and Pear amongst the students, and now we had an Apple.

"彼得，快把地图拿出来，说不定地图上标了咱们所在的位置。"我嘀咕道。

他拍拍口袋，看看包里，低头说道："被我落在的士里了，我随手把它放在脚边，下车时忘记捡起来了，对不起！"

没有了地图，我俩举步维艰。地图上标着中英两种文字，这对我们很重要，我们说不来要去的地方，但的士司机看得懂上面的中文。我拦住一个可怜的学生模样的男孩，他也不会说英语，我只好打电话给一个中国老师，玛丽。我们进行了三方通话，玛丽和男孩说中文，和我说英语。实在没辙的时候，我们偶尔会使出这一招。

"朝左走一小段路就能看到那家店了。"玛丽说。

才走了不到一分钟路，我告诉玛丽："没错，我看见了，太棒了，多谢了。"

这家书店不大。我们在书店里慢慢看，见到中意的书就买，感觉还是很惬意的。这时已是午饭时间，我们只完成了清单上的一件事。如今没有了地图，我们失去了指南，根本不知下午打算去的地方在哪儿，而此时风已经越刮越烈了。

我从酒店拿了一份宣传手册，上面登了一家能接外团的旅行社。我们没招了，一心只想找到一家本地旅行社，找个会说英语的人，管他是谁。我们又叫来一辆的士，把地址给司机看。司机摇了摇头，嘴里嘟哝了几句汉语。

"他不知道这个地方。"彼得说。

"不应该呀，手册上写的都是中文呀。"

司机坐在车里一边嘀咕一边摇头，然后打了一通电话。突然，我们像坐火箭一样，嗖的便到了一条小巷边的一个门店，这家店就开在五星级大酒店马克波罗背后。

"你们好，有什么需要我帮忙的吗？"我们一进到门里，一个年轻姑娘操一口漂亮的英语问候道。

"噢，你的英语真漂亮。噢！能找到一个英语这么好的人真是太高兴了。"我舌灿莲花。

她笑着说："我的员工英语都很好，我们的客人来自世界各地的都有。我叫艾帕儿（Apple，指苹果）。"

We introduced ourselves and chatted for a while asking for her business card and told her we'd be delighted to use her for all our travel.

"No problem, contact me anytime. We'll make all your bookings and email you back."

"Where did you learn such good English?" I asked.

"Self-taught," she replied, "but my husband speaks good English too. We lived in Australia for a few years."

What a gem! She spoke wonderful English and knew her job.

"As you're teachers I can get you 50% discount with Xiamen Airlines," she told us.

"Wonderful, fabulous, terrific," I gushed again.

Other teachers came in, made bookings and left. On hearing about losing our map, Apple gave us another one and wrote some instructions for us in Chinese. We were delighted to have met her and her staff and headed off for our next port of call, a much larger book shop.

Xinhua (said Shin wha) book shop was a huge four floor shop. Book shops in China are a hoot. You have to pick your way across the floor which is littered with people sitting and standing reading books. Let's face it, why buy it when you can come in and read it for free? They had a good selection of English books for our students to read so we bought a few of those.

As we came into the street again, we could see the weather had deteriorated drastically.

"We need a Bank of China," I said to Peter, "to withdraw some money. Have you seen one?"

"No. Don't remember seeing one at all."

"Well, this is the main street there must be one somewhere."

Isn't it always the way? You don't want something and there are heaps of them, you want something and there's not one to be found.

We walked the length of the main street again, and found an ATM lurking behind a pillar. We withdrew what we needed. By now it was nearly dark, the rain was coming down in buckets, and we had one umbrella between us.

听到她的名字，我觉得有点儿好笑。在我的学生当中有叫橘子和梨子的，现在叫苹果的也有了。

我们介绍了自己，和她聊了几句，向她要了张名片，告诉她以后我们旅游都找她。

"没问题，随时联系我。我们负责订房订票，再写邮件通知你。"

"你的英语这么好，是从哪儿学来的？"我问。

"自学的，不过我先生的英语也很好。我俩在澳大利亚生活了几年。"她回答。

太难得了！这姑娘不仅英语好，还懂行。

"因为你们是教师，我可以从厦门航空公司拿到五折机票。"她告诉我们。

"太好了，棒极了，超赞。"我又忍不住满嘴好话。

又有几位老师过来，订了票便走了。听说我们丢了地图，艾帕儿送了一张给我们，并在上面用中文写好路线。穷途末路之中遇见了她和她的员工，让我们喜出望外。我们高高兴兴地前往下一站，一家更大的书店。

新华书店是个四层楼的大书店。中国的书店都是闹哄哄的。你得小心地穿过或站或坐的捧书阅读的读者。说实话，有时间看免费的书，干嘛要掏钱买呢？书店里，不少英文书籍适合我们的学生阅读，我们一口气买了好多本。

再次来到街上时，天气已经坏得不行。

"我们必须去一趟中国银行，取点儿钱。你看见哪里有中国银行吗？"我对彼得说。

"没有呢，记不得了。"

"那里就是大街了，可能大街上会有。"

事情是不是经常这样矛盾？你不想要什么东西，那个东西却随处可见。可当你想要一样东西的时候，却满世界都找不到。

我们又走了一遍大街，看见在一根大柱子后面藏了一个ATM提款机。我们取了一笔钱。此时，天空黑压压的，下着倾盆大雨，我俩只能共撑一把伞。

"Think ahead, be prepared" is my personal motto. As always, I was prepared. I'd written a list of very basic phrases in a handy little notebook. I was going to unleash my terrible Chinese on some poor unsuspecting taxi driver. But we weren't the only ones looking for a taxi. Every taxi we saw was full. We got wetter and wetter waving down taxis that just ignored us.

The notebook was at the very bottom of my bag and as it seemed impossible to get a taxi we looked for the No. 21 bus stop. Sure enough up the road and around the corner was the stop. By now it was pitch black, the wind was howling and the heavens had opened.

We clambered on board to find the bus was going the wrong way! All these buses go there and back, so we knew it was eventually going to go past our hotel. But this one went to Xiamen University and stopped. It was the driver's tea time and everyone had to get off and join the queue in the pouring rain for the next bus.

We showed the driver our card with the hotel's name on. He understood what we wanted. He took us part way down the bus and pointed at the route which was marked out in Chinese. With emphatic gestures he said "one, two' in Chinese. We smiled and nodded knowingly.

"Second stop," Peter said. "Be back at the hotel in a jiffy."

As we neared the second stop I squeezed my way towards the back exit.

"No," yelled Peter. "This isn't right!"

"You sure? This is the second stop."

"No! I'm sure it's not right. Now what?" he yelled back to me.

Everyone stared, but we had got used to looking foolish. We just nodded and smiled at everyone. As we approached each stop Peter tried to work out where we were. We were hopelessly lost and the bus went for miles as the typhoon made landfall.

"Okay, get out," he yelled.

"You sure?"

"Yes, quick, get out. This is right."

We squished our way out the door into the violent wind and horizontal rain. Our clothes were saturated and using the umbrella was futile in the wind. We made it back to the hotel, dribbled our way up to our room and collapsed with relief.

HOLIDAYS AND TYPHOONS
假日与台风

"未雨绸缪，有备无患"是我的人生座右铭。我像以往一样，有备而来。我在一个小笔记本上写了许多基本词汇。我打算用糟糕的中文麻烦某个可怜的没有戒心的的士司机。可是，想打的士的人并非只有我们两个。每辆的士都载了客人。我们不停地冲的士招手，身上越来越湿，可是一辆辆的士都对我们视而不见。

我把笔记本放到包的最下面，看来是没有希望打到的士了，我们想找21路公车站点。确实，大路上方和拐角路口都有公交站点。此时街上已经一片漆黑，台风呼呼刮着，天空像裂开似的，大雨如注。

我们跟跄地上了一辆公车，却发现坐错了车。因为所有的公车都会按原路返回，所以我们知道21路车会经过我们的酒店，没想到车开到厦门大学就停下不走了。这个时候恰好是司机换班的时候，所有的乘客都得下车，加入在大雨中候车的队伍，等下一班车发车。

我们把写了酒店名字的卡片给司机看。他看明白了，领我们走到车内的路线示意图前，极为夸张地打着手势，用中文说"1、2"。我们笑眯眯地点点头，以示明白。

"第二站下车，一会儿就能到酒店了。"彼得说。

快到第二站的时候，我赶忙朝后车车门挤去。

"不对，错了！"彼得大叫。

"你确信？这就是第二站呀。"

"不对！我敢肯定错了。怎么办？"他冲我大叫道。

一车的乘客都盯着我们看，不过我们已经习惯人前丢丑了。我们只能冲着大伙儿点头、微笑。每到一站，彼得都要想办法搞清楚这一站是什么地方。我们彻底迷路了，汽车一直往前开了好远，而台风已经登陆了。

"行了，下车。"彼得叫道。

"你确定？"

"是的，赶快下车，就这一站。"

我们挤出车门，来到狂风暴雨之中。我俩的衣服已经湿透了，肆虐的狂风之下，

We cursed the bus driver for giving us the wrong information. I talked to Linda, the Manager the next morning. Ah yes, I got it wrong again! The driver was right. Of course I didn't understand he was telling us we needed the second stop from the end. That was mostly our mistake for thinking we understood something simple, when we didn't have a clue what he was really saying.

The typhoon passed overnight and the weather improved enough for us to spend the next day walking for miles exploring. Our legs were little stumps by dinner time. We returned to Longyan happy with our few days away.

Check out Apple's web page, their service is second to none.
http://www.appletravel.cn/ or email them at apple@appletravel.cn

雨伞是不顶用的。我们走回酒店，一路滴滴嗒嗒地回到房间，累得一塌糊涂，但心里却如释重负了。

我俩大骂司机误导我们。第二天早上，我把这事儿告诉酒店经理琳达。没错，这回又是我冤枉了人家！司机是对的。当然，我们没有搞清楚，他是叫我们在倒数第二站下车。我们老是犯这样的错误，总以为事情简单，我们能够明白，而实际上却稀里糊涂。

台风第二天便走了，天气转好了不少，于是我们又到处转了转，到午饭时间时，我们的两条腿已经成了两根木棍，毫无知觉。几天之后，我们开开心心地返回了龙岩。

请查阅艾帕儿的网站，她们的服务绝对一流。

www.appletravel.cn 或者写邮件给这个地址：apple@appletravel.cn

CHINESE CUISINE, CANTEEN-ESE STYLE

Many a person has written books on Chinese cooking and I don't intend to do that here. But I have to say that eating at a Chinese restaurant in the West is not an authentic experience with Chinese food. In Longyan, we got the "genuine article".

On several occasions the school hosted banquets for the senior staff and foreign teachers. At first, so much of the food was strange, and we were somewhat suspicious of everything. It was rare to find a mushroom there that looked like a mushroom, and because meat was very expensive when you bought for a school full of starving students, it only came in small portions along with other stuff to "flesh it out". On the whole they didn't eat large portions of meat. But the "real deal" was eating at the university canteen.

I went through several phases in the canteen. I started off with the general run of the mill stuff, which was vegetables, some of which was easy to recognise, such as pumpkin, carrots and greens, but there was other food which was unrecognizable. Slabs of rice the size of a pound of butter was the key ingredient. The students all consumed vast amounts of boiled white rice, with several helpings of vegetables and small quantities of meat. They ate three substantial meals a day, and seldom anything in between.

My first visit to the canteen was unnerving to say the least. We went about six o'clock in the evening and found out later that the food arrived about five o'clock, so everything was cold and greasy. If the students got to the canteen late they just ate it cold, they seemed to be used to it. But I couldn't face that, so I started cooking in our apartment for a while. It then occurred to me to take a container and take it back to the apartment to reheat in the microwave. That turned out to be a good plan.

食堂就餐记

许多人写过书，介绍中国的厨艺，我不想步人后尘。不过我得说，我们在西方国家中餐馆吃到的菜式并不正宗。在龙岩，我们尝到了"地地道道的中国菜"。

学校做了好几次东，宴请外教和老教师。第一次面对这么多陌生的菜品，我们心里没谱，不大敢尽情享用。在中国的餐桌上，很难见到蘑菇的本来模样。因为这里肉价很高，又有一学校饥肠辘辘的学生等着填饱肚子，因此食堂总是把肉切成小片，和其他菜一起煮"提鲜"。但在学校食堂，你吃到的是"真货"。

对在食堂吃饭，我经历过不同阶段。一开始专挑普通菜式，也就是蔬菜。蔬菜，像南瓜、胡萝卜、青菜什么的，容易辨认，但还有一些就不知为何物了。米饭是主食，分成一块一块的，跟一磅重的黄油差不多大小。学生们一般会买上一大份米饭，配上几样青菜和一小碟肉。一日就早、中、晚三餐，中间很少吃东西。

我俩初次在食堂的用餐经历，用"望而生畏"一词来形容，当不为过。晚上6点，我们来到食堂，发现饭菜全都凉了，油腻腻的，后来才知道食堂五点钟就开放了。学生们要是来晚了，就只能吃冷饭冷菜。对此，他们好像已经习以为常了，可我却难以接受，于是亲自下厨煮了一段时间的饭。后来，我心里闪过一个念头：何不拿个饭盒，到食堂把饭菜买回家，再用微波炉加热食用？这个办法果然极好。

We did keep an eye on the canteen though, and at lunchtimes, when we came straight up from class, the food was hot. Once we knew their schedule we went there regularly. The food was brought out in large stainless steel bowls to a bain-marie type counter, but without the hot water to keep it warm. The range of food was impressive, about twenty to thirty selections. The problem was identifying the stuff. Chinese people ate a huge amount of tofu, but they disguised it, so I didn't know what it was. They chopped it, diced it, fried it and used it in many dishes, but I never enjoyed tofu, it seemed like tasteless edible rubber.

Growing up in New Zealand with vegetables plentiful and being rather wasteful we discarded most of the stalk. But not there. They eat the whole thing, so, often a serving of cabbage was ten per cent cabbage and ninety per cent stalk. Carrot was recognizable as was the pumpkin which they diced and served along with quite a bit of the cooking juice. There were all sorts of greens which I'd never seen before. I tried some but they were often very bitter and chewy, not my thing at all.

They served green peas sometimes. The first time I saw them I thought they looked okay, but no, they were old and dry and as hard as bullets. They had green beans, which were good, and lots of cauliflower and broccoli. They also did something quite unusual with potato. I don't know how they cooked it, but it tasted not unlike baked potato that had been cooked again with some sort of juice. It looked a bit odd, but it tasted delicious, so I often chose that.

The system was that you walked into the canteen, helped yourself to a stainless steel tray and soup bowl, got your chopsticks and a spoon and worked your way along the line pointing to what you wanted. You could choose as much as you wanted, and they charged a little more if you got extra helpings. Some of it I was never game enough to try, but the students tucked in and devoured tons of food every day.

Chinese people love to eat fish, but I never ate them at the canteen. They were small and full of tiny bones, and anyway we didn't know their origin, maybe a dirty river. Chinese people learn at a very young age the knack of eating only the flesh and leaving the bones behind. They also loved tiny shrimps that the locals considered a delicacy. They put the whole thing in their mouth, work the shell from the flesh, spat the shell onto the table, and swallowed the rest. The table was the place for any rejects, so beside each place there was a little pile of bones, skin or other inedibles, that just got spat onto the

不过，对食堂的情况，我们的确一直都很上心。中午，要是一下课就去食堂吃饭，饭菜都是热乎乎的。一旦摸清了食堂的开放时间，我们就成了那里的常客。我们把外带的食物装在一个大不锈钢碗中，再搁入一种水浴保温器里，容器内没放热水，因此无法保温。食堂里有二三十种食物。麻烦的是，里面的原料是什么，我们不知道。中国人很会吃豆腐，变着花样煮，搞得我认不出来。他们把豆腐剁碎、切丁、油炸之后放入许多菜中，可我一直不爱吃这东西，总觉得它跟可以食用的橡胶一样，寡淡无味。

新西兰这个国家从来不缺蔬菜，可能是打小在那儿长大的缘故，我们很浪费，一般只吃菜叶，不吃菜梗。中国人却不一样，他们连梗带叶一起吃。因此一份白菜中往往十分之九是菜梗，只有十分之一是菜叶。胡萝卜容易识别，南瓜也一样好认，切成了小方块，打菜的时候，他们还会舀上大半勺南瓜汤给你。这里有许多蔬菜，都是我以前没见过的，我吃过一些，大都又苦涩又难嚼，不对我的口味。

有时食堂会煮豌豆。第一次看到豌豆的时候，我觉得卖相不错，其实我看走眼了，这东西又老又干，硬得跟子弹一样。这里也有青豆，味道不错，花菜和西兰花几乎餐餐皆有。他们还会用土豆做出很不一样的菜式，我不知道具体煮法，吃起来有点儿像烤土豆加汤汁回锅再煮过的味道。瞧着挺奇怪的，但非常美味，我常吃。

食堂的用餐程序如下：进食堂先取一个不锈钢托盘和汤碗，拿好筷子和汤勺去排队，想吃什么菜用手指一下就行。想吃多少就点多少，多点多算钱。有些菜我一直没敢尝试，但学生们却大口大口地往嘴里塞，每天都要消灭掉一大堆食物。

中国人爱吃鱼，但我从未在食堂吃过鱼。因为这里的鱼很小，很多细鱼刺，我们又不知道它们的产地，说不定来自一条肮脏的小河呢。中国人很小就学会了吃肉吐骨头的本领。他们也喜欢吃一种小虾，当地人视其为一大美食。他们把整条虾放进嘴里，剥去壳，将壳吐到桌上，然后把虾肉吞进肚里。桌子就是放剩物的地方，因此每个座位边，都有一小堆他们吐出的骨头、肉皮等不能吃的东西，等餐厅服务员收拾桌子时再清扫。

table for the cleaner-uppers to remove as they wiped down the tables.

There was a wide variety of meat. Fatty pork was chopped up and cooked in a delicious soy-based sauce. Beef chunks, chicken stew, and other varieties of meats were also available. Some of it looked pretty awful, but it tasted surprisingly good. The portions are big enough, served by girls behind the counter who slopped large spoonful's into your tray willy-nilly. These girls didn't speak any English, so it was just point, point, and nod.

Soup was a must. I rather think this was a Longyan-ese thing, rather than a Chinese thing, but we were told you must have soup with every meal. The rice could be quite dry so they were partial to some juice to wet it down. I think this is where the vegetable juice comes in. Anyway, soup is a big deal. There was only one soup I enjoyed, made from sweet white carrots. They also made seaweed soup that tasted like boiled grass, and a lentil soup that made my taste buds revolt.

It took us some time to find out about the hotpot meals that were available in the back corner. These were "made to order" meals. This was Peter's favourite lunch time meal and I ate them often. We could go to a counter right at the back of the canteen, and there a pretty girl with beautiful long hair walked around giving and taking orders and delivering to the tables. She was efficient, but had the voice of a fishwife. You could hear her from one end of the canteen to the other, and that was some achievement with hundreds of students, who all possessed wonderfully developed lungs, exchanging the news of the day. So we ordered "chow fan" or "chow mein". Chow fan is fried rice with stuff added and chow mein (said me-in) is fried noodles with stuff added.

After a while we educated the staff and they prepared good hotpot noodle meals for us, adding vegetables, spices, meat and eggs. This was a very hot, tasty, filling meal cooked directly on the gas cookers in earthenware pots.

They also made a different soup. We'd get a very large bowl with mushrooms and a bit of beef and vegetables. We normally ate with Deneice and another teacher, Mary, and we shared one bowl between the four of us. They used to add tofu to this too, which we asked them to omit, but the fishwife didn't speak a word of English, so sometimes the message didn't get through.

The price at this restaurant you may ask? A full meal at the "choose your own poison" counter was 2.5 Yuan, about 45 cents Australian. The bowl of white carrot soup,

食堂准备了很多种肉菜，肥肉切块用酱油红烧，味道好极了。烧牛肉、炖鸡等荤菜，食堂一应俱全。有的菜样子难看，但吃起来味道却好得不可思议。每块肉都很大，负责打菜的姑娘总是不由分说地往肉里添一大勺肉汤。姑娘们不会说英语，我们都是靠手指、点头完成打饭任务。

汤自然必不可少。我以为喝汤只是龙岩人而非所有中国人的习惯，可是有人告诉我们，中国人的餐桌上每顿饭都少不了汤。因为米饭很干，所以他们得配点汤才好吞咽。我想，也是这个理由，才有了蔬菜汁吧。总之，汤是一定得有的。我本人只喜欢喝一种汤，就是那种清甜的白萝卜汤。他们还会煮海带汤，这东西让我感觉像吃煮熟的青草一样。还有一种扁豆汤，我喝了直倒胃口。

过了一阵子我们才知道，食堂背后的一个角落里，有砂锅煲，想放什么料自己点。这个是彼得最爱的午餐，我也常买。我们走到食堂正后面的一个餐柜前，那儿有个俊俏的服务员，有一头漂亮的长发，点菜、下单、上菜，忙里忙外，手脚非常利索，嗓门极大，在餐厅另一头都能听见她的声音。她这副大嗓门是这里的环境给练就的。食堂里黑压压几百个学生，每个学生的肺部发育均没问题，个个说着自己的大事小事，有多嘈杂可想而知。我们常点炒饭或炒面。炒饭即加了配菜的炒米饭，炒面是加了配菜的炒面条。

后来，我们请这里的厨师给我们做好吃的瓦罐面，里面放了蔬菜、香料、肉片和鸡蛋。瓦罐放在煤气灶上直接煮，热腾腾、香喷喷的，而且管饱。

这里还有一道与别处不一样的汤。一大碗汤，里面放了香菇、青菜和几片牛肉。我们经常是跟戴妮丝和玛丽一起吃饭，因此四人合吃一份汤就行。有时候他们也会加豆腐，我们说不用，可是"大嗓门"不会说英语，所以有时没明白我们的意思。

可能你会问，饭菜价格如何？在"自选柜台"饱餐一顿是 2.5 元，约 45 澳分。一碗白萝卜汤大概是 0.5 元一升，约 8 澳分。而瓦罐面加大碗汤共 3 元，约 50 澳分。

后来我极少下厨了。走到一个地方点完菜就可以坐下享用，用餐完毕抹抹嘴巴就可以走人，何乐不为？唯一的不便是，得下104级台阶，走一小段路，再爬两层楼

about a litre was 0.5 Yuan, 8 cents Australian, and the hotpot meals and large bowls of soup were 3 Yuan, about 50 cents Australian.

My cooking days became few. Why cook when you could just walk in and order, sit and eat and leave them to do all the washing up afterwards? The only problem was, you needed to go down 104 steps, along the road a little way, up two flights of steps, eat, then down two flights of steps, along the road and back up 104 steps again.

Not far from the gate there were other "restaurants" and we ate at these quite often. We gave each one a name so that if we texted each other we knew where to meet. There was the "floppy fish" restaurant, so named, because when Deneice was there the first time, a fish jumped out of the holding tank and flopped and flipped all over the concrete, out the front door and onto the street.

Out of deference to the haute cuisine, ambience, price and service, the canteen was called "The Ritz".

There was the "porridge" shop, where they made rice porridge, sloppy stuff with vegetables and a bit of meat, not my style at all, priced at 2 Yuan.

There was the "round rice with pork chop on top" shop. Here the meal consisted of a plate of quite tasty rice with a piece of deep fried flat pork schnitzel on top, vegetables and a very nice soup for 3 Yuan. The girl there could speak some English which was very helpful as all the menus were in Chinese.

Then there was the "noodle shop", similar to the canteen noodles, 2 Yuan.

On the corner there was "The diesel shop", named due to the fact that when you sat on the little plastic stools at the little plastic tables, all the diesel fumes rolled in like a London fog. We didn't go there much, we hated the fumes.

Over the road was the "chicken sandwich" shop, which resembled a cheap version of MacDonald's, but not as nice. The chicken was very stringy and tough, but they made nice chips and good coffee, which we enjoyed on a regular basis. It was the most expensive place locally, about ten Yuan each, about $1.80 per person for a wrap, chips and drink.

So now, we could eat, slurp and gobble with the best of them. There's no dainty way to eat some of this food, it's head down and shovel.

Fancy a bit of tucker?

梯，之后又得下两层楼梯，走一小段路，再爬 104 级台阶回家。

离校门不远处，另有几家"餐馆"，我们常到那里吃饭。我们给每家餐馆都取了个名字，这样短信联络起来方便。有一家叫"跳跳鱼餐馆"，因为戴妮丝第一次到这家餐馆吃饭时，看见一条鱼儿跃出鱼缸，在水泥地板上啪嗒跳了一阵，突然跃出前门，飞到街心，所以取了这个名字。出于对高档美食、用餐环境、价格和服务的尊重，我们把学校食堂誉为"利兹大饭店"。

校门外还有一家"粥店"，卖稀粥，就是那种稠乎乎的东西，里面搁了蔬菜和一丁点儿肉丝，2 元一份，我是完全吃不惯的。

另一家店叫"卤肉饭店"，一份套餐包括一碗米饭，上面放了一块红烧肉，相当可口；一碟蔬菜和一份非常美味的汤，总共 3 元。这家店的女服务员会说几句英语，能帮我们点菜，因为菜单是中文的，我们看不懂。

还有一家"面馆"，跟食堂卖的面条差不多，一份 2 元。

街角那家就是"柴油餐馆"。只要一坐入塑料小桌边的塑料小凳，一股浓浓的柴油尾气，随即像伦敦的大雾般迎面扑来。因为受不了尾气的侵扰，这家店我们大都过门不入。

大路那边有一家"鸡排三明治店"，出售的东西类似于肯德基，但价格更便宜，味道也更差。鸡肉又硬又老，不过薯条和咖啡不错，我们常买。这家就是当地最贵的店了，一份三明治、一包薯条加一杯饮料，共计 10 元，大约 1.8 澳元一人。

现在，我们大可以不顾斯文，专捡好吃的部分下口，砸吧砸吧地咀嚼。吃这些东西高雅不起来，尽管低下头来大快朵颐。

你也嘴馋了吧？

A BOIL UP TO END ALL BOIL-UPS

For those Aussies who have not heard the term, a "boil up" is a famous Kiwi (New Zealand) stew. The Maori's (indigenous New Zealanders) put a big soup pot on the stove and add bacon bones, potatoes, water cress, green vegies, and anything else you want to throw in.

The Chinese are famous for their "hotpot" meals. (When you live in China you soon learn that they are famous for many many things). This is similar to a Kiwi "boil up" but a little different. There are special restaurants for "hotpot", and they seem to call them different things, but maybe the technical term is a "Chaffing Dish". Quite early on in our year in Longyan, when we were still getting used to the local food, we were taken by some local Longyan-ese to the best one in town.

The first thing that grabbed us as we walked in was the noise. There were about 300 people in a smallish room, squashed around tables, all talking at once, and to be heard over their neighbours they talked at the top of their voice. The next thing to hit us was the smell.. This was going to be a "boil-up" extraordinaire. In the middle of every table was the equivalent of the soup pot; a great big bowl with the gas going underneath and full of boiling soupy stuff.

With food, we have learned that if you can see it boiling, it probably will not upset our stomachs, because we could determine the length of the boiling process. The dish started off with the soupy stuff, with what looked like mutton joints. There was no meat on the bones, but lots of fat and gristle. In with that there was 'seafood' which could have

吃火锅

许多澳大利亚人没听说"boil up"一词，其实这是指著名的新西兰炖菜，源于毛利人（新西兰原著民），也就是在一个炉子上放一个大汤锅，然后把熏肉骨头、土豆、水芹、青菜等任何想吃的菜扔进锅里煮熟。

火锅（Hot Pot）是中国流行的美食。（到了中国你就会知道，这里流行的东西很多很多）。火锅跟新西兰炖菜相似，但略有不同。中国有许多风味火锅餐厅，但叫法各异，不过它的专业术语可能是叫布菲炉（Chaffing Dish）。刚去龙岩没多久，我们还吃不太惯本地菜，有人请我们下馆子，吃全龙岩最好的家乡菜。

一进餐馆，给我们的第一印象就是闹哄哄。不算大的一个地方，塞了三百多人，挤在桌边，高声谈话。为使自己的声音盖过邻桌，一个个都扯着嗓门。另一个印象就是味儿大。这里简直就是火锅荟萃之地。每张桌子中间，都搁着一个汤锅，其实是个巨大的碗，碗下面是燃气，碗里装满了沸腾的汤料。

那时，我们对吃东西已经有了一点儿经验，只要看得到食物在热水中翻滚，十有八九吃了不伤胃，因为煮多久时间我们说了算。首先上的是汤底，底料看着像羊大骨。骨头上没有肉，都是筋和肥油。一起做汤底的还有海鲜，什么海鲜都可以。我捞了一小块出来吃，味道很怪。小蟹模样的东西浮在上面，还有一些我从未见过的海鲜。你可以捞出大骨头，啃上面的肉筋和肥肉吃，咬起来挺带劲的。（我的牙口不行，

been anything. I tried one piece but it was pretty horrible. Little crabby looking things floated around in it, along with other completely unknown seafood items. You took out of the bowl these muttony joints and with great relish chewed on the fat and gristle. (Not for my teeth I'm afraid.) Then you could add your own food to the pot bit by bit.

Everyone was supplied with chopsticks, a bowl, a glass, a spoon and the usual copious supply of rice.

We had no control over the food on the table. It had been pre-ordered by our hosts and consisted of a wide variety of fish, meat and vegetables. Firstly went in lumps of tofu. Peter tried that and said it was okay. Then went in other lumps of fried tofu. Peter said it was a bit like tasteless sponge cake. A special kind of pure white Chinese mushrooms were added, that look a bit like long white octopus shaped things, small, and chewy, but edible.

Our hosts added shaved pieces of lamb or beef, which gave the soup a muttony/fishy/beefy/ taste, a rather weird combination. There were plates of other food that I had not seen before. I had no idea what most of it was. While all these bits and pieces were being added, (and we were encouraged by our hosts to add what we wanted), we used our chopsticks and fished out of the pot what we wanted. We could also ladle out and drink the soupy stuff which slowly got thicker and thicker.

One of the vegetables on our table was lotus root, a very exotic sounding vegetable. This is about the shape of a kumera, white, and when it was sliced it looked a bit like a wheel with spokes and bits missing from the middle. It has the consistency of exotic firm potato and the exotic flavour of nothing much at all.

As the stock boiled away the quantity reduced and a waitress did the rounds adding more stock to the pots as necessary. It also helped to thin it down again. Other vegetables were added. They cook their lettuce here! Ugh. And other greens go in and come out, some of them very bitter, and other leaves that are obviously food, but not as we know it.

Peter tried some largish dumpling things, he was quite adventurous with his food and tried almost everything but I was much more conservative and stuck to what I knew. They also had other shaved, raw meats, cigar shaped, I had seen it in the shops and not known what it was. Once that is cooked you lift it out with your chopsticks and gobble it down.

I ate very slowly, looking as if I was eating a lot, and got through quite a bit of soupy stuff which wasn't too bad, and several slices of lotus root, which was not fabulous but

A BOIL UP TO END ALL BOIL-UPS
| 吃火锅

吃不动。）之后，想吃什么食材自己往锅里放。

每人一副餐具，包括一双筷子、一个碗、一个玻璃杯、一把汤勺，以及一大碗米饭。

对桌上的菜品我们没有发言权，都是主人事先点好的，菜很多，鱼呀、肉呀、蔬菜呀，十分丰富。先上桌的是豆腐。彼得尝了一块，说味道还行。接着是一碟炸豆腐。彼得说，跟没放味道的松糕一样。然后又加了一种纯白色的中国蘑菇（凤尾菇），模样像长长的白色章鱼，个儿小，不易嚼，但可食用。

主人又加了一些羊羔肉或肥牛肉，这下子汤的味道夹杂了鱼、羊肉和牛肉的味儿，很是古怪。还有几碟菜，我以前没见过，不知道是什么东西。这些东西慢慢地被放进锅里煮，（主人一个劲儿叫我们把自己爱吃的菜放进去，）我们拿筷子夹出自己想吃的东西。也可以拿勺舀汤喝，汤慢慢地会越来越浓。

桌上有一碟蔬菜是莲藕，很稀奇的一样蔬菜，模样像红薯，白色的，切成片后，看着像中间少了辐条的轮子。吃在嘴里像奇怪的硬土豆那样，怪怪的，没什么特别味道。

汤越煮越少，食物也越吃越少，需要的话，女侍者会一遍遍加汤，这样也能稀释一下底汤。后来，又放了一些蔬菜进去。他们竟然用莴苣烫火锅！呃。又加了一些青菜，捞出来一吃，有的很苦，有的叶子显然被当成了食材，但就我们所知，不是。

彼得吃了几个大饺子，他这个人比较胆大，什么东西都敢吃，而我比较保守，非熟悉的东西不吃。他们把生肉也削成薄片，卷成雪茄状，我以前在超市见过，但不知是什么东西。肉煮熟了要马上用筷子夹出，现吃。

我吃得很慢，瞧着好像吃了很多，喝了不少汤，味道还蛮好的，还吃了几块藕片，虽然称不上美味，但不难吃。

后来，他们送来了甜玉米，好像每次都是在饭局结束的当口，我爱吃的东西才上桌。他们把玉米棒切成薄薄的"车轮"，放进火锅，鱼、羊肉、牛肉汤里又多了一种独特的甜玉米味儿。自然，玉米没有加盐和胡椒，但味道依旧很好，我真的很爱吃。

okay.

Then they brought around some sweet corn. It seemed that they always brought out the things I liked at the end of the meals. They sliced up the cobs into thin "wheels", and in they went, adding a distinctive sweet corn flavour to the fish/mutton/beef soup. Of course there was no butter salt or pepper for the corn, but never-the-less, it was very tasty, and I really enjoyed it.

After a substantial meal we left our kind hosts with many "xie xie"s, and I am happy to say the meal had no ill effects on our tummies. We were so wary of some of the stuff we saw eaten, it's enough you make your hair stand on end. As time went on we got used to the huge variety of foods the Chinese people eat, and although I couldn't bring myself to eat some of the bugs and beetles they devour, in time I ate chickens feet, and other things that I would never have tried at home. I learned not to be so fussy.

During the evening I couldn't help thinking of my daughter-in-law, Powhiri, and how this would be Powhiri heaven. She is an accomplished "boil-up" cook. She would have had a ball, and would have loved chewing her way through the mutton bones with Peter.

A BOIL UP TO END ALL BOIL-UPS
吃火锅

　　饱餐了一顿后，我们对友善的主人说了不少"谢谢"，然后与他分开了。我很高兴，这顿饭没给我的肚子带来麻烦。当地人吃的一些东西，看着都毛骨悚然，我们一直敬而远之。随着时光的流逝，渐渐地我们适应了许多中国人的食物，但我依然不敢吃某些虫子和甲虫，虽然当地人吃得很欢。后来我吃过鸡爪等食物，若在国内，这些东西我这辈子都不会碰。我学会凡事别大惊小怪。

　　那晚，我老是想起儿媳妇波华丽，想到她在这里会多么如鱼得水。她是做新西兰炖菜的好手。要是她也来吃火锅，会很享受，也会和彼得一起津津有味地大啃羊大骨。

CURL UP AND DYE IN CHINA

The hazards of visiting a hairdressing salon in China were numerous. I'd put a colour in my hair just before I left home, but after two months it needed a touch up. I decided to test out a hairdressing salon close to the university gates by getting the cut done first. Peter had his hair cut there and they did a good job, but he was quite bald so they couldn't go too wrong with him.

I thought I could manage on my own without an interpreter. That was my first mistake. I went about 8.30am. Three girls were there but none of them could speak English. I tried to explain that I wanted a haircut. They all looked at me and burst into giggles, which is what happened when they didn't have a clue what you wanted. With my usual but erroneous confidence, I thought I could manage this on my own.

I was shown to a seat and the three girls giggled and pushed each other nervously, until one of them felt compelled to do something with me. Using my fingers, I showed her how much I wanted cut off. Second mistake. I don't think she understood sign language either. She picked up her razor and starting at the back began a razor cut, slicing slowly. Some came off the back some off the top. So far so good. But then she really got into the swing of it. At the back it was coming off at a great pace, and then I realized that she thought my one inch off, was leave one inch on! It was getting shorter and shorter and I was starting to panic. I looked like a shoddily shorn sheep and the floor was covered with all my hair. She stopped to catch her breath, so I made the face of a very satisfied customer, said thank you, thank you, thank you and got off the chair. I paid my 5RMB,

美发记

到中国的发廊做头发，得步步小心。出国前我刚染过头发，但一晃就过了两个月，头发需要重新打理。我决定到校门口的那家发廊，先剪个头发看看。彼得在那儿理过发，看着不错，可他的头上已经没剩几根毛了，再怎么剪，都糟糕不到哪里去。

我一开始就犯了个大错误，以为不带翻译，自己也能对付。大约八点半，我走进发廊，里面有三个姑娘，可三个人都不会说英语。我试图告诉她们我想剪发。她们大眼瞪小眼地看着我，嘻嘻直笑，每当这里的人们听不懂你的话时，就是这种表现。我一向自信，心想自己能够搞定，但我想错了。

我被领到一张椅子边坐下，三个姑娘呵呵笑着，不好意思地你推我让。有个姑娘推脱不过，只好挺身而出。我用手指比了比我想剪短的长度。我又错了，没想到她连我的手势也看不懂。只见她拿起刮刀，开始从脑后慢慢得削。脑后削一缕，头顶削一缕，我觉得还行。可是，紧接着她便大胆了起来，抓起后面的头发大刀大刀地剪。到后来我才恍然大悟，她误会了我的意思：我要她剪短2.5厘米，她却以为我想留2.5厘米的短发！看到头发越来越短，我开始如坐针毡。我就像只被剪过毛的绵羊，满地都是我的头发。她停住想歇口气，我赶紧做出满意状，一个劲儿地对她说"谢谢"，起身离开座位。我付了5块钱，不到一澳币，夺路而逃。

less than $1 and took off.

The lesson learned the hard way was, always take a translator to the hair dresser. After this I knew I couldn't arrange a colour without an interpreter so I spoke to one of the English speaking Chinese teachers.

"Can you tell me where there is a good hairdresser?" I asked.

"You want a hairdresser?"

"Yes. Where do you go? Are they any good?"

"Oh, my hairdresser lives a long way away. But she doesn't speak English."

"Can you suggest somewhere I could go?"

"But your hair is already so short, you want to get it cut some more?"

"No," I said, "I want to have a colour put through it."

"Oh!" She understood. Everyone has their hair dyed, even the men. Very few people in China have grey hair.

"I don't think your hair will look very good black," she said.

"No, I want it light brown. Where should I go?"

"Brown? Oh I don't know if anyone can do it brown."

"Can you suggest somewhere I could go?" I asked again.

"Maybe you should just look around and if you find a nice modern looking shop go in there."

That wasn't very helpful. So I decided to ask our ever helpful student Twilight. This girl was a pearl among pearls. She'd lived in Longyan for all of her twenty years and knew the city very well. She found us all sorts of places that existed up stairways, on first or second floors, in alleyways we would never normally go down, or tucked away in the most unbelievable corners of town.

"I know a good hairdresser," she said. "It will be my honour to take you there."

"Oh wonderful. Thanks so much. Can we go tomorrow afternoon?"

"Yes, I'm free. Meet me at the gate at three o'clock."

The gate was the general meeting place. Everyone met everyone there.

"We can get a number 7 bus, the shop is close to MacDonald's," Twilight said when we met the next day. Everything was relative to MacDonald's, it's a very central point in town. We walked a block or so and then up a flight of stairs to a very modern looking

这次我买了一个大教训，知道以后上发廊一定得带上翻译。我知道染发没有翻译在身边帮忙，肯定没戏，于是我向一个懂英语的中国老师求助。

"你知道哪一家发廊比较好？"我问。

"你要剪头发？"

"是。你平时去哪里做头发？手艺好不好？"

"噢，我去的那家发廊比较远，而且理发师不会说英语。"

"你能推荐一家发廊吗？"

"你的头发已经这么短了，还想剪短？"

"不是的，我想染发。"

"噢！"她这才明白过来。这个地方人人染发，甚至男的也染。满头银发的中国人难得一见。

"我觉得你把头发染成黑色不大好看。"她说。

"没有呀，我想染成浅棕色。我该去哪家发廊呢？"

"棕色？可我不知道谁会染这种颜色呢？"

"告诉我，哪家发廊比较好？"

"或许你可以到处逛逛，看到哪家店时尚，就进去。"

这个主意我可不大喜欢，于是我决定向学生特莱特打听，她总是能帮我摆脱困境。这个女孩是珍珠中的珍珠。她今年20岁，从小到大一直住在龙岩，因此对这个城市了如指掌。不管什么地方，她都找得到，比如一楼或二楼的楼梯间，我们平时不敢去的巷子里的小店或某个谁也料想不到的几角旮旯。

"我认识一个很棒的理发师，"她说，"陪您做头发是我的荣幸。"

"噢，太好了，太谢谢了。明天下午去，行吗？"

"行，没问题。三点钟在校门口见面。"

校门是大家会面的地方。不管是谁，与谁见面，都约在校门口碰头。

"我们坐7路公交车，那家发廊就在麦当劳的附近。"第二天我们一见面，特莱

salon. Twilight knew all the staff.

"This is my teacher," she said to the boss. "She wants to have a colour, light brown."

"Welcome to our salon," the young man said in Chinese. He and Twilight chatted away in Chinese so I couldn't follow much of it.

"Please come and choose your colour," Twilight said. The hairdresser showed me the normal book of colours available in hairdressing salons.

"Oh good," I thought, "something familiar." I looked through the colours but was dismayed at the limited choices. There was no dark blonde, my normal colour. The choice went from medium blonde to dark brown, with nothing in-between.

"Twilight, I don't know what to do, my usual colour is not here." I thumbed through the book and decided on medium blonde. Twilight made this known to the boss.

"Come tomorrow and they will take good care of you," Twilight said. "They know what you want."

I arrived at the appointed time and was greeted as if I was royalty. I was the only client so escorted to a chair by the entire staff, brought a drink of water (they don't drink chilled water, it's bad for you, it's always lukewarm… yuk!) as one put the cape around my shoulders.

Here I will digress a little. A Chinese hair cut usually included a wonderful relaxing head, neck and shoulder massage that started at the fingers, went up one arm around the back of the neck and down to the other fingers. This could last up to twenty minutes and was part of the cost. The head massage sometimes came with a deep moisturizing head massage, finished off with a thorough hair wash.

Everyone hovered around me, poked, prodded, pulled, checked and had a hands on experience with my unusual "foreigners" hair, while the boss mixed the colour which he gently applied.

They left me for a while then came back, sprayed water and massaged the hair again. It was so relaxing! Hair washing takes place on a padded bed that you lie down on. This was the only soft bed I'd seen in the whole country up to this time. There was a large square basin at the head of the bed, with a sort of padded head rest that poked up from the bottom of the basin and you rested your head on it. After another thorough wash and massage I was herded back to the mirror.

特便说。在这个地方，不管找哪个地方，都以麦当劳为准心，因为它恰好位于城中心。我们走了一小段路，爬了一层楼梯，来到一家相当时尚的发廊。里面的人特莱特全认识。

"这位是我老师，她想染发，浅棕色的。"她对老板说。

"欢迎光临。"年轻男子用中文招呼我。他和特莱特用中文说了一会儿话，我听得稀里糊涂。

"请您过来挑选颜色。"特莱特说。理发师把发廊中常规色系拿出来给我看。

我心想："还好，挺眼熟的。"翻完色卡后，我觉得颜色不全，感觉有几分气馁。没有暗金色，我平时用的颜色。只有中等金色和深棕色备选，且两者之间没有过渡色。

"特莱特，怎么办呢，我平时染发的颜色这里没有。"我翻着书，决定用中等金色对付，但特莱特已经把我的问题反馈给了老板。

特莱特说："您明天再过来吧，他们会给您好好做的。他们已经知道您想染的颜色。"

按照约好的时间我准时来到发廊，受到皇家成员般的礼遇。我是唯一一个获得此等待遇的客人：被全体员工簇拥着来到一张椅子边坐下，然后有人递上一杯水（他们不喝凉水，这对你们来说有点儿麻烦，他们喝的水都是温的……呵呵!），这时有人帮我披上了一件围布。

请允许我跑题一下。在中国理发通常包括头、颈、肩按摩，从一只手的手指开始到手臂，再到颈后部，一直按摩到另一只手的手指。大概要花去20多分钟，按摩费用包含在理发费用中。有时头部按摩是边洗边按，等按摩好了，头发也彻底洗干净了。

理发师们一起俯身看着我，用手戳、挑、扯我的头发，都想感受一下我这个老外不一样的头发。老板在一旁忙着调颜色，然后走到我身边，小心地给头发上色。

上完了色，他们就走了，让我一个人呆着。过了一阵子，有人过来往我头发上喷水，又开始按摩我的头发，舒服极了！洗头是躺在铺了床垫的床上进行的。这是我来到中国后睡到的第一张软床。床头放了一个大水盆，从盆底向上立了一个供头枕放

"Hell's bells!" I mumbled. "It's too fair! It's really blonde! Not at all what I wanted. But I can't change it, it's a done deal." He also gave me another haircut, trimming up the razor cut bits that were all straggly. I looked at myself with this very blonde and very short hair.

Of course when I went back to school everyone commented on the change. I was not happy with it.

After two weeks I went back to the salon and asked for a darker colour, so they gave me the book of sample colours again. Now as you will know, the pages in these colour books overlap with all the little sample colours poking out the side.

"I don't know what to do," I said to myself. "The dark colours are too dark. What's this?" I asked myself amazed. I flicked all the pages back and forth, checking all the English wording.

"All their spelling is wrong," I muttered. "They've got bronde [sic] instead of blonde. I saw the dark br last time and assumed it was dark brown! They've got dark blonde after all!"

Some of the other colours were spelled in terrible English too. I giggled to myself.

"I'll have dark bronde please," I said pointing to the colour I wanted in the first place.

They repeated the whole process doing their usual very gentle application. Today was busier, there were other clients so I didn't have the whole staff hovering, quite miffed I was, but the boss-lad was there, keeping an eye on proceedings. I enjoyed another twenty-minute massage.

Once they'd finished pummelling, it was back to the head. They removed the towel.

"Oh! Much better. Yes, this is good, my usual colour. Thank you so much," I said in Chinese.

So they combed, primped, blow dried and fussed around, then whipped off the cape like a matador.

"Okay?" he asked me.

"Okay," I said with a big smile. "Very good."

Today's effort cost me the princely sum of 100RMB, equal to about $15.00 AU. Not bad eh?

的地方,上面铺了个垫子,你把头靠在上面。头发被再次冲洗干净和按摩后,我又被领到了镜子前的座位上。

"完了!"我嘀咕道,"这么黄呀! 纯金黄的颜色! 这哪儿是我想要的效果,现在想补救都来不及了,颜色都已经上好了。"老板又替我修了修头发,把散乱的头发都削短了。我看着镜子里的自己,头发短短的、金黄金黄的。

回到学校,自然所有人都对我的新发型,评头论足了一番,我心里很是不悦。

隔了两周,我又找上门去,说我要重新染发,用深一点儿的颜色。他们又把那本《染发颜色大全》拿给我看。这下你该知道了吧,其实书上介绍的颜色和书中所配的颜色样本是一模一样的。

"真不知道该怎么办?"我自言自语道,"深色又都太深了,这是什么东西?"我惊异地自言自语道。我把书从头到尾飞快地翻了一遍,看书里的英文介绍,嘴里嘀咕道:

"单词都写错了呀,金黄(blonde)被写成了bronde。上次我看到了"dark br"时,还以为是深棕色(dark brown)! 得了,有深金色就行!"

另有一些颜色的拼写更是错误百出,我忍不住嗤嗤地笑出了声。

"请给我染深金色。"我指着自己情有独钟的颜色说。

像上次一样,他们对我的态度特别温柔。这一天店里比较忙碌,还有其他客人在做头发,因此没有像上次一样,全部理发师都围着我,好像我是一只米菲兔,不过老板守在我身边,帮忙照看我的头发。我又享受了25分钟的按摩。

最后理发师轻轻敲了敲我的肩背,然后回头看了看我的头发。他们解开毛巾。

"嗯,好看多了。没错,很好,这才是我习惯的颜色。多谢了。"我用中文说道。

他们拿起头梳,把我的头发梳顺,又仔细地摆弄了一番,然后吹干,还是觉得美中不足,又摆弄了一遍,最后吹去围布上的碎发,那围布有点儿像斗牛士的斗篷。

"行吗?"老板问。

"行,很好。"我笑容满面地回答。

这一次染发花去我整整一百元人民币,将近15澳元。不过,还是挺值的吧?

CHEAP TAIWANESE JUNK

We have a saying that has persisted in our family for some years. It's "Cheap Taiwanese Junk". It came from the time when Jonathan was buying his first expensive camera. It was made in Taiwan and faulty from the day he bought it. But we think that saying needs to change. The Taiwanese do not corner the market on junk, but the Chinese do a good job too.

After a couple of months we bought a radio/cd player/tape deck combined. We missed our Aussie music, and wanted something we could use for lessons too. We walked all over the town trying to find something suitable. There were plenty with tape decks but almost none that included a CD player. We did find one, that for some reason Peter turned his nose up at, I don't understand why. Seeing him walking around the campus with a very girly pink plastic player would have been fine. But he didn't think so.

We finally found one he liked and gave it a very thorough checking over. It did everything we wanted, including having an inbuilt microphone so that we could record the students speaking and play it back to them, as many of them had never heard their own voices. We took it home and it was lovely to have John Williamson and Slim Dusty pounding out their songs.

The next day, Peter tried to record from the CD to the tape recorder. No go. He pushed every button but it just would not work properly. He managed to get it to tape one song, and then the buttons went on strike permanently. He was not (as the Aussies say) a happy little camper.

便宜货

有一句话我们家人念叨了好几年，就是"台湾便宜货"。说起"台湾便宜货"，应该追溯至我的儿子乔纳森买的第一台昂贵的相机。这台相机是台湾制造的，从买回家的那一天起便故障频仍。但我们以为，应该换个脑筋了。毕竟，台湾人又没有把便宜货堆满市场，而且中国制造的产品质量也不错。

在中国呆了两三个月后，我们买了一台收音机/CD/磁带多功能一体机。当时我们很想听澳大利亚音乐，也想找点上课的材料，于是遍访全城，寻找自己想要的机子。卡带机很多，但没有磁带/CD双用机。后来，我们总算找到了一台，可不知何故彼得看不上眼。我以为，一个大男人拎一台女孩用的粉红塑料机子，走在校园里，没什么见不得人的地方，可他老人家不肯苟同。

最后，我们总算找到一台他中意的机子，并彻底地检查了一遍。这台机子拥有我们想要的一切功能，包括内置麦克风，这样我们可以录下学生的发言，回放给他们听，因为许多学生从未听过自己的声音。我们拎着机子回到了家，满心欢喜地听着约翰威廉逊和史里姆达斯丁的歌声。

第二天，彼得想把CD上的东西翻录到磁带上。不行。他把每个按键都按了一遍，就是不好用。勉强录了一首歌曲到磁带上后，按键们便集体"罢工"了。彼得可不是一个乐天派，用澳大利亚人的说法，一个快乐的小营员。

We asked our ever useful Twilight to accompany us as an interpreter. She spoke good English and first rate Chinese, which is what we were lacking. The man in the shop of course recognized Peter at once, they don't sell much stuff to foreigners (remember there's only about a dozen of us in a town of 350,000 people).

"This player has been bumped or dropped," the shop assistant said after Twilight explained the problem for us.

"No, I don't think so," said Peter.

"There's a mark on the case here, look," the assistant replied.

Peter looked at it. There was a mark although he was sure he hadn't done anything to it.

"Because of this, the warranty will not apply," he told Peter.

"Really?" Peter said. "That's not fair." He thought for a minute and asked, "Well, what do I do now? I need something for classes on Monday."

"I'll have a look at it tomorrow. Come back and maybe I can fix it for you."

"Okay, I'll do that," Peter said. "I'll come about 1pm. If I can have it tomorrow (Sunday) that will be good."

We went back the following day at the specified time, again taking Twilight.

"Is the player fixed?" Twilight asked for us.

"No, I can't fix it. I've phoned the factory but they don't have any more of this model. If you want to, you can choose another one."

Twilight and the shop assistant began a long convoluted conversation in Chinese.

"The only thing you can do is buy a different model," Twilight eventually said. "It will be another 20RMB. Is that okay with you?"

"Will it play CD's and record onto tape too?" Peter asked. "If so, then I will buy it."

"This one will do what you want," Twilight assured him. Peter tried all the buttons, but he didn't think to try recording a CD in the shop.

We took it home about 4pm, and Peter tried to record Slim Dusty singing Waltzing Matilda, a song we wanted to sing at the University President's party at the end of the week.

All was not well. Steam started rising, and I could tell he was getting just a tad wound up. Peter could get the tapes turning then the machine chewed them up and spat

我们叫来小帮手特莱特，跟我们过去当翻译。她英语不错，中文更是顶呱呱，我们缺的就是她这个本领。店员自然一眼便认出了彼得，因为他们很少卖东西给老外（别忘了，35万人的城市中就我们十几个老外。）

特莱特把机子的问题告诉了店员。他说："这台机子被人砸了，不然就是摔到了地上。"

彼得赶紧说："不对，没有的事儿。"

店员说："瞧，机身有个印迹。"

彼得瞧了瞧。虽然他敢保证自己什么也没做，但机身上的确有个印迹。

店员告诉彼得："这个问题不在保修范围之内。"

彼特急了："什么？这不公平。"然后想了一下又问："那我该怎么办？我需要录材料，周一上课好用。"

"明天我帮你瞧瞧。你们明天再过来，说不定我能修好。"

"好，我下午一点过来。要是明天（星期天）能修好，还来得及。"

第二天按照约定的时间我们来到店里，同样叫上了特莱特。

特莱特和店员用中文你来我往交涉了好一会儿。

最后，特莱特告诉我们："现在最好的办法是买另外一种型号的机子，多加20元钱，怎么样？"

彼得问："也能播放CD，把CD上的东西录到磁带上吗？要是能，我买。"

特莱特宽慰他，道："这台机子有您想要的功能。"

彼得试了试所有的按键，可就是没想到当场录一下音。

下午四点，我们拎着新机子回到了家。彼得想把达斯丁的《跳华尔兹的马蒂尔德》录到磁带上，我们想在周末的晚会上唱这首歌，这次晚会校长也会参加。

一切都不对劲。麻烦开始升级，我感觉到彼得越来越焦躁了。他能让磁带转动，可没转几下就会绞带，"啪嗒"一声停了，没法录了，气得彼得火冒三丈。

这时已经是傍晚五点了，我们已经来来回回爬了好几趟六层楼，看来还得重复一

them out, and the machine refused to record. He was getting very agitated.

At this stage it was 5pm, and we'd been up and down our six flights of stairs several times, but it was obvious we were going to repeat the performance and go back to the shop without another minutes delay. By now Peter was on a mission and we flew down those stairs, got a taxi at the gate and walked into the shop again. You can imagine the look on the shop keeper's face as he saw us coming in. I'm sure he was wishing we'd never entered his little shop.

We did not take a translator this time, so Peter with arms flying used sign language, and showed him the tapes all chewed up, and how the buttons didn't work all the time. In desperation the shop assistant brought out a different model, brand new and reading his body language, this one was top of the range. No cheap Taiwanese junk here, was his message.

Peter took it out of the box, tested every possible combination of buttons and checked the CD player and the tape recorder to his satisfaction. We said a final farewell to the shop and taxied home, climbed back up our six flights of stairs and almost dying of starvation, I started a late dinner while Peter got out his new toy.

Oh dear! At 8pm guess where Peter was? Yes down the stairs again and back at the shop. Slim Dusty was reclining in the machine we returned. He needed this CD for class tomorrow.

He experienced a torrid time with a different person in the shop, a young woman who spoke no English and didn't know about the previous events of the day. She suspiciously followed Peter right round the shop as he poked into every corner trying to find this elusive CD. She suddenly thought that he might want to buy a CD player so she got down the broken one he'd just returned and tried to sell it to him! It had been put back up on the shelf as is, for resale. Inside was Slim Dusty. Peter grabbed the CD, waved it at the girl, said goodbye and exited that store like a train, swearing never to return, and staggered up our 104 stairs again, exhausted at 8.30pm.

We emailed the family to advise them that on our return we had for sale, one first class, top notch, best quality Chinese CD/tape recorder/radio. Any offers to be made by return email at any time.

次，得抓紧时间把机子送回去。这一次，彼得可是有话说了。我俩飞快地冲下楼梯，在校门口拦住一辆的士跳了进去，再次赶往那家店。看到我俩走进店里，店主的表情你不难想象。我相信，他肯定正在祈祷，祈祷我俩不要再进他家的店。

这一次我们没带翻译，彼得挥舞着双手，打手势告诉他，机子会卡带，按键不灵。万般无奈的店主取出另一种机子，崭新的，从他的身体语言来看，这款机子是最好的了，好像在说：这个不是台湾便宜货。

彼得打开盒子取出机子，测试了所有的按键，仔仔细细地检查了CD机和磁带录用功能。我们告别了店主，坐上回家的的士，爬上六楼时，差点儿饿昏了过去。我赶紧下厨煮饭，彼得忙着折腾他的新玩具去了。

噢，天啊！晚上八点钟的时候，你们猜猜彼得跑哪儿去了？没错，又下六楼去那家商店了。达斯丁的CD忘了取出来，还在刚才那台坏机子里，可他明天上课要用呢。

彼得在店里度过了一段艰难的时光，因为看店的人换成了个年轻女子，不会说英语，而且对前面发生的事情一无所知。彼得在各个角落东看西看，希望能找到他那不知何去的CD，姑娘一脸狐疑地跟着他。突然她好像明白了，以为彼得要买CD机，赶紧拿出那台坏机子，想卖给他！原来机子又被放到待售的货架上了，达斯丁原封不动地躺在里面。彼得取出CD，向姑娘挥了挥手，说了声"再见"，快步出了店门，像一列发誓永不返回的火车，跟跟跄跄地再次爬完一百零四级台阶，于晚上八点半回到家里，累得一点儿气力都没有。

我们给家人写了封邮件，告诉他们等我们一回国，就把这玩意儿给卖了，就说我们有一台一流的、高级的、质量上佳的CD、磁带、录音、收音多功能一体机出售。有意购买者随时回邮件联系。

WHEN THE CHIPS ARE DOWN

The headmistress of a small local private school asked us to take some extra weekend classes with her younger students. She employed Chinese teachers, but needed a foreign teacher to take classes once a month with a group of ten year olds, and a class of older ones aged fourteen to eighteen years. It was only once a month for three months and the money was good so we agreed.

On the first Saturday, Peter went and took the younger group. He came home exhausted. It took him a week to recover! He said they were uncontrollable. On the first Sunday I took the class of older students. Their English levels varied but I got through the two hours and was prepared to go and teach them again in another month's time. Peter was NOT going back to the young ones.

When the next month came I went along and taught the younger ones instead of Peter. WELL! Naughty? They were little rotters! There were about 5 or 6 girls and the same number of boys. The girls on the whole were manageable, some were quite sweet, one or two wanted to learn, and their speaking was pretty good for their age. But the boys! Well, they were just the pits.

Of course, I needed to remember that this was a Saturday afternoon. They were there for two hours which was far too long, having already endured a long week of lessons, and were now ready to let off some energy. And let off energy they did. The boys especially, were loud, rude, and unmanageable. They ricocheted all over the room, behind the curtains, running everywhere, up and down, pulling and fighting with one

兼职记①

一所民办学校的校长请我和彼得周末去她学校上课。她手下有中国教师，但需要一个外教给两个小班上课，一个班是10岁左右的小孩子，另一个班级是14到16岁的大孩子。一个月只要各上一次课，连续上三个月，报酬也不错，于是我便答应了。

一个周六，彼得去给年龄小的班级上第一次课，回到家里，他彻底崩溃了，用了整整一周时间才恢复！他说那些小孩根本不服管教。周日，我去给大孩子上课，学生的英语水平参次不齐，但这两小时给我对付过去了，准备下个月再度前往，而彼得却坚决"罢课"了。

第二个月，我代替彼得去给小朋友上课。果然够呛！一群小淘气？错了，是一群小无赖！班上有五六个女生和五六个男生。女生总的来说还算听话，有几个还蛮乖巧，有一两个还挺想学，就她们这个年纪，英语算不错的了。可是男孩就别提了！妈呀，简直顽劣到了极点。

当然，我得提醒自己，现在是周六下午，他们已经上了整整一周的课，这额外的两小时对他们而言肯定无比漫长，正打算释放一些能量。他们真的是在释放能量。尤其是男孩又吵闹又粗野，完全无法驾驭。他们在教室里、窗帘后上窜下跳，跑来

---

① 原文题目"When the Chips Are Down"意思是"在关键时刻"，此时"chip"指的是赌场的筹码。但本文中还指薯条。

another.

After about fifteen minutes, I was ready to walk out. But my stubbornness prevailed. I wasn't going to let these youngsters get the better of me, so I stayed. It became a supreme battle of wills. I won the battle of lasting the two hours, but they won the battle of "will I sit in my chair? NO!" I have to say, that I was stunned at the dreadful behaviour, being used to the older students who were models of decorum in comparison.

I did my thing, sang songs, played games, covered pre-prepared exercises on the board, talked, etc, but it was hopeless. If anyone learned anything I would be surprised. A few had books, but they were all different, so there was no uniformity there. Some of them didn't have anything, except a big mouth and a fog-horn voice.

I was provided with a helper for the full two hours. I was not left to face the lion's den alone. The problem was, that this incompetent helper sat down at the back of the class taking notes of what I said and did, and just let the kids run riot. She was also a teacher, but she didn't seem to understand much of what I said to her. How she taught any English was beyond me!

I went home and said to Peter that now I understood his reasons for not going back. I wrote to the headmistresses explaining that I was prepared to come and teach the older class, but I refused to take the young ones again.

She phoned me a few days later asking me please to go once more for their final class of the year. She said she would be so appreciative if I could help with the younger class at their end of year treat at MacDonald's. She explained that another teacher would be in charge, games had been organised and she really wanted me to attend too.

Muggins me! I agreed to go this last time thinking they would just go for a feed, run riot round MacDonald's and then we could all head home. Not quite!

The new teacher, who had recently graduated from Fuzhou Teachers University, spoke very good English. This was her first teaching job since graduation so was young and energetic with lots of ideas, so I left the class in her care. I expected an easy couple of hours. Peter came along for the fun too, thinking that if things got out of hand, he might be able to help a tiny bit.

All the little darlings arrived and the parents were delighted to be introduced to Peter and I, two foreign teachers. Our group occupied one end of the restaurant, partially

跑去，拉扯打斗。

15分钟之后，我差点儿就想甩手离去，好在不服输的个性占了上风。我不能让这些坏蛋骑在我头上作威作福，于是我留下了。接下来就是双方意志的大较量。最终我赢得了胜利，但小家伙们也守住了一块阵地，"要我乖乖坐在座位上，没门！"说实话，他们的行为如何恶劣，让我瞠目结舌。相较之下，那些大孩子个个都是讲文明的"模范学生"。

我使出了十八般武艺，唱歌、对话、玩游戏、做黑板上的练习等等，但全都毫无用处。在这样的课堂上，要是有谁能学到东西，连我都会觉得不可思议。一些孩子带了课本，但每个人的课本都不一样，说明没有统一教材。而另一些孩子空手而来，只带了一个大嘴巴和一副大嗓门。

学校给我配了一个随堂助手，并非我一个人独闯虎穴。问题是我的助手太无用了，就知道坐在后面，记录我上课的过程，小孩子们四处撒野，她却不理不睬。她也是一个老师，不过好像听不大懂我给她说的话。我想象不出，她到底怎么教英语！

回家后我对彼得说，现在我知道他不肯去上课的原因了。我给校长写了封信告诉她，大孩子的课我会去上，但小孩子的课就另请高明吧。

几天后校长打来电话，请我帮个忙，上完本学期的最后一次课。她说期末的时候她会请小孩子们到麦当劳上课，我若肯前去帮忙，她将不甚感激。她解释说，另外一个老师负责教课，游戏已经安排妥当，真心希望我也能到场。

瞧我这个大蠢蛋！居然答应最后再去一次。我以为小孩子们在麦当劳吃饱喝足之后，不过跑一跑、闹一闹，就会散伙各自回家。这完全是我的一厢情愿！

新老师刚从福州师范学院毕业，英语说得很不错。这是她毕业后的第一份工作，因此她很年轻，有精力，想法也多，所以我把活动内容全权交给她去安排。我心下认为，这几个小时我应该很轻松。彼得觉得好玩也跟了过来，他想如果活动失控了，兴许他能帮上一点儿小忙。

小宝贝们一个个到达了麦当劳，家长们很高兴能认识我和彼得这两个老外。我们

separated from the rest of the dining area. The new teacher pulled out handfuls of printouts and handed me three pieces of paper explaining that these were the games she had planned. So far so good.

The new teacher stood up, and then turned to me asking me to start the first game. Aha! They wanted me to run the show after all. She handed me a bunch of flash cards with pictures and words for the children to learn. Guess what they had to learn? How to pronounce all the items on the menu! Good grief, I was a stand-up teacher of propaganda for MacDonald's!

There wasn't much I could do, I was stuck there, so I started on the first game.

"Big Mac," I said.

"Big Mac," they replied.

"Chicken wings," I said.

"Chicken wings," they dutifully repeated.

"Chocolate shake," I intoned as the nudging and poking started.

"Chocolate shake," some of them replied.

By the time I'd got through fries, ice-cream sundae, sweet corn and soup, I'd lost them. MacDonald's was a bit different from home. They catered for the Chinese tastebuds, including Chinese type foods too.

By this time, the students had developed a massive hunger and one by one got money out of their pockets and headed for the counters to buy food. Amongst the group were several little darlings resembling well-bred barrels, and they certainly didn't need any more cheeseburgers, hamburgers or fries! They needed a bit more rice and noodles and a good deal of running around, followed up by some intensive discipline.

After the twenty or so students had refuelled, I was asked to start the second game, still on the food theme. It was a stupid game, where the students were supposed to put their hands over their ears while others mimed the name of a food. None of them followed the rules, they just listened to the words, sort of repeated them, and slowly the whole thing dissolved into chaos again. Apparently someone won that game as I handed out some prizes at the end of the afternoon.

By this time I felt a proper fool, waltzing around MacDonald's making these horrible noisy little kids learn how to say "cheeseburger" in first class English. I tried to shrink

这群人在麦当劳的一头，跟其他就餐区有部分隔断。新老师取出一叠打印材料，递给我三页纸张，说这是她准备的游戏。到目前为止一切顺利。

新老师站起来，转身对我说，可以开始第一个游戏了。我说呢！还是要我出来作秀嘛。她递给我一叠抽认卡，上面是孩子们学习的图片和单词。猜猜他们学的是什么？如何念麦当劳菜谱上的所有菜名！悲催呀！我竟然成了替麦当劳站台的老师！

如今，我人已在此，不好退出，于是硬着头皮开始第一个游戏。

"巨无霸。"我念。

"巨无霸。"他们跟读。

"鸡翅。"我再念。

"鸡翅。"他们听话地跟读。

"巧克力奶昔。"看到他们开始推推搡搡、戳来戳去，我拉长了声调。

"巧克力奶昔"。部分孩子在跟读。

等我念到薯条、冰淇淋圣代、甜玉米和菜汤的时候，已经没有一个人跟读了。这里的麦当劳跟国内的不一样，是根据中国人的口味烹调的，还有中式快餐。

这时，学生们已经饿慌了，纷纷从口袋掏出钱，上柜台去买东西吃了。其中几个小宝贝，因养尊处优，已经状若酒桶，自然不应再吃芝士堡、汉堡和薯条！他们需要的是米饭、面条和大量的跑步锻炼，外加严格的管教。

大约20分钟后，学生们吃完饭了，新老师叫我开始第二个游戏，游戏的主题依旧是食物。这是个很弱智的游戏。游戏要求部分学生们双手捂住耳朵，部分学生小声说出一种食物名称。没有一个人遵守游戏规则，都是在听人念词，然后重复，渐渐地他们又闹开了。显然有人胜出了，因为在活动的最后，我分发了一些奖品。

此时，我觉得自己是个十足的傻瓜，在麦当劳走来走去，用字正腔圆的英语，教这群可怕的、吵闹的小孩儿学念"芝士堡"，我尽找人多的地方站，希望别和大学同事不期而遇。我的样子可狼狈了。

等孩子们吃完第二顿饭，又到了第三个游戏的时间。我们一起唱英文歌曲"小小

into the "ambience" and hoped no one from the university was there. It would not have been a good look.

After a second bout of refuelling it was time for the third game. We did "Twinkle twinkle little star". They knew the tune and we worked with flash cards for "diamond", "twinkle" etc. The game was as fatuous as the others, but someone won it, because I gave out some more prizes.

Oh dear, what a comedown! From well behaved twenty to twenty-five year olds, to proper little toads of about ten to twelve years old. Their behaviour was dreadful and by the time you added the ton of sugar-hype included in the food they munched during the entire two hours, well, they were right off their trees!

At the end of the two hours, I'd managed to avoid the worst of the confrontation, the poor new teacher was hoarse from screaming at them all the time, and Peter just sat there nibbling chips, watching and grinning from time to time.

The principal then did the rounds of the whole restaurant trying to enrol more students for next year, boasting about the two wonderful foreign teachers working for her.

The parents arrived to pick up their offspring, who by this time had succeeded in hi-jacking the entire dining area. They shook our hands again, and we reciprocated, encouraging an immediate departure so we could also leave. The principal was thrilled with the afternoon's success and Peter and I took ourselves over the road for a strong coffee in a quiet child free Western restaurant.

Would you like fries with that?

星星亮晶晶"。他们知道调子，我们用抽认卡教他们认"宝石"、"眨眼"等词儿。这个游戏跟前面一个一样愚蠢，但有人赢了，因为我又分了一些奖品出去。

我的学生从彬彬有礼的 20 到 25 岁的年轻人突然变成了无法无天的 10 至 12 岁的小坏蛋。老天，多大的落差啊！这些小孩的行为真的太可恶了，在这两小时里，他们的嘴巴就没停过，一直在吃东西，又摄入了不少糖分，如今正精力充沛着呢！

活动最后，我成功地克制住了脾气，没有跟他们正面冲突。可怜的新老师，嗓子都喊哑了。彼得坐在那儿，边吃薯条边冷眼旁观，不时做个鬼脸。

校长在餐厅里走来走去，为明年的招生造势，还大言不惭地吹嘘，她的学校聘请了两个优秀外教。

家长们来接孩子回家了，此时这坏蛋们已经成功占领了整个餐厅。家长们一个个过来与我们再次握手，我们也赶紧握了握他们的手，希望他们马上离开，这样我们也可以尽快开溜。校长非常兴奋，觉得这次活动无比成功。之后，我和彼特迅速逃进一个没有孩子的西餐厅，各点了一杯浓咖啡压惊。

你还想要薯条吗?

A STITCH IN TIME

One of the best parts of being in Longyan was the fact that everything, including clothes and shoes were cheap to buy, as is fabric, to have made up by a dressmaker.

There were quite a few dressmakers around town, and within just two streets of the university there were at least five. Many of them worked in a little "cupboard" space with a sewing machine, a fluorescent light above, room for a seat and that's about it. On arriving in Longyan it didn't take long for me to realise that the shops did not stock things my size. I'd brought along plenty of clothes, but still, with the prices being so cheap, I decided I wanted go home with some "Chinese" clothes.

On one of my sojourns along the local streets I found a fabulous dressmaker. Deneice called her "the seamstress," as that was her American term. But I called her "my dressmaker" and we got to be good mates.

My dressmaker owned a big shop in comparison to the others. It was the size of a small single garage, the entire front open to the road, with several very Western looking mannequins lined up along the street, real mannequins, probably pretty old, but mannequins none the less.

There were clothes hanging up along the walls waiting for customers to collect them. A rack at the back was crammed with some wonderful lengths of fabric. Her creations looked very professional; in fact she used very complicated patterns, not just plain styles.

I'd found two other fabric shops in the centre of town. I went to both shops with the

做衣服

住在龙岩最大的一个好处就是所有的东西，包括衣服、鞋子在内，都很便宜，买布料请人缝制新衣一样花钱不多。

城里有不少裁缝店，单单校园内的两条街上就有五家。多数裁缝店都很小，差不多只放得下一个衣橱，除了一台缝纫机、一盏白炽灯和一张椅子，别无他物。到龙岩不久，我就发现本地商店没卖我穿的衣服号码。我带了不少衣服过来，但是一看到价格如此实惠，便蠢蠢欲动了，决定回国的时候带上几套具有"中国特色"的衣服。

有一次逛街，我发现了一家非常棒的裁缝店。戴妮丝用美国人的叫法，称店家为"裁缝师傅"，我喜欢叫她为"老板娘"，我俩后来关系可好了。

老板娘的店铺与其他人的相比算是宽敞的了，有一个小车库那么大，店面对着马路，门前放了几个西方人长相的人体模型，虽然比较旧，但的确是人体模型。

店铺里的墙上挂了一排成衣，供客人挑选。店铺后面有一个货架，上面堆了好多漂亮的布料。老板娘的手艺看起来相当精湛，衣服款式大都挺复杂的，不走简单的路子。

我在市中心找到了两家布店，这两家我都进去过，但都空手而归。一家布店紧挨着麦当劳，布料很多，花色齐全。我是一个人进城的，以为这样的事情用不着带翻

success rate of these visits being a big fat zero. The first one was close to MacDonald's where they had a large range of fabrics. I went down town on my own, thinking I might be able to do this without a translator, but this was not a good idea. I walked in, looked around then tried to make conversation with one of the girls there who fell all-of-a-heap in giggles, which is what they do if they don't know what else to do with you. So I tried to make myself understood, using sign language or drawing, but I walked out completely frustrated, thinking that I was dopey to even try.

The second shop was a men's tailor, up six flights of stairs and he spoke no English. I toddled down the six flights of stairs and home again, somewhat frazzled around the edges.

So having found "my dressmaker" down the road, I was really excited, again taking ever helpful Twilight to translate. The first visit was a great success. I attacked the rack of fabric with glee, picked out about four different pieces and proceeded with great gusto to explain what I wanted made up.

I drew the designs for each piece of material and because she was very good at her job, she soon caught on. I went home with high expectations of some lovely new clothes.

About four or five women worked for her, as well as her husband who was a very clever man who worked at a tiny table. She showed him my drawings and he drafted them on some old newspaper. One day I asked him about his training and he said he was self-taught. Once the pattern was outlined, he handed it to another girl who stood at a long table and cut out the material. She had a pair of scissors, a tape measure and a big brain. She snipped and snapped and all of a sudden a garment was cut out.

These pieces then got put into a plastic bag waiting for the machinists to make them up. Some days later, the machinist took out all these unnamed and unnumbered little snippets of material, and with only the initial drawing proceeded to put the whole thing together. Lo and behold, a complicated pattern was made. These were clever people! Then it was pressed and hung ready for the customer.

The cost you might ask? For 240 Yuan, close enough to $40 Australian, I owned six new garments, and that included the cost of fabric for three. No-one is going to call that extravagant.

The real marvel of it all was the machinery they used. Mrs Noah must have used

A STITCH IN TIME
做衣服

译，但我想错了。我走进布店，看了看四周，想和里面的一个姑娘说话，她却一味地笑而不答，中国的姑娘们遇到不明白的事情，总是这样。我又是打手势又是画画，想让她明白我的意思，最后还是只能灰溜溜地走出店门，觉得自己好傻，白费了这么大劲儿。

第二家布店在六楼，店主是男的，完全听不懂英语。我蹬蹬地走下六楼，再次打道回府，感觉极其挫败。

所以，当我在学校附近不期然找到这家裁缝店时，兴奋极了，我再次带上能干的特莱特当我的翻译。第一次进店我们就满载而归。我一边挑着货架上的布料一边啧啧称赞。我选了四种不同面料，满心欢喜地对老板娘描述我想要的款式。

我把每一种布料想做的衣裳式样画了出来。老板娘是行家里手，一看便知。我带着对漂亮新衣的憧憬回到了家里。

老板娘雇了四五个女工，她丈夫也在店门帮忙。她丈夫很机灵，在一张小桌子上做活。她把我的图样交给丈夫，他比照着我的图样画在一张旧报纸上。记得有一天，我问他手艺是从哪儿学来的，他说是自学的。他把画好的衣样交给一个站在一张长桌边剪料子的姑娘。那姑娘有三大宝贝：一把剪刀、一个卷尺和一个好脑子。只见她东剪一刀西剪一刀，没一会儿工夫，一件衣服的样子就成型了。

接着，这些布块被放进一个塑料袋里，等车工缝纫。几天后，车工从袋子里拿出这些没有名字、没有标号的小布块，比照着那张原始图样，把衣服缝好。瞧瞧吧，这么复杂的一款衣服，他们可真聪明！最后再把衣服熨平挂好，剩下的就等客人取货了。

做这些衣服要花多少钱？总共240元，差不多40澳元，我就拥有了六件新衣，包括三块布料的费用。不会有人称这个为奢侈吧？

真正令人称奇的是店里的设备。也许远古的诺亚妻子替家人缝制衣裳时用的就是这些工具吧，我根本猜不出这些东西到底使用了多久。这家店使用的电工缝纫机，但我想原来是台旧脚踏缝纫机，用早被淘汰的八号电线改装而成的。我还在一个地

these machines for her family, and I couldn't even guess how old they were. The ones in this shop were electric machines, but I think they were old treadle ones that had been converted with number 8 wire. I'd seen another place with treadle overlockers! How's that for ancient?

The working conditions would have ACC or OSH (New Zealand and Australian government departments that oversee safe workplace conditions) on their doorstep in a second, but here, such things don't exist. They sat at these tables on little old backless plastic stools, with fluorescent lights overhead, working about eight to twelve hours a day. Whether I went early morning or late afternoon they were all there beavering away.

I must say they all seemed to get on very well together, and often staff became almost like extended family. I think that if they worked long hours they would make good money, considering the average wage for an unskilled person might be about 800 Yuan a month, which was about $100 Australian. I think the girls got paid thirty or forty Yuan a garment, so if they made two garments a day that was about eighty Yuan a day, 480 Yuan a week for six days, perhaps 1800 Yuan a month. Big money compared to some people's incomes.

My dressmaker definitely increased her profits while I lived in Longyan, and I acquired some very nice one-off clothes. Some of the fabrics were unique and came from Shanghai, Hong Kong or Shenzhen.

So if you want some fabulous clothes save your pennies and go and see "my dressmaker".

A Stitch in Time 做衣服

方看见了脚踏锁边机呢！把这玩意儿拿给古人用如何？

这样的工作条件要是在新西兰或澳大利亚，负责工作条件安全的政府部门早就找上门了，但在中国，没人管这种事情。裁缝店的工人们坐在无靠背的破旧塑料小凳上，房顶垂着几盏白炽灯，在桌边一干就是8到12个小时。不管我到裁缝店的时间是清晨还是傍晚，他们都在里面埋头苦干。

我得说，工人们之间似乎非常和睦，亲密得几乎像一家人似的。我想他们加班加点地干活，应该收入不错，因为非技术工的月薪在这里大约是800元，相当于100多澳元。我私下算了算，姑娘们做一件衣服大概能挣30或40元，如果一天能做两件衣服，大概就有80元的收入，按一周工作六天计算，每周收入约480元，那么一个月大约能挣1800元。比起一些人来说，收入算是相当高了。

我自然给老板娘带来不少利润，但我也得到了几件独一无二的漂亮新衣。有些布料风格独特，是从上海、香港或深圳进的货。

要是你想添置一些美丽的衣裳，赶紧省钱，去老板娘那儿，保管你不虚此行。

EVER BEEN FRAMED?

As our year came to a close I wanted to buy gifts for the students we were going to entertain for our "last supper" party, about 15 of the students we were especially close to. It was very hard to know what to get the boys, a nice necklace or something for the girls would be fine, but the boys were a bit difficult. I had seen some nice photo frames up town and thought I could put some of the photos I had taken in the classroom into the frames.

Alone, tempting fate again without a translator, I sallied forth to the downtown. I went into the first shop that had very nice Perspex type frames. Price? 35 Yuan each. Ouch, too dear! Another shop close by had nothing suitable. Then I went over the road to the shop where we bought our camera. It took a minute for me to explain that I wanted photo frames. They pulled out a few really tacky things, but then a lovely one, at only 15 Yuan, which would really fit the bill. It was quite classy looking and I was happy with the price.

So I made it clear that I wanted it. But then I had to tell them I wanted 14 of them and this was the tricky part. I tried to ask them if they had more. Nope, that didn't work, they didn't know those words. Numbers are okay here, they use the same numerals, but words really confuse them. I wrote down "Do you have more?" No go. I wrote down "14". That didn't help. I tried using lots of versions of "this is one, give me more" in sign language. Nope. Then I used my noggin. Of course, count in Chinese. Well, that is fine if you can count. I still can't get past three. And then I get muddled with one and

买相框

　　转眼，一年期约将满，我想给学生们买些礼物，学生们为我们准备了一场晚会，邀请我们参加"最后的晚餐"，与我们特别要好的学生大概有15个。真的不知道该买啥礼物给男生，女生好办，一条漂亮的项链就能令她们欢天喜地了。以前，我在市里看见过一些精致的相框，可以挑选几张我在课堂上给他们照的相片，放在相框里，送给他们当礼物。

　　没带翻译，独自一人前往市里，想再次试试运气。我看见一家店里出售一些精美的有机玻璃相框。价格呢？一个35元人民币。天哪，这么贵！旁边还有一家店铺，但里面的东西都不合我意。于是，我继续前行，找到了以前买相机的那家店。我费了一番工夫才解释清楚我的来意。他们取来几个相框，看着大都很俗气，不过最后拿出的那个物件相当漂亮，只要15元钱，价钱很不错。这款相框样式经典，价钱也好。

　　我告诉他们，我要买这款相框，可是我还得告诉他们，我想要14个相框，这可难坏了我。我想问他们，还有这样的相框吗。不行，他们听不懂我的话。说数字应该行，数字都是相同的，但说话不行。我用英文写道："还有这种相框吗？"这招没用。我又写了"14"，还是不行。我试着打手势告诉他们："我就要这东西，再拿几个来。"通通不行。我只能亮出自己唯一的小本事了，用中文数数。要是懂得数数，自

two, is it ar ee or ee ar?

After a minute they started to realise that I was counting. Then my brain really got into gear and I wrote down the number 14 in Chinese. This I could do. A large plus sign for ten and a rather wriggly sign for 4. They understood that. But then they stood looking at me and I stood looking at them, and nothing happened. I was so frustrated, it seemed they had not understood at all!

By this time the girl in the shop had bought up Baidu on her computer, a sort of Google search engine. She was typing in the message I wrote "Do you have more" and seeing what other messages it came up with, because it would have it in English then in Chinese. In the end, she got on the screen "1 piece".

"Yes," I said, "yes, 1 piece, times 14". But, because the computer had no idea exactly what I was trying to say, and because it was a very smart computer, it came up with variations on the word "piece". These were the options it listed.

"They saw a piece of material. She played a piece from Chopin. There was one piece of fruit left. "

Nope, that made it muddier not clearer.

I thought I would try the sign language thing again, but it was hopeless. They just could not understand me. In desperation I resorted to phoning someone who could speak Chinese. It would only take someone five seconds to tell them, "She wants 14 frames". All the students and teachers I tried were not answering. Poor Alex was suffering from some awful allergy and in the hospital getting treatment. So I put it in the too hard basket and got ready to leave.

"Sit, sit, sit", they said. Actually they didn't say a word, but they gestured emphatically. So I sat. They waved their arms around, chattering in their fluent Chinese, and I think they were saying that they were getting someone who could speak English. So I waited and waited, while heavy rain set in. I had been there about 45 minutes by now. Then someone came in with a box containing 15 of these frames.

Oh the excitement! "Yes, yes, that's exactly what I want! Fabulous! That's just right! Well done!" I gushed. Ah, they knew they had got it right.

Aha, now I had to tell him I only wanted 14 not 15. They just got more and more confused, so I thought it was better to quit while I was ahead, and take the 15. I did the

然好了，可我数到三便数不下去了，从头再数时就连"一"和"二"都分不清了。

过了一会儿，他们才恍然大悟，我在数数来着。这时我脑子突然灵光了起来，用中文写了个"14"。这一招好用。一个大加号当数字十，外加一个歪歪扭扭的四字。他们看懂了。可是接下来我们又开始大眼瞪小眼了，他们好像还是不知我的用意，我泄气极了。

这时，一个姑娘在电脑上打开百度，类似谷歌一样的搜索引擎。她把我写的"Do you have more"打在百度上，查找这句话的意思，因为百度会先显示英文，再出中文。电脑上出现了"1 piece"字样，我连忙说："对的，1 piece，再乘以14"。可是，电脑并不懂我说的话，而它又是如此的聪明，于是一下子跳出了一大串"piece"一词的相关用法。下面就是电脑给出的参考选项。

"They saw a piece of material. She played a piece from Chopin. There was one piece of fruit left."

（"他们看见了一样东西。她弹奏了一曲肖邦的曲子。还剩下了一个水果。"）

不行，电脑是在帮倒忙。

我想，再试试手势吧，可是任凭我如何比划都无济于事，他们就是不明就里。绝望之下，我只好打电话求助一个懂中文的人。这么简单的事儿只要五秒钟就搞定了。"她想要14个相框。"可是，那么多学生和老师，没有一个人接我的电话。可怜的亚历克斯又全身过敏，正在医院治疗呢。无奈之下，我决定作罢，打算走人。

他们却一起说："坐坐坐。"其实他们没有说话，只是一直打着"坐下"的手势，于是我坐下了。他们挥舞着胳膊，操着流利的中文，彼此交谈，我想他们在说，他们会找个懂英文的人来帮忙。于是我坐在店里，等了又等，这时天空突然下起了一阵急雨。我已经来了大约45分钟了。接着，有人抱了一个盒子进来，里面装了15个我想要的相框。

我高兴坏了，一个劲儿地说："没错，没错，我就是要这个东西！太棒了！对极了！你们好能干！"原来，他们知道我的意思呀。

international signal for money by rubbing my thumb and fingers together. He writes 100 Yuan down, so I hand over my 100 Yuan note and he packs them into a bag and I skedaddle out of there quick smart. 100 Yuan is roughly $15 Au, so $1 each for a nice 5 ×8 photo frame. A successful purchase and as we would say at home, "cheap as chips".

When shopping in China there was something about DIY that gives a certain sense of accomplishment. How the poor shopkeepers felt I had no idea, but I felt good.

好了，还有一个麻烦，现在我得告诉他们我只要 14 个相框，不是 15 个。我越说他们却越糊涂了，于是我决定还是识相点儿，不再解释，15 个全要。店主在纸张上写了个 100 元钱，我拿去一张百元人民币给他，他收入钱包。我赶紧脚底抹油溜出店门。100 元人民币，差不多 15 澳元，也就是一澳元一个漂亮的 5×8 相框。划算极了，要是在澳洲老家，我们就会说："跟薯条一样烂便宜。"

没带帮手靠自己的本事在中国买到了东西，我心里特别得意。可怜的店家会怎么想，我不得而知，但我本人感觉很好。

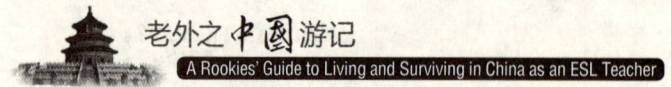

OUR FIRST WEEK IN CHINA

Our plans were right
We booked our flight
Packed clothing of different styles
In bags stacked books
And clothes hanging hooks
Off to the land of the Chinese smiles.

Our plane touched down
In Xiamen town (said Shar-min)
The hotel was several miles
The taxi cabs
Were all quite mad
In the land of the Chinese smiles.

The room was good
Bed made of wood
If I sleep here I'll be surprised!
In actual fact
Was good for my back

在华第一周的日子

制订好了计划
预定好了航班
打包好了春夏秋冬的衣裳
书籍和衣架搁进了行囊
奔向中国——一个远在天涯的地方

飞机徐徐降落异乡
陌生的厦门市就在前方
酒店位于几公里远的地方
出租车载着我们
像疯子一样
一路呼啸，在中国的道路上

舒适的客房
硬梆梆的大木床
我能睡着肯定是天方夜谭
这样的床啊
其实可为我的脊背疗伤

Slept well in the Chinese style.

His pocket picked
Pete felt real sick
With his Yuan and credit card swiped
Police involved
Small hope they hold
In this land of the Chinese wiles.

We make the trip
To Longyan-Yip
We arrive on campus in style
Paul's photo's not right?
Round building-no sight
That building is being devised!

Apartment quite nice
Cold water and ice
In the fridge white and new soon resides
Rice cooker it's true
Gas burner times two
In the land of the white Chinese rice.
We're finding our way
Tho' the sky's always grey
Round this town of considerable size
The kids all seem good
Take naps when they should
In the land of the shy Chinese smiles.

The taxis are bad
The drivers are mad

OUR FIRST WEEK IN CHINA
在华第一周的日子

让我像中国人那样进入梦乡

彼得的钱包丢了
他感到十分心伤
钱呀卡呀究竟去往何方
警察们也抓狂
希望渺茫
怎样才能让扒手无处可藏

惜别厦门，带上行装
前往龙岩学院方向
如同初见，校园陌生的模样
莫非错了，彼得图片上的形象？
圆圆的大楼在何处躲藏
原来她隐匿于人的想象！

住所温馨
凉水似冰一样
崭新的白色冰箱
退位给了电饭煲中的米饭
煤气灶出了状况
白花花的大米派不上用场？

我们在想办法
尽管天空灰濛阴暗
小城不小，我们差点迷失了方向
孩子们可爱良善
困了便睡，哪管他人眼光
羞涩的中国学生满脸灿烂

出租车破旧不堪

Though no accidents yet to advise
Their horns they toot toot
On their scooters they scoot
As they travel the long Chinese miles.

So, settled we are
At least-well, so far
We're finding the heat makes us tired
But we're ready to teach
And the young minds to reach
Of the students with shy Chinese smiles.

司机个个疯狂
虽然没出交通状况
喇叭一路响了又响
好像驾驶的是小小滑板车
漫漫长路任他横冲直撞

终于，我们住进了"新"房
至少目前无事可烦
炎炎夏日我们疲惫异常
只能强打精神走进课堂
悉心滋润那些年轻的心房
年轻的学子，羞涩的笑容挂在脸庞

THE CITY OF LONGYAN

I have been grappling for some time with the problem of describing Longyan in words. It's not an easy task. I can only compare it with New Zealand and Australia, and I guess with a few other cities I have been to, Xiamen, Hong Kong or Bangkok. I don't think there is a word that will adequately convey the ambience of Longyan.

There are words like, messy, grubby, dirty and filthy. And then I got stuck. What came after filthy? Very filthy doesn't do it justice. Can you have superlatively filthy? Filthy beyond compare? I think that multiplying filthy by ten and adding another dollop on top for good measure would give you some idea. In other words, it ain't clean. Peter's description was, "the pits, which is only exceeded by the smells".

The university grounds were well kept. The only detraction was the open drains, of which there were a few, with a sort of dirty scum on top, water running hither and thither and the smell ranging from an "Oh dear" to a "gag". Otherwise the grounds were fine.

When you stood at the university gate however and looked out, it was a different matter. There was a fairly wide tarsealed street with constant traffic. A security officer was in charge of the university entrance twenty four hours a day. The gates were locked at midnight I was told, so if you came in later than that you had to climb the gate or wake up the sleeping all night attendant in the office. Next to the attendants office there was an ATM which had an English option so we tried to use that one. The main problem was that it was often out of service.

There were small shops along the street that sold everything from stationery, clothes

小城龙岩

我纠结了很久,都不知道该用什么词语形容龙岩这个城市。真的不容易。我只能拿她跟新西兰和澳大利亚比照,或者跟一些我曾去过的几个城市,比如厦门、香港或曼谷相较。但我一直觉得,找不到一个恰当的字眼描述龙岩的风貌。

在我的词库里有乱、闹、糟、脏几个词儿,接着我便词穷了,比脏更严重的词儿是什么呢? 用"很脏"一词形容仍不够到位。你能找到表达最脏的一个词儿吗? 无与伦比的脏? 我想把你对脏的印象放大十倍,再添一堆垃圾,方才接近真貌。换言之,就是距离干净十万八千里。用彼得的话来说,就是"乱糟糟外加臭烘烘"。

大学校园倒也井井有条。唯一不雅之处是几处明沟。上面漂着一些脏兮兮的浮渣,污水四溢,散发的味儿有的让你惊呼"老天",有的让你掩鼻而过,臭味程度不等。否则,校园的卫生还是可圈可点的。

可是,如果你站在校门口,向外张望,情况就大不一样了。宽宽的柏油街道上,车水马龙。学校大门口一天24小时都有门卫值岗。据说,晚上12点关闭校门,你要是返校晚了,要么翻门而入,要么就得叫醒在办公室睡觉的夜班门卫。保卫处办公室隔壁有一台ATM机,上面有英文选项,我们试用过那台机子,可它三天两头出故障。

街道两旁小商店林立,卖什么东西的都有:文具、衣服、发夹、食品、饮料,应

or hair clips to food and drink. There were several hairdressers in this little street, which was about a hundred yards long. They did a roaring trade when school was in, but their tills were bald during holiday times. There were also quite a few food shops, little restaurants, permanent, grubby, busy, and a bit smelly. They were not restaurants as a Westerner knows them. We ate at one or two of the cleaner looking ones and never got sick. But in Longyan terms, they were busy little restaurants. About half way down this little street the open drains started again. They were about 50 centimetres square, half full of scummy water, muck, decomposing vegetables, and any rubbish you cared to chuck in. They were also very convenient for men to urinate in and to hold babies over to do the same thing.

Sitting alongside this drain sat an elderly man who used to be a teacher. I called him the "fix-it man". He worked there day in and day out and he fixed anything; shoes, bicycles, baskets. If it was broken he mended it for a miniscule amount. You've heard of men with gnarled hands and weather beaten faces? He had those too. You know the little tables and chairs you can buy for toddlers? His cane chair was about that size, held together with bits of wire and old bicycle tube inners. No one there threw anything out until it had been fixed at least ten times, so he was a busy man. He fixed my umbrella when the knob fell off the end. He had a whole string of old umbrella knobs to choose from.

Then you got to the corner of the street. This is where it became a little trickier. There were more "restaurants". The entire front of these stores were open so all the dust came in from the very busy, dirty, dusty road that was constantly being travelled by cars, bikes, buses and very big trucks. There were great cracks in the footpath, well, large concrete slabs sat over the drains, and rats the size of small cats scurried hither and yon. There they cooked in woks over gas, and fed many a hungry traveller or local body in need of sustenance. I wasn't game to try these ones. They washed their dishes in cold water in large bowls on the footpath, and reused them. The patrons sat on little plastic chairs or stools at little plastic tables. All the scraps were tipped into large square kerosene type tins to be emptied. Someone emptied these into mobile kerosene type tins on motor cycles and the waste was taken away somewhere.

Can you see this in your mind's eye? Not quite the Ritz. We didn't know such places existed until coming here. Most days we'd wander down this street and after a while

有尽有。小街上有几间美发店,占据了近一百米长的街面,学生在校期间,生意非常火爆,但一到放假时候,店里便十分冷清。还有不少食杂店和小饭馆。饭馆永远门庭若市,吵吵闹闹,散发着浓浓的油烟味儿,不像我们西方人眼中的餐馆。我们在一两家比较干净的小店里吃过饭,回家后安然无恙,一点问题也没有。在龙岩人眼里,这些小店就是生意红火的小餐馆。大约在小街的半道上,有一处排水明沟,四四方方的,口径约五十厘米,蓄了半池的污水、秽物、腐烂的蔬菜和废弃的垃圾。这里也是有些男子偷懒方便的地方,也有人抱着小孩往里面尿尿。

　　明沟的旁边坐着一位老者,他以前也教过书,我叫他"巧手先生"。他整日坐在那里,修修补补:鞋子、自行车或篮子都不在话下。破东西交给他修,价格非常便宜。你可曾见过长满老茧的双手和饱经风霜的面容?看看这位老者,你便心中有数了。又可曾见过那种给学步婴孩用的小桌子和小椅子吗?他坐的小竹椅就那么大,用电线和旧自行车内胎捆扎结实。这里的人们从不舍得丢弃旧物,缝缝补补不下十次,才会弃之不用,所以老人的生意很好。我的一把伞柄头丢了,就是找他修好的。他存了一大串备用的旧伞柄头。

　　来到街角,这里的情况便开始复杂了。所谓的"餐馆"更密集了。一家家餐馆大门敞开,灰尘便飘飘洒洒地从那条肮脏繁忙、尘土飞扬的马路上飞入其中。大路上,汽车、自行车、公共汽车和大货车来来往往,永不间断。人行道上裂痕处处,下水道口盖着大块的水泥板,小猫般大小的老鼠在街上横冲直撞。他们就在这样的地方在煤气灶上忙碌着,填饱了许多饥肠辘辘的游人或需要充饥的当地百姓。我仍不敢上那些地方用餐。他们在人行道上放个大脸盆,用冷水洗刷碗筷,接着又拿去盛饭装菜。人们就坐在塑料小椅子或小凳子上,在一张塑料小桌边吃饭。剩饭剩菜一律倒入一种方形的煤油桶状的大铁罐里。铁罐中的东西被环卫工人倒入摩托车后的大铁罐中,送往什么地方处理掉了。

　　我能想象出这一幕吗?这可不是利兹大饭店哟。要不是到了龙岩,我们也不知道世界上还有这样的餐馆。我们常在小街上溜达,没过多久也就见怪不怪了。这里还

it became something we just accepted. There were also many fruit vendors with their barrow stalls selling a huge variety of fruit. Often in the evenings we'd wander down this street and buy our fruit there.

Turning to the left, further up the street, there were more shops, almost like Western shops, supermarkets that had a wide variety of goods. These were government run, clean, and we were given receipts for our purchases. Further along again there was a wet market, which was back to the filthy times ten plus a dollop. They sold everything from fish that may have died weeks ago, to boxes and bags of dried everything you can think of. They had about a hundred different types of rice and noodles. There I bought vegetables and made early morning trips to buy pork or beef.

I didn't have the heart to buy a live chicken and get the poor thing killed, but I could buy frozen drumsticks in town. I became well known by the stall holders there and they got to know me. I went to one stall for eggs, another for vegetables and another for meat. Seeing I was only one of two (the other being Deneice) white people who went there, it was easy to pick us out. Not far from the corner there was a bakery that made very good buns with pink icing on and a little blob of mock cream. I shopped there often.

The centre of town consisted of a large shopping area, with some nice clean Western restaurants that served excellent food. One had fabulous modern, clean, Western toilets. MacDonald's and KFC resided there along with shops that sold everything you could think of. But the streets were filthy times ten with a dollop on top, people just chucked their rubbish anywhere.

And yet you know, I think that on the whole, the people themselves were clean. When they walked up the street, they were well dressed, their hair was clean, their clothes and shoes were clean, and although I didn't do the horsey test and physically check it out, I think their teeth were clean. The insides of houses I have visited were spotless. It's a puzzle as to why their streets were so dirty.

They also seemed to be content with their lives. To be true, they don't know much different. Education and the government opening its door to the West meant there was change in the air, but on the whole I think people were content. Materialism was rearing its ugly head, but for now they seemed to be satisfied with their lives.

Despite all the minuses, I fell in love with that grubby city and its wonderful people, and cried like a baby when I had to leave.

有许多水果小贩，推着手推车兜售各种水果。我们经常晚上到这里买水果。

左拐往上走，商店还要更多，跟西方国家的差不多。超市里，货物琳琅满目，应有尽有。这些都是国营商店，干净整洁，购物有小票。再往上走，有一家菜市场，里面的状况就是我最前面提到的光景：将你对脏的印象放大十倍再加上一堆垃圾。菜市场里卖什么东西的都是：从死了几星期的鱼，到各类大小包装的干货，无一不全。还有上百种大米和面条。我都是到那里买蔬菜，还会一大早过去买猪肉或牛肉。

我没勇气买活鸡，因为要叫人杀死那个可怜的东西，我于心不忍，但我会上城里买冻鸡腿。我在那些商贩里可有名气了，他们都认识我。我会在一个摊位买鸡蛋，到另一个摊位买蔬菜，然后再换一家买肉。会进菜市场买菜的白人只有两个（另一个是戴妮丝），所以他们一眼就能认出我们来。角落旁边有一家面包坊，他家的小面包非常美味，上面撒了些许粉色糖衣和一小团奶油。那是我经常光顾的地方。

市中心有一大片商业区，那里有几家西餐厅相当不错，很干净，东西也好吃。其中一家餐厅有个干净而现代的西式卫生间。麦当劳和肯德基就开在商店旁边，商店里商品种类齐全，应有尽有。但是街道却着实肮脏，到处都是人们随手乱扔的垃圾。

但是，话又说回来，市民们给我的感觉都非常清楚整洁。他们逛街的时候大都收拾得清清楚楚，头发干干净净的，衣服和鞋子也整整洁洁，虽然我没有凑近查看，但我感觉他们的牙齿也是洁净的。我走访过的人家，全都纤尘不染。怎么街道会这么脏，我很是费解。

他们好像很满意自己的生活。说真的，他们并不了解外面的世界。虽然教育的普及和政府的开放政策意味着变化即将来临，但总的来说，龙岩人是安于现状的。尽管丑陋的拜金主义已经探出了脑袋，但至少目前，他们似乎对自己的生活状况是没有意见的。

尽管这个城市存在不少瑕疵，我却爱上这个乱糟糟的地方和那些了不起的人们。不得不告别龙岩的时候，我忍不住像婴孩一样，嚎啕大哭。

LONGYAN?—NO LONG RAIN!

Wherever you live, you have weather. Sometimes it's good, sometimes it's bad and sometimes it's fabulous. When we were looking for a place to live, we thought Longyan's weather patterns would be similar to home. As it turned out, the weather was a little hotter than we were used to.

The geographical placement of Longyan was a little different than expected too. It sat in a sheltered basin in quite a mountainous area. We had high mountain peaks all around giving a lovely outlook.

When we first arrived it was autumn and still hot, mostly in the low 30's, very humid, and we needed the air conditioner and fans on all the time. After a while it cooled off, and around November the temperatures were very comfortable. Then winter arrived with a vengeance. And I mean Winter! It brought back memories of our cold New Zealand winters, the ones we'd escaped by moving to Queensland.

It doesn't snow there, but it must snow somewhere close by, the wind had a very snowy feel to it. We rushed out and bought winter clothes. I also had a lovely scarf knitted at a store by the gate. It was pink and white, long and wide enough to wear like a hood-cum-scarf all around my head and shoulders. It was very warm and greatly admired by all the girls. At the end of the first term, the classes gave us some gifts of scarves, gloves etc. which were very welcome.

Getting out of bed and going to early morning class by 8am was a pretty cold start. It made us realize that we were warm weather people rather than cold weather people.

多雨的龙岩

不管你住在哪儿，总免不了跟天气打交道。天气时好时坏，也有时阳光明媚、舒适宜人。我们当时物色在华生活的地点时，还以为龙岩的天气跟我们在澳大利亚老家的差不多。结果呢，这个地方还要更热，我们不大适应。

龙岩的地理位置也跟我料想的不大一样。它地处盆地，四周是起伏的山峦。放眼望去，座座山峰高耸入云，十分美丽。

我们初抵龙岩之时已是秋季，但暑气依然未消，气温徘徊于30度左右，我们整天开着空调和风扇度日。稍后，天气开始转凉，大约十一月份之际，天气便十分清爽怡人了。可是接着凶神恶煞的冬天便上场了。我说的是寒冬！这不由得让我想起了新西兰的寒冷冬季，就是为了逃避它，我们才搬到澳大利亚的昆士兰居住的。

龙岩城区没有下雪，不过附近的山区肯定下了雪，因为寒风之中带着雪的气息。我们赶紧冲出去购买冬衣。我曾在学校大门口的一家小店里，买了一条漂亮的针织围巾。这条围巾粉白相间，又长又宽，可以既当帽子又当披肩，将脑袋连同肩膀一起围住，非常暖和，女学生们见了都赞不绝口。在第一学期末，学生们送了一些围巾、手套给我们当礼物，我俩好生感激。

要在寒气袭人的早上八点之前起床去上课，真的很不容易。这时我俩才明白过来，我们是适合温暖气候的人群，不适应寒冷气候。那台空调也可以当暖气使用，公

The air conditioner was also a heater and there was a free standing floor heater, but it got quite cold inside, especially when you consider that the whole place was lined with ceramic tiles, so there was nothing there to hold any warmth. It was like living in a huge bathroom. Looking back we should have asked for extra heaters.

We missed a large part of the winter by going to Thailand for a month during the Spring Festival holiday break. That proved to be a wise move, because the weather was warm and sunny for the whole month. We enjoyed a fabulous holiday, and returned as brown as berries.

We came back to very warm weather even though it was still only February. But there were cold spells here and there when we got out the winter clothes again. Then it started to rain. They said spring was the wet season, and they were right. One of the best things about the rain there is that it seldom came with wind. So the rain just fell down from the sky, and when you walked with an umbrella, it kept you fairly dry. Umbrellas there are a large part of life. You either need them for the rain or for the hot sun.

The rain started around early March, and lasted all month. We started April off with those "April showers" and it rained for most of April. There were no torrential downpours, we could get down to class and back and not get wet. It was miserable, the sky was always grey, but it was liveable. When May came, it was just the same as April, wet. Still no downpours, but misty light rain, interspersed with cloudy periods. I do remember the sun coming out occasionally, and now and then a sunny day gave us the chance to do the washing.

One of the students told us that the rain normally continued for a while yet, and that around her birthday, April 20th the first thunder storm would arrive. Sure enough on the 20th April our first thunder storm made its appearance. Chinese mythology says the storms are sent to wake up the sleeping animals and tell them summer is on the way.

By the end of April, we'd seen enough rain to last for a very long time. But it just didn't let up. For the entire month of May it rained, and it got worse and worse. I do remember the sun coming out, I can't remember which day now, but it came out on a Tuesday for one hour between 11am and noon, because I was walking from the dressmaker back to school and nearly cooked! But by 1pm the rain was back.

Soon things started getting serious and during the early part of June there was serious

LONGYAN? NO LONG RAIN!
多雨的龙岩

寓里还有一台立式电暖器,可是屋里依旧冷飕飕的,尤其是整个房间地板铺的都是磁砖,根本不保暖,就像是住在一间巨大的浴室里一样。回想当年,应该再向校方申请几台暖气才对。

寒假的时候我们跑到泰国玩了一个月,躲过了大半个最寒冷的时节。此举是明智的,因为泰国那里一整个月都阳光明媚,暖洋洋的。我们舒舒服服地度了一个假,晒得黑不溜秋地返回学校。

回来之时虽然才二月,但天气已经相当暖和了。可以脱下厚厚的冬衣,可冷空气又时不时光顾。接着就开始下雨了。这里的人们说,春天是潮湿的季节,此话不假。这里极少既下雨又刮风,算是一大优点吧。所以,雨是笔直地从天空落下,撑了雨伞,基本不会被淋湿。雨伞几乎成了我们形影不离的伙伴。

这样的雨大约三月初开始下,一直到三月末才结束。可一到四月,阵雨又上场了,春雨忽下忽停,几乎延续了整个四月。突如其来的暴雨倒是不曾下过,我们从家中去课堂,从课堂回家,都不曾被雨打湿。天空永远是灰蒙蒙的,日子真的不好过,但我们挨得住。五月的龙岩跟四月一样潮湿。依旧不下大雨,多为如烟的细雨,偶尔夹杂几个阴天。我记得太阳的确露了几次脸,正好让我们洗晒衣服。

一个学生告诉我们,通常这样的雨会一直下着,等到她生日4月20日左右,才会迎来第一次雷雨天气。果然,在4月20日那天,雷雨如期而至。根据中国神话故事,雷雨是被派去叫醒蛰伏的动物们,告诉它们夏季就要来临了。

到四月末,我们已经在雨水的陪伴下度过了好长一段时光,可雨呀,依旧无休无止,整个五月都在下雨,而且愈来愈厉害。我的确记得出过一次太阳,但记不得确切的日期,只知道是在某个周二,11到12点之间,天空放晴了一个小时,因为那时我正巧从一家裁缝店出来准备回学校煮饭。可刚到下午一点,雨又夺回了领地。

很快事态便开始严重起来,六月初福建省的许多地方发生水患。中国根据灾情不同设有不同级别,级别越高灾情越严重,此次洪灾级别为三。五月初来过一次台风,当时级别为五,情况真的很吓人。狂风暴雨折腾了整整一宿,好在第二天风雨便

flooding in many parts of Fujian. They have a grading system here, and the flooding got to category 3, which is as high as it goes. A typhoon went through in early May, and it got to a category 5, which is bad as it gets. We had one night of very high winds and very nasty rain, but by the next day the worst was over. The coast which is two hours away by bus was affected more than we were, so by the time typhoons got to us, they'd dissipated somewhat.

Another of the problems was the dampness in the air. When we put on our clothes, they felt damp. When we went to bed all the bedding felt damp. All the paper felt limp and soggy. I started using the air conditioner, not so much to keep the house cool, but to try and reduce the dampness in the air. I planned some outdoor activities for my classes but needed to postpone them till the weather improved.

On the television weather map there was a huge bank of cloud sitting over the country dropping rain, similar to the tropical lows we see over the top end in Australia during the monsoon months. But the locals said this was very unusual weather for this time of the year. They had not seen it like this for years. Ah well, we got to see it! Now all I wanted to see was the sun!

In May, while the weather forecasters were continually forecasting precipitation, we decided that it was time to change the name of this country. Everybody reckoned China was so named because it made so much china, plates and pottery. But we thought it should be named after the interminable mist or fog that had hung around for so long. Since we got back from Thailand in the middle of February, it's been fog, rain, fog and more fog. I decided we should now call it Chog.

One rainy night in May the school held a singing contest. The students were required to sing an English or a Japanese song. Japanese was also taught there, and there were quite a few students learning Japanese. Some of the songs were not too bad, and some were not too good, but it was a nice evening, and seeing we were considered English experts, we were part of the judging team.

Very funny things happened at times. We were told how to judge them on pronunciation, tunefulness etc. and we had to give them a score out of ten. After the first few songs, some of which we gave generous scores of six or seven, we were sent a little note to say that we were not allowed to mark anyone with a mark less than 8.5, to save

LONGYAN? NO LONG RAIN!
多雨的龙岩

小了许多。离龙岩两小时车程的沿海一带，台风造成的破坏比龙岩要严重得多。因为台风到达我们这里的时候，风力已经减弱了不少。

多雨的天气带来的另一个问题是潮湿的空气。我们穿在身上的衣服，摸着总是潮潮的。睡觉的时候被褥也是潮潮的，纸张大都软软的、湿湿的。我打开了空调，不是为了降温，而是为了除湿。我给学生们设计了几项户外活动，不得不全部推到天气转好之后再开展。

根据天气预报图，中国的上方有一大团雨云，类似于处于最高点的热带低压，那种热带低压我们在澳大利亚季风季节见得到。听当地百姓说，今年的天气很反常，这么多雨水，百年不遇。好呀，竟然给我们撞上了！现在我最渴望一见的是太阳！

时至五月，天气预报仍在预报降雨量的多少，这时我们决定给这个地方改个名字。人人都认为中国之名的由来是因为她以瓷器闻名。我们以为这个地方雾霭氤氲如此之久，当以此为名。自从我们二月中旬从泰国回来，天气预报报的就是雾、雨、雾或大雾。我决定从此叫它为"雾城"。

五月的一个雨夜，学校举办了一场外文歌曲大赛。参赛选手必须唱英语或日语歌曲，我们这所学校也有日语专业，学日语的学生人数还不少呢。有些选手唱得相当不错，另有一些就差强人意了，不过晚会现场气氛很好，因为我们是英语专家，所以被邀请为评审团成员。

在中国时不时便有趣事发生。我们被告知如何从发音、音准等方面评分，我们以十分制打分。前面几首歌曲演唱完毕，我们非常慷慨地给其中一些歌手评了6或7分，结果有人送了一张小纸条告诉我们，为了选手的面子，最低分不要低于8.5分。老天，即使他们五音不全，全部跑调，至少也能从10分的总分中拿到8.5分。我们也写了张条子，说我们打算按照我们认为公平的方式打分，即根据选手表现评分。

他们邀请我和彼得作为"嘉宾"献唱。于是乎，我和彼得，这个总认为自己是音盲加跑调大王的彼得，站到了台上，唱了首澳大利亚乡村歌手史里姆·达斯丁的歌曲。彼得忘乎所以地站在台上，面对黑压压的观众，像摇滚明星一样又跳又唱，真的

205

face. Oh dear, even if they couldn't sing a note, they were still supposed to get at least 8.5 out of ten. We sent the note back and said we would mark them how we felt was fair, and we gave marks according to their performances.

They asked Peter and I to sing a song, as "guest singers". So there was Peter, a self-confessed tone deaf and off key crooner, with me, up on the stage singing a Slim Dusty song. It was hard to believe that Peter happily stood on the stage and sang in front of an auditorium full of people, pounding it out like a rock star.

That evening we got a text message from one of our students. Unfortunately I have deleted it, so I can't repeat it verbatim, but it said how wonderful our singing was, and that I was more beautiful than flowers, and Mr K more handsome, that it was wonderful to hear our English song, and that she enjoyed our performance very, very much.

Elvis, eat your heart out!

叫人难以置信。

  当晚我们收到一个学生的短信,可惜短信被我们删除了,不能字字复述,但大意是我们唱得非常棒,我的模样比鲜花还美,彼得帅呆了,我们唱的英文歌曲太好听了,她很非常喜欢我们的表演。

  亲爱的猫王,你天上有灵,该羡慕死我们了吧!

WHO'S BEEN MUCKING ABOUT WITH THE SUN?

Someone's been playing games and not told me. I'm pretty sure about that.

Peter and I lived in New Zealand for much of our lives. New Zealand is in the south of the southern hemisphere, pretty much at the bottom of the world. The next stop is Antarctica.

Winters were quite cold there, although it rarely snowed in our part of the country. However, we knew that the sun lived at the top end of the world and so we never bought a house with the main entrance to the house facing the bottom end of the world because that is where the howling southerlies came from and invaded your warm home every time you opened the door in winter. Therefore we looked for houses that had doors facing north, east or west and that was very sensible. Our homes were designed for outdoor living in the summer, but more importantly to keep warm in the winter. We always knew which was east and west, and even though the sun moved around a bit up and down the globe, we knew it rose in the east and set in the west but lived up the top. No problem.

Then when we moved to Australia, we found that houses were designed to stay cool. In Queensland because even the winters are warm, there is a whole new mindset involved. So they have doors, and lots of large windows that open in any direction so that any breeze will wander into your house and keep you cool. Very sensible.

Even so, the sun still rose in the east and set in the west, and spent most of its time up in the top of the world.

是谁对太阳暗动了手脚？

有人一直在"捣鬼"，只是没让我知道，不过我心中有数。

我和彼得一生大部分时光是在新西兰度过的。新西兰位于南半球，几乎直抵世界最南端，再往下便是南极洲了。

虽然我们住的地方极少下雪，但冬天奇冷无比。我们知道，太阳住在世界的北部，因此我们从不买大门超南的房屋。若是大门朝南，冬天只要一开大门，南风便趁势呼啸而进，占领你温暖屋子的每个角落。所以我们看的房屋，大门都是朝北、朝东或朝西，这样选择是有道理的。我家的设计既要方便夏季户外生活，更要考虑到冬天保暖问题。我们对东西方向感一向很强，尽管地球绕着太阳转，但我们知道太阳是东边升起西边落的。

后来，我们迁居澳大利亚，发现这里的房屋讲究的是如何防暑降温。因为昆士兰的冬天亦是温暖的，我们只能抛去旧习接受新想法。这儿的房屋门很多，四处都是大窗，这样才能让每一缕微风吹进房屋，保持屋内的凉爽。这么考虑是极其明智的。

即使这样，太阳依旧东方升起西方落，大部分时间在北部逗留。

可是，等我们来到中国生活的时候，有人"暗中搞了些名堂"。不是移动了中国的

But about the time we came to live in China, someone made some changes. Either someone moved China or else someone has been mucking about with the sun. The Bible says that faith the size of a mustard seed (a really tiny seed) could move mountains, but I'm not sure about moving a country as big as China.

However, somehow, China seems to have been turned one quarter of a turn on the globe, because, and I kid you not, here the sun rises in the south and sets in the north. I have always had a really good sense of direction, and generally could find my way anywhere, (within reason). In Napier, the hill was north, the sea was east and everything else could be worked out. In Australia the sea is east, the storms come from the west and you can work out the rest. But not so here.

For some reason I have yet to find out, China generally builds all its houses facing the same way. There are rows and rows and rows of these high rise apartment buildings, usually built in housing estates, and some of them a huge. They have the long side of the building usually facing south and the short end of the building facing east and west. My limited research says it's to do with feng shui. But it seems to have completely messed up my sense of direction, because, it is an absolute fact, that the sun is now rising in the south and setting in the north and it does the same thing every day.

Of course, here in Longyan you can go for days without seeing the sun, just a mist everywhere, all day every day. Sometimes you get the see the sun as a giant red ball as it rises and then a giant red ball as it sets, but that is all you see of it all day. In fact the first time we saw the sun set we were absolutely convinced it was the moon rising! It took us a while to figure it out; it was just too red for the moon.

Living in China now, I realise that I am at the top end of the world and things will be different. For those of you who have lived or travelled from the bottom bit of the world to the top bit of the world, or vice versa, you may have noticed the same thing. How did you deal with this? At the moment the sun is whirling around directly over poor old Rockhampton, causing heatwaves and such. It definitely is not close to China because our highs here are 10 to 15 degrees and our lows are 3,4,5,6, etc. In Beijing, (who would want to live there?) they are having lows of minus 15 and highs of minus 5. What joy! And I am told Longyan gets much colder in February, so course we are really looking forward to that!

位置，就是对太阳动了手脚？《圣经》上说，信念犹如芥菜籽，细小如沙，却能移动大山。但是，要将中国这么幅员辽阔的疆土移动，我是心存疑虑的。

可是，中国好像被谁生生扭转了60度，我没开玩笑，因为在中国，太阳是西边升起北边落下。我的方向感向来很好，一般到哪里都能认识路（在合理范围内）。比如，尼泊尔这个国家，北面是山东面是海，其他方向皆可分辨。或在澳大利亚，东面是海，风向为西，其余方向自可判定。可在中国，这些辨别方向的方法通通派不上用场。

原因我至今不明，中国的房屋一律朝向一方。在中国，高楼大厦鳞次栉比，多属于同一个小区，而有些小区规模巨大。房屋的稍长一端通常向南，略短一方朝东或朝西。根据我有限的调查，这样建房是跟风水有关。但我的方向感一下子全被打乱了，因为这样一来，太阳变成了从南升起往北降落，而且日复一日，周而复始。

当然，在龙岩这个地方，常常一连几天见不着太阳一面，天空整日灰蒙蒙的。有时，你能看见太阳像一个巨大的红球升起，又像一个巨大的红球降落，一日之内，仅此两个照面。我们第一次在中国看见落日时，竟然深信不疑地把它当成了刚刚升起的月亮！过了好一阵子，我俩才恍然大悟；因为月亮怎么可能如此通红通红。

如今我已人在中国，我知道在地球北部生活，情况会有所不同。如果你原来生活在南半球，现在来北半球居住或旅游；或者原来生活在北半球，现在来南半球居住或旅游，可能就会有我这种感觉。那么，我们该如何处之呢？此时此刻，太阳正在可怜的昆士兰首府老洛克汉普顿上空盘旋，将阵阵热气倾入该市，而中国却完全不同。因为龙岩此刻最高温度在10至15度之间，而昆士兰的最低温度都在3至6度之间徘徊。北京（谁会想在那个地方生活？）冬日更冷，最高温度不过零下5度，而最低温度却可低至零下15度。好没意思的地方！有人告诉我，二月的龙岩还要寒冷得多。没关系，我们还真想会会它！

Anyway back to the subject. I am still confused about east west north and south, and all that stuff and as my sense of direction is usually really good, I am quite sure someone has been playing games with the sun, and if it was you, please could you put it back again. Or if someone actually has turned China one quarter of a turn on the globe, please could you undo it for me? Thanks.

To use one of Peter's latest words, I am somewhat discombobulated.

WHO'S BEEN MUCKING ABOUT WITH THE SUN?
是谁对太阳暗动了手脚

让我重回旧题吧。如今，我依旧分不清中国的东西南北。因为我的方向感一直很好，所以我很笃定，是有人对太阳动了手脚。如果恶作剧者是您，烦请您将太阳归位。如果真有人将中国挪动了60度，可否看在我的薄面上，把它复位？万分感谢。

用彼得最近常说我的一句话结束这篇文章：我这个人神经兮兮的。

POLLY WANNA CRACKER?

(Email to the family)

It is 9 pm on the 12th of February, one lunar month after the Chinese New Year and an important day in China. It's the night of the Lantern Festival. The aim is to scare off evil spirits.

They not only have lanterns, they have fireworks.

Remember those snotty nosed little kids down the road, who, around November 5th lit a big Tom Thumb and stuck it in the letter box behind you, and frightened you to death? Well that's what it's like here just now.

We were woken up at 6 am this morning with Tom Thumb type crackers, not just one or two, but great long strings of the things, several hundred at a time. They sounded like bullets ricocheting off the walls, leaving the paths littered with the superfluous red paper covering.

The buildings here are tall and close together. They are also covered with ceramic tiles, so it's similar to being in a bathroom. Nothing absorbs the noise, which thunderously reverberates and echoes everywhere. This has been intermittent all day.

However about 4 pm it started in earnest. These strings of crackers were going off everywhere, you could hear them constantly. When it's close to home it's deafening. You can't do anything; just put your fingers in your ears to deaden it a bit.

As it got dark the real fireworks started. So far they have been going for about two hours nonstop, and I don't mean the little rockets we used to have when we were

放鞭炮

（给家人的一封邮件）

现在是2月12日晚上9点，中国新年后的第一个农历月。这一天对中国人来说是个重要的日子，因为今晚是元宵夜，元宵节的原始目的之一就是驱逐鬼怪。

家家户户不仅挂灯笼，还放鞭炮。

还记得那几个爱流鼻涕的小孩吗？他们就住在马路另一头。大概是11月5日吧，他们点了一个闪光炮，扔进你们身后的信箱，吓得你们四处逃窜？我们现在的情形就跟那时差不多。

清晨六点，我们就被鞭炮声惊醒。像闪光炮的声响，但不是一两个炮响，而是一长串的鞭炮，几百副同时噼啪作响，如同子弹射向墙壁，留下一地的红色碎纸片。

这里的房屋高大密集，都贴了瓷砖，人在里面仿佛置身于浴室一般。没有消音的设施，因此鞭炮的回声在屋里震天动地。鞭炮时断时续地响了一整天。

可是，到了下午四点左右，突然炮声大作。整个城市，到处都是噼里啪啦的鞭炮声，没有片刻的停顿。要是住家附近有人在放鞭炮，那响声震耳欲聋。对此，你束手无策，只能捂紧耳朵，减弱点声响。

暮色降临时，真正的烟花粉墨登场了。一口气燃放两个小时，从不间断。这里的烟花不是我们小时候玩的那种小火箭，是那种轰隆作响的大家伙，就是在悉尼大桥

kids, but the great big whopping boomers they use for displays on the Sydney Harbour Bridge. The skyline is constantly alight, and the air is full of acrid smoke drifting across the city.

I calculated that the booms were happening about three per second from the area around the university. We went up on top of our building, so had a panoramic view over the city and into the hills. But sitting here now, three per second is a major underestimate. There are people on the roof tops all around us lighting these massive fireworks. The noise is unbelievable.

We saw some of these fireworks for sale today in all sorts of shapes and sizes. Remember, fireworks are made here in China. The biggest were very large round fireworks that sold for about 600RMB, about $100AU. They looked like great big hat boxes. Peter thought that they were put together in a series so you just sat the thing on the ground and lit one wick and it was timed to set off about twenty of the big boomers. They must have sent millions of dollars up in smoke and there will be an enormous pall of smoke over the town tomorrow. But what a sight! As I send this email to you they are still going at a hundred miles an hour. WOW!

上烟火表演燃放的那种。天际夜空绚丽明亮,空气中弥漫着一股硝烟味儿。

我粗粗计算了一下,校园内差不多没隔三秒就有烟花响起的声音。我们爬到楼顶,此处观景,既可俯瞰整座城市的夜景,有可将四周的山影尽揽入怀。坐在楼顶的时候,我才发现自己刚才算少了,怎么可能才三秒一响呢? 四周,每座楼顶,都有人在燃放那些"巨无霸"。此等喧闹,无可名状。

今天,我们看见了卖烟花的地方,摆着各种大小不同、形状各异的烟花。别忘了,这些烟花都是中国当地制造的。最大的家伙是圆形的,一个大概600元,约100澳元,很像一个巨大的帽箱。彼得以为,每个"巨无霸"都是由一组大烟花捆扎而成的,燃放的时候,只要把它放在地上,点燃一个引子,时间一到,二十来个大烟花便会齐声炸响。这里,肯定有数以百万的钞票化成了天空中的青烟,明日的天空定将烟雾迷蒙。不过,多么壮观的景象! 就在我给你们写邮件的当口,一个个烟花依旧以每小时一百英里的速度飞向空中。哇!

WALKING ON WATER

Walking on water is not done very often, but the equivalent was done today, here in good ole Longyan.

In another story I have told you about meeting Roger and Alex at English corner, a weekly free for all, where we English teachers, and only the foreign ones, went and spoke to all and sundry, supposedly improving everyone's spoken English.

We got to know these young men quite well but Roger got a job and moved away to another city. He asked us to visit him one weekend. Mary and I went to the train station to buy the tickets.

Well!!!!!

We thought buying tickets at Shenzhen was hard, but that was a piece of cake in comparison. We arrived at the train station and made our way up the queue.

"We need tickets to Fuzhou for the overnight train on the eighteenth please," Mary said in Chinese.

"There are no tickets for the eighteenth," the lady replied. "I can give you tickets for the seventeenth."

"No, that's no good," said Mary, "We need them for the eighteenth. Is the train full already?"

"I don't know. All my tickets for the eighteenth are sold."

"When should we come back then? When will we be able to buy them?" Mary asks.

购票奇事

在现实生活中，我们很少水上行走（walking on water），但像耶稣一样能行于海面上的奇事今天却降临到了我身上，就在龙岩这个美丽而快乐的小城。

在前面的一个故事中，我曾说过，在一次英语角活动中，我们遇见了罗杰和亚历克斯。英语角一周举办一次，大家都可以参加，要求英语老师到场，跟参加者聊天对话，希望借此提高大家的口语水平，而实际上只有我们几个外教会去。

不久我们与他俩交上了朋友，可是罗杰找了份工作，搬到了另一个城市。一个周末，他邀请我们去他那儿玩，于是我和玛丽一块儿去买火车票。

好一番周折呀！

我们原以为在深圳买票已经够折腾了，但没想到与此次经历相比，深圳的波折根本不值一提。我们到了火车站，排队到售票窗口。

"我们想买18号去福州的车票，晚上的火车。"玛丽用中文说。

"18号的车票没有了，不过有17号的车票。"女售票员回答。

"不会吧，太糟糕了，我们要买的是18号的票，火车已经满员了吗？"玛丽问。

"不知道，我这儿18号的票全都卖光了。"

"那我们应该什么时间再过来？什么时候能有票？"

"不知道。"

"I don't know."

"There must be tickets available," I said to Mary. "Today is the first day we can buy them." (The system, which has now changed, was that you could not buy tickets until four days before travel. Our timing was just right.)

The lady couldn't help us, but I wasn't happy with this.

"Let's just stand here for a minute and ask again," I said to Mary. "Let's make it clear we are not giving up so easily."

"You should go to a different office, there might be some seats there," we were told after a few minutes.

It was 2pm, and the other office was not due to open until 2.30pm. The office lady was asleep and no one was going to wake her up just to sell us some tickets.

At 2.40 the office opened. Mary and I expectantly went to the counter, smiled nicely at the lady explaining what we wanted, but a heated exchange in Chinese soon got under way and I couldn't follow a thing.

"The problem is, that we want soft sleepers and she says we can't have them until four days before travel," Mary said to me.

"But it is four days before," I said, getting a little annoyed.

"Tomorrow will there be some tickets available?" Mary asked.

"I don't know," was the reply.

"When will you know?" Mary asked.

"I don't know."

"Can you tell us when we should come back?"

"I don't know," said the office lady.

I could feel the tension rising, and Mary knew there was something suspicious about the whole thing.

"There must be tickets available," I said to Mary. "If no one can buy them until today they must be for sale. They can't have sold them all this morning."

This was obviously a time when logic was not going to work. Sometimes, "don't know" is a perfectly good answer when you don't want to do anything. Mary continued to question her and got lots of "don't knows" in return.

Then this kind lady suddenly said, "If you leave your name and phone number I'll

我对玛丽说："肯定有票，今天是允许购票的第一天。"（按照那时的规定，火车票预售期为四天，现在的规定又变了。我们是踩着点儿来的。）

售票员不愿帮助我们，但我没有死心。

"呆会儿再问问，咱们不能就这么随便被打发走。"我对玛丽说。

这会儿是下午两点，其他售票点要到两点半才开始售票。售票员在午休，谁也不会起床卖票给我们。

两点四十分，售票窗打开了。我和玛丽满心期待地走到窗口，陪着笑脸对售票员说我们想买的票，很快她和玛丽就用中文唇枪舌战了起来，我一个字也听不懂。

玛丽对我说："麻烦了，我们要买软卧，可她说只卖发车前四天的票。"

"可今天就是发车前四天呀。"我说，心里有点儿不悦。

"明天会有票吗？"玛丽问。

"不知道。"对方回答。

"那你什么时候会知道呢？"玛丽又问。

"不知道。"

"你告诉我们，我们该什么时候过来买票？"

"不知道。"售票员回答。

我感觉到两人的话语中开始有火药味儿了。玛丽知道这其中肯定有猫腻。

"票指定是有的。要是今天大家都买不到票，她们的票也卖不出去。不可能才一个早上，所有的票就卖光了。"我对玛丽说。

显然，有时候逻辑判断毫无用处，因为有时候，当一个人不想做某事的时候最好的回答就是"不知道"。玛丽还在拼命追问，可对方就是一问三不知。

突然，售票员大发善心，说："要不，你们把名字和电话号码留下，有软卧的时候我打电话给你们。我相信很快就会有票的。"

我看着玛丽说："没错，是有票，但不知为什么她不愿意卖给我们。不能放弃，我们就在这里等，什么时候有票什么时候买。"

call you when there are soft sleepers. I am sure there will be some available soon."

I looked at Mary. "Right, there are seats then, she just doesn't want to sell them to us for some reason. I'm not giving up. Tell her we'll wait here until there are some soft sleepers we can buy."

Mary repeated my message in Chinese and we both went and sat a short distance away, but right in her line of vision. After a while she called out to Mary.

"I could sell you hard seats for the eighteenth", she said. "Then on the eighteenth you could come down and if there are any soft sleepers free you can just pay the difference and have your cabin."

I was horrified! "Hard seats! All night?" I squeaked to Mary, "Peter would kill me if he had to sit all night on a hard seat for ten hours, no sleep or anything." The lady in the office got the message.

These hard seats need to be seen to be understood. They are slightly padded bench seats, set in pairs facing each other, and each seat takes three people, so that you have three people on one side and three opposite staring you in the face with a little narrow table in between, where, one by one, they flop their arms and heads to sleep. There is very little room. They take all their baggage with them, chooks, goods, and anything at all, eat and chuck all their rubbish on the floor, I mean, this is traveling in the raw. Our three hour trip from Changting was manageable, but doing this all night was not a good idea at all.

Continuing my horrified voice I said, "What will happen if there are no soft sleepers available when we want to travel? No I couldn't possibly do that!"

We maintained our vigil. Suddenly she piped up. "If you buy the hard seats now, I could give you your return tickets now too."

Now this was the walking on water bit. No one, I mean, no one, ever, ever, can buy a return ticket. The rule was you must buy your ticket from the city you were leaving from, and getting return tickets is just unheard of.

"Mary, ask her what would happen if we bought the hard seats now, but there were no soft sleepers on the eighteenth. Could we get a refund?" I said.

"Yes," the lady told Mary. "A refund was available, but less fees of twenty per cent."

玛丽把我的话用中文转述给了售票员，然后我俩离开窗口，找了个她看得见的地方坐下。过了一会儿，她叫玛丽过去。

"我可以卖18号的硬座票给你们，你们18号再过来，如果车上有软卧，只要补上差价就行了。"她说。

我一听吓得尖叫道："硬座！一整晚上？叫彼得坐十小时硬座，没法睡觉，他会杀了我的。"售票员听懂了我的话。

只有亲眼目睹过的人，才知道硬座是怎么回事儿。所谓硬座，就是一些长凳，上面放了一条窄窄的垫子，二组乘客面对面坐着，每条长凳上可坐三个人。因此一边坐三个人，另一边坐着三个人，对面有六只眼睛盯着你看，中间隔着一张小桌子，大家纷纷把双手往桌子上一靠，头枕在手上就睡下了。几乎没有多余的空间，乘客带了很多行李，小鸡、货物，什么都有。吃东西的时候，垃圾随手扔往地上，给我的感觉，就像与原始人一同出行一样。从长汀回来坐三个小时的火车，我们尚能勉强对付，但要坐上一整宿，恐怕不行。

我余悸未消地说："要是等我们快上车了，还没有卧铺票该怎么办？不行，太不靠谱了！"

我们依然心存戒心。突然她松口了，说："你们买硬座票的话，我现在就卖回程票给你们。"

好奇怪呀！我是说，在那个时候，从来没有人能够在当地买到回程票。按照规定，只能从出发地购票，在当地买到回程票闻所未闻。

"玛丽，问问她，要是我们现在买了硬座票，到18号没有软卧，该怎么办？可以退票吗？"我说。

"是的，可以退票，但要扣除20%的手续费。"售票员告诉玛丽。

我一听，声音马上高了几度："20%？不行，没的事儿！明明是她们拿不准要不要卖票给我，反而还要我赔上200元。"

售票员对玛丽说："买不买，赶紧决定。再等下去，我可不敢保证你们还能买到

My voice went up another couple of notches. "Twenty per cent? No fear, not for this mug. I'm not giving them 200 Yuan just because they can't decide whether to sell me a ticket or not!"

"It's a matter of urgency," the office lady said to Mary. "If you wait there's no guarantee that you'll still get the return tickets, you know other people could snaffle them up in a flash and there'll be no tickets at all."

Talk about put on the pressure!

"No," I said to Mary, "I'm not falling for that. If the seats aren't available yet, then no one will have bought them, it's all a great big story."

We continued our vigil.

"Wait a moment," she called out to Mary, "I'll make a phone call."

Those phone lines ran red hot for about thirty minutes.

"Yes, I can get you the soft sleepers now for the eighteenth and I can also give you soft sleepers for your return trip."

Yay, after about two hours, we might get some tickets. She gave Mary a piece of paper with a number on it, and we trotted back to the first counter again. There was quite a queue, but we got through, and lo and behold, in my hot little hand I held soft sleeper tickets, and the absolutely unbelievable "walking on water" return tickets too.

Mary was stunned. "I have never known anyone to get a return ticket," she gasped. "I don't know why she gave them to you!"

We think that maybe this is what happened. Because there was a "shortage" of seats, they asked people to buy the hard seats with the promise of getting a soft sleeper when boarding the train. They knew there would be soft sleepers available. Then the passenger paid the difference when boarding the train, and some happy little train attendant pocketed the difference, putting them into a soft sleeper, no one in authority is any the wiser, and everyone is happy. Not a bad little scam really!

回程票。到时被一抢而光，半张票也剩不下。"

给我们施加压力！

我对玛丽说："不行，我不吃这一套。如果票还没放出来，那么谁也买不到，都是糊弄人的。"

我们依然没有松口。

"等一下，"售票员对玛丽喊道，"我打个电话看看。"

这一通电话她打了足足半小时。

"行了，我可以卖18号的软卧给你们，连同回程的软卧。"

太好了，熬了两个小时，车票总算有着落了。她递给玛丽一张纸条，上面写了一个号码，我们一路小跑地回到第一个窗口。好长的队伍，但我们挺过去了，看看吧，本人热乎乎的手掌心里握着软卧票，和叫人难以置信的仿佛神赐的回程票。

玛丽傻眼了，喘着气儿说："我还没见谁买过回程票呢，真不知道她们为什么卖票给你！"

我们猜可能是这么回事儿。因为卧铺票"短缺"，她们就叫人们买硬座票，同时承诺可以上车补票，而实际上她们知道有余票。等乘客上火车付了差价，某个幸福的小乘务员，便可神不知鬼不觉地将这笔钱揣进口袋。各取所得，岂不皆大欢喜？！

好聪明的小伎俩！

MY DAILY BUS RIDE HOME FROM SCHOOL

At the moment I am working at Xiamen University, at a new campus. I have an hour's journey there and back each day, by bus and boat. The last part from the ferry home at night is a very squishy experience.

I take the underground tunnel to the other side of the road and enter the bus station. I need a number 28 bus to get home. It's bedlam, my bus is not here, and there is already a long queue. There is a buzz as the old yellow and black bus rattles in, and everyone talks at once, jostling for the first place.

A Chinese bus is not like an Australian bus. It has single seats down the windowed edges and some seats at the back, but most of the bus is used by standing passengers who hang on to anything they can grab.

Each seat has a hand hold, there are hand holds swinging from the roof and quite a few poles from floor to ceiling. The front double hinged door opens, and it's mayhem with everyone trying to get on first, young and old grab and push and shove, using elbows and knees putting their 1 rmb into the money slot, and running for a seat.

I am not lucky enough to get a seat, and with my backpack on I'm feeling really tired and hot. I look around and marvel at these buses. They must have come off the ark, split plastic seats, floor covered in metal sheets, no luggage racks, no air conditioning, the ceiling looks like it has been worked on by a patchwork quilter, rust here and there, and you would think a gust of wind would tear it apart.

This bus would be on the road from 6 am until midnight with rarely a stop, puffing

下班乘车记

2008年的夏天,我在厦门大学的新校区教书,每天上下班都很折腾,又是公车又是轮渡,一趟都得用去个把小时。晚上下课出了轮渡坐公交车往家赶的那段路程着实拥挤不堪。

我穿过地下通道来到大路另一端的公交车站。我得坐28路公车回家。车站十分喧闹,28路车还没进站,但候车的人已经排成了长龙。终于,那辆黄黑色的破公车咣当咣当地进了站,顿时所有的乘客都嚷开了,争着抢第一个上车。

中国的公车跟澳大利亚的不大一样。这里的公车沿窗两排放着单把座椅,后部有几排椅子,但大多数乘客都得站着,看有什么可抓的东西便抓牢。

每个座位上都有把手,车厢顶棚也垂着一些拉环,顶棚和地板之间还安装了不少立杆,都可以供乘客抓握。每次只要车前门一打开,外面的乘客便一涌而上,谁都想第一个上车,无论老幼,都是又推又挤,手挡脚抵,抢先上到车里,赶紧把一块钱投入收费箱,便跑着找座位去了。

我运气没那么好,找不到座位,背着双肩包站在车里,感觉又热又累。我环顾了一下四周,甚是诧异:这些车子肯定大有年头了,塑料椅子都开裂了,地板上不少地方都用金属片打着补丁,里面没有货架,没装空调,车顶的样子像是被修修补补了不少回,到处锈迹斑斑,让人感觉只要一阵大风,车子就会四分五裂似的。

这趟车打清晨六点发车起便要马不停蹄地工作到午夜时分,一路上对着毫无戒

out black exhaust fumes to all the unsuspecting pedestrians nearby.

The bus moves off stopping frequently to let more people on, then some get off and I grab a seat. I try to get a seat near the back door. I MUST exit out the back doors; I cannot get out the front. The bus fills quickly at this time of the day, and I gradually get more and more squashed. People gradually cram backwards as new ones enter.

I can't move my legs or feet. I have my nose stuck in some Chinese mans nether regions; I don't look up to see whose face is at the top. Up there, it is armpit city! The bus is still taking on passengers, now the driver leaves open the back doors so they can stand in the stair well, and its just as well, we need some air movement in here! Mid summer with about 70 people crammed in makes for near fainting conditions.

We come into the train station and a few get off, but more get on. At this point I stand and like a piece of wet soap try to slide through the mass of people to stand by the back door. The bus takes off again, and jams on its brakes as it almost hits a car. Everyone on board jolts, moving as one, everyone pushing their neighbor, hanging on for dear life. We are like a huge tin of oily sardines, all standing on their tails trying to keep their balance.

We take off again, and the next stop is mine. I pull my backpack behind me and try to sidle closer to the exit. The bus stops, the back door opens, a couple get out but I am too far away. "Excuse me! Look out! Make way mate! "I yell. (I have no idea how to say this in Chinese), and then the bus starts to move again. "Hoi hoi, wait a mo, hang on mate, whoa!" I yell at the top of my voice. Others, closer to the driver yell so he can hear and the doors open again. I ooze out of the bus, down the steps onto the footpath. (You now understand why I can't exit at the front?)

I straighten my clothes and grin to myself. This is taking life by the horns and doing something. This is pure adventure, and I love it.

I take a few deep breaths to make sure my lungs still work, and head for home. This is the easy bit, along a broken undulating paved path, round the corner along a short lane to my apartment block, up five flights of narrow, concrete, almost dark stairs to my lovely apartment, to the peace and quiet and a homemade dinner.

心的行人喷着黑乎乎的尾气。

　　车子过了一会儿就停一下，好让更多的乘客上车。见有人下车，我赶紧抢了一个座位坐下。其实我特别想找个靠后车门的座位，因为乘客只能从后门下车，前门不准下车。此时，车内已经装满了人，我感觉越来越拥挤了，不停地有乘客上车，人们都慢慢挤向后面。

　　我的腿脚无法动弹，鼻子顶到了一个中国男子的下身部位，我没有抬头看那人的脸。脑袋上方竟然成了胳肢窝的世界！公车仍在放乘客进来，最后司机为了让乘客可以站在门口，后门都没关上。这样也好，车内急需通气。大夏天的，里面挤了七十多个人，个个都闷得快要晕倒了。

　　车子驶到火车站，下了几个人，但上车的人数却更多。此时，我站在里面，像块湿漉漉的肥皂，想挤过拥挤的人群，站到后车门附近。车子又开动了，有的人被挤到刹车边上，害得我们的公车差点儿撞上了一辆轿车。乘客被晃得失去了平衡，慌乱中你推我、我推你，想抓住什么东西以防跌倒。众乘客如同一大听油腻腻的沙丁鱼罐头，紧贴在一块儿，想着方子站稳脚跟。

　　车子再次开动了起来，下一站就轮到我下车了。我扯了扯背包，想方设法往门口挤去。汽车到站了，后门开了，下了两个人，但我还卡在里面出不来，急得我用英语大叫："各位，对不起！让一让！小心了！"（因为我说不来中文）。这时车子又发动了，我着急得扯着嗓门叫："司机，等一下，等一下！"司机附近的乘客见状，帮着我一同大喊，司机听见了，又打开了后门。我挤到门口，下了车来到人行道上。我整了整衣服，忍不住冲自个儿扮了一个鬼脸。这时候搭这路车回家，得勇往直前，不怕苦不怕累才行。好刺激呀，但我乐此不疲。

　　我深深吸了几口气，看看肺部能否正常工作，之后朝家中走去。相较而言，接下来的路程完全是小菜一碟：只见我走过一条坑坑洼洼、处处裂缝的柏油路，转弯进入一条短短的小巷，来到了自己的公寓大楼前；接着爬五层又黑又窄的水泥台阶，回到了温馨的公寓，逃离了喧嚣，静静地享用一顿自煮的晚餐。

BOOKING TRAIN TICKETS IN ADVANCE

Let me tell you about buying our train ticket from Shenzhen back to Longyan after our second trip to Hong Kong.

We arrived in Shenzhen from Longyan by train. We were meeting friends from Australia for a few days in Hong Kong. We disembarked and went to the ticket office to buy our return ticket to Longyan for May 5th. It took us a while to find the sales counters, and when our queue got to the ticket office we got a lady that couldn't speak any English. Valiantly we tried to explain what we wanted.

"Two tickets to Longyan please. May 5th. Lower bunks. Soft sleeper. Thank you."

She looked at us blankly then held up her hand with her thumb tucked in, meaning the number 4. I had no idea what she meant.

"Longyan. May 5th. Two people. Soft sleepers please," I repeated.

Again wordlessly she held up her four fingers.

A third time I repeated myself, only to get another handful of "4".

Frustrated I stood there, and she just sat and looked at us. Deciding that we weren't going to make any progress we stood aside while she served others. A young man approached.

"Can I help you?" he asked in English.

"Yes, I am trying to buy tickets for Longyan but she doesn't understand me."

He talked to the lady behind the glass then explained to me. "You are too early. It is six days until you travel and you can only buy your tickets four days before you travel.

购票记

BOOKING TRAIN TICKETS IN ADVANCE

我们第二次去香港旅游的时候，打算从深圳坐火车回龙岩，购票经历相当曲折。我想把当时的经过说给你们听听。

我们从龙岩坐火车抵达深圳后，打算去香港小住几日，与几个从澳大利亚来的朋友见面。我们一下火车就想直接到售票处，买5月5日回龙岩的火车票。我俩转了几圈才找到售票处，排队走到窗口，替我们服务的女售票员一句英语也听不懂。我们鼓足勇气，告诉她我们想买的票。

请给我们两张到龙岩的票，5月5日，软卧，下铺，谢谢。

她一脸茫然地看着我们，然后冲我们举起一只手，拇指内扣，摆了一个数字"4"。我不懂她的意思，又重复了一遍：

"龙岩，5月5日，两个人，软卧。"

售票员再次一言不发地伸出四个手指头。

我再一次重复了自己的请求，对方回敬我的依然是四个手指头。

我站在窗口，一脸挫败，而她呢就坐在里面看着我俩。我们知道再努力也是白费劲儿，于是退到一旁，让别人买票。一个小伙子朝我们走来。

"我能帮你们什么忙吗？"他说着英语。

"是的，我们想买去龙岩的火车票，可她听不懂我的话。"

You must come back in two days."

This was one of the humbugs about buying tickets for train travel. What a pain! We needed to go back in two days.

We went through customs and on to Hong Kong, met our friends and I found a travel agent and asked about buying a ticket in Hong Kong. If we wanted to go from Shenzhen to Fuzhou, the entire length of the train trip we could buy our ticket in Hong Kong. But as we wanted to get off part way to Fuzhou, in Longyan, we could not buy our ticket in Hong Kong. After this very complicated explanation we realised that a trip to Shenzhen for tickets was inevitable. We could, of course, pay for the full trip and get off at Longyan, but that was a very expensive proposition.

Two days later we went from Hong Kong, through customs into China again. As we entered the railway station we were accosted, in the gentlest manner, by a young Japanese lad who was lost and wanted to buy a ticket too.

"Follow us," we said, taking pity on him. "Where do you want to go?"

"I am not sure," he said in halting English.

We got into the queue and waited. This queue did not move one inch. After about ten minutes I was getting impatient. I checked the other queues thinking it might be a good idea to switch, but none of them were moving. All the queues were getting longer and longer, even out the door into the courtyard outside, and not one window was open, no tickets were being sold, and on closer inspection, there were no salespeople at the twenty or so counters.

I did what I often did in such circumstances; I looked around and said out loud, "does anyone speak English?"

"Yes, I do," said a young girl standing close to me in the next queue. I talked to her for a while to find out what was wrong.

"Oh, its lunchtime," she said.

"Lunchtime?"

"Yes of course. They are all having their lunch. They will be back at noon when they have finished eating."

"Don't they just send half off for lunch and then the other half go for their break?" I asked amazed at such a schedule.

BOOKING TRAIN TICKETS IN ADVANCE 购票记

小伙子与窗后的女士说了几句话，然后告诉我们，"你们来太早了，你们六天后才要离开深圳，但这里只能预售发车前四天的票。你们得两天后再过来一趟了。"

坐火车出行购票时会遇见许多啰嗦事情，这就是其中一件。太麻烦了！我们两天后还得再来一趟。

我们通关来到香港，见到了朋友，找到了一家旅行社，向他们咨询了如何在香港买票。如果我们想从深圳到福州，就可以在香港买到全程票，但同样是这列开往福州的火车，中途在龙岩下车的火车票，却买不到。我们磨了好久的嘴皮子，终于明白了，唯一的办法就是回深圳买票。当然，我们可以买全程票，途中在龙岩下车，但费用太高，很不划算。

两天后我们从香港过关又回到了中国大陆。快到火车站的时候，身边多了一个极其温文尔雅的日本小伙子，他迷路了，也想买火车票。

"跟我们走吧。你要去哪里？"我们同情地问。

"我不大清楚。"他用英语结结巴巴地回答。

我们排队等待。队伍一动不动。等了10分钟左右，我不耐烦了。我看了看其他队伍，暗忖是不是应该换个队，发现所有的队伍都静止不动。人越来越多，队伍越来越长，都排到了门外的院子里了，可依旧没有一个人前来打开窗口售票。我仔细瞅了瞅，发现20多个售票窗后，没有一个售票员。

我又使出常用的招数。我环顾了一下四周，大声问道："有谁会说英语的吗？"

"我会呢。"隔壁队伍中一个离我很近的年轻姑娘应道。我跟她说了一会儿话，想知道究竟出了什么问题。

"噢，现在是午餐时间。"她说。

"午餐时间？"

"是呀，售票员都去吃饭了，等他们吃完饭了，12点就会回来的。"

"为什么不错峰安排呢，一半人先吃，另一半人后吃？"这样的安排让我万分惊讶。

She laughed. "Oh, no. They all must go at the same time."

There was nothing to do but wait, so we chatted. She was a very interesting young lady, having worked in America and England. I told her about the young lad who was with us.

"I'll try and help him too, I have time. Where does he want to go?"

"He doesn't seem to know," I said. "He's got it written on a piece of paper though."

The young lad pulled out his piece of paper with the address. The girl looked very puzzled. "This isn't Chinese. Maybe it's Japanese."

"No," the young man said. "I am Japanese. This is not Japanese. But I must go here." We were all baffled, including the young Japanese man, who had no idea where he was supposed to go. He spoke no Chinese either.

"I think he needs to go to Guangzhou," the Chinese girl said after some thought.

"You need to go to a different counter for that," she told him. "Wait with us and I will help you."

Once the staff's appetites are sated, they come back and all the windows opened at once. The queues started to move. I looked at the lady behind the counter. Guess what. I have got the "4" lady again.

She recognised us, and talked to the lady sitting at the next window. Of course, I had no idea what she was saying but the tone of voice and the body language indicated something akin to, "Here they are back again, these crazy white people who can't speak Chinese and want to travel and I can't understand a single word they say. I don't know what they want. Can anyone help me?"

The wonderful young Chinese girl heard her, and spoke to her for us. We got our lower level soft sleepers. It was just as well we went back to Shenzhen that day because the train was almost fully booked.

As for the Japanese lad, the Chinese girl took him off somewhere else to get a ticket for Guangzhou. We hoped that was where he wanted to go, because that was where he was going to end up! Then we went shopping at the Lo Wu shopping centre.

姑娘大笑道:"噢,不行的,必须在规定的时间一起去。"

除了等别无他法,我俩乘机聊起天来。这个姑娘在美国和英国工作过,相当有趣。我把同行的日本小伙子的情况告诉她。

"我看看能不能帮上他的忙,反正我不赶时间。他要去哪儿呢?"

"他自己好像也不大清楚,不过他有一张纸条,写着要去的地方。"我说。

小伙子拿出写着地点的纸张,姑娘看了一眼,满脸困惑:"这上面写的不是中文,说不定是日语吧。"

"不是日语。"小伙子说,"我就是日本人,不是日语,可我必须去那个地方。"我俩顿时无语,小伙子也一样,不知自己该前往何处。他也不会说中文。

姑娘想了想说:"我想他要去的地方是广州。"

"你得去另一个窗口买票,"她告诉小伙子,"等我们一下,我会帮你的。"

售票员们填饱了肚子回来了,所有的窗口一下子全打开了。队伍开始移动。我看了一眼窗口的售票员。猜猜是谁? 我又碰见了那个冲我摆四个指头的女士。

她认出了我们,对坐在隔壁的女士说了些什么。我当然听不懂她的话,但从她的口气和身体语言里,我能猜出大概意思:"他们又来了,这些老外真好玩,中国话都不会说,还来这里旅游,他们说的话我一个字也听不懂。我不知道他们要做什么。能不能帮我一下?"

热心肠的年轻姑娘听到她说的话,替我俩与她沟通。我们买到了软卧下铺票。还亏得我们回深圳买票了,我们想坐的那列火车没剩几张票了。

至于那个日本小伙子,被姑娘领去了另一个窗口,购买去广州的车票。希望广州就是他真正要去的地方,因为他即将落脚的地方就是那里! 买到票后,我们直奔罗湖商城购物去了。

购物

有人告诉我们,有机会一定要去罗湖商城走一趟。这个五层楼的超级大商城,

Shenzhen Shopping at Lo Wu Mall

We were told, if possible, we should visit the Lo Wu Commercial City Mall. This huge sprawling mall on five floors is an amazing place. The shops are not named but numbered. The general advice is that when you find something you like, ask for their business card and make notes on the card for future reference. We allowed half a day to look around this mall, which was in reality the minimum time needed.

Coming from Hong Kong you must go through the border control and as you exit you are on the south side of a huge square. On the Western side is the main Shenzhen train station. To your immediate right, on the eastern side of the square is this shopping mall. You can also do this forty minute day trip by train from Hong Kong Central but you will need a Chinese visa to enter.

This is a place where extraordinary skills in bartering were required and expected. We had honed our skills at bartering in Longyan, so knew that the general rule was to pay about half the asking price.

Touters of the highest order were in full force, and they pestered us to death. We got quite good at just ignoring them. If they got pushy and wanted me to offer a price on something I didn't want, I offered the ridiculous price of 1RMB. Then they gave up.

This mall sold everything you could imagine including clothes, shoes, handbags, linen and fabrics. We didn't take a bag with us but bought one there and filled it during our day. Lo Wo is a maze with escalators going all over the place. The shops are small and jammed to the gills with goods.

Many malls in China are built in a similar manner. Our method in a new mall was to go to the top, and slowly work our way down floor by floor, finding things that interested us. Once on the ground floor again we'd return to those places of interest and start haggling.

As we walked the corridors touters called to us, encouraging us to "lookee, lookee see here". Once inside a shop, they are convinced you are there to give them your very last penny, and getting out again, is a bit like the proverbial camel through the eye of a needle.

In one shop I made the fatal mistake of asking to see a catalogue. That seemed to

真是个不错的地方。店铺没有名字只有标号。我有一个常识性的建议：看到自己喜欢的东西，向店家要一张名片，在名片上加注，方便以后使用。我们可以在商城逛半天，其实半天也只能走马观花。

从香港出来，必须经过边检，出了边检口，就到了一个大广场南部。广场西部就是深圳火车站。在你右侧的广场东边就是罗湖商城。也可以在白天从香港中环坐四十分钟地铁过来购物，不过须有到大陆的签证才行。

这个地方需要高超的砍价本领。我们在龙岩练过讨价还价的功夫，因此知道一般作法是砍去报价的一半。

巧舌如簧的店家各个使出浑身解数招徕顾客，使劲儿缠着我们不放。我们已经学乖了，对他们不予理睬。遇到死缠烂打的，硬要我对一样我不中意的东西出价，我就出一个低得可笑的价钱，比如一块钱，让他们知难而退。

商城里，各种商品，只要你想象得出，应有尽有。服装、鞋子、提包、织品以及布料，无所不有。我们没有带包出来，就在商城买了一个，买了东西就往里装。这里就像个迷宫，到处都是扶梯。店铺不大，塞满了货物。

中国的商场大都是这样的格局。我们每到一个新商场，都是先上最高一层，从上往下慢慢逛，寻找喜欢的物品。逛到一楼后再回头，找到有自己中意商品的地方，悠着劲儿砍价。

走在过道里，店主殷勤地招呼我们："瞧一瞧，看一看，过来看看吧。"只要你进了店，他们便认准了，你今天肯定会把口袋里的每个子都掏出来买他们的东西。想空手出去，就像《圣经》中所说的那样，宛如骆驼穿过针眼一样困难。

我在一家商店犯了一个大错，叫店家把目录拿给我看看。我的举动在他们眼里似乎就是购物的前兆，可我只想看看而已。他们冲出去给我取样品，可我懒得等，继续逛往别处了。在前面的一家店里，他们找到我们，非常恼火，说我们等一会儿都不肯。我赶紧道歉，说给他们添麻烦了，但我真的不想买东西。

在这个地方，你能看到世界上所有的名牌。不过，千万别上当，这里的名牌都是

be the prelude to buying, but I was only looking. They rushed off to bring me some samples, but I didn't bother waiting and wandered on. They found me a few shops further on, insulted that I hadn't waited. I apologised for upsetting them but said I didn't want to buy anything.

These places sell every brand name on the planet. But don't be fooled, they are all fakes, fabulous fakes, but fakes nonetheless. Many shops sell the same items so it's important to check the prices.

However, we did find a shop with men's suits. Did Peter need another suit? No of course not. Well, maybe yes. Of course he does! So we looked. They seemed to be well made from good quality lightweight fabrics. The colours were just what Peter wanted, so he tried on a jacket, then the trousers. They fitted perfectly. He decided on one and asked the price. They wanted about 900RMB, or $150AU. He put on a horrified face and said it was far too expensive, it was impossible to pay that much!

So the bartering started. We got them down to about 500RMB, which was a fabulous price so I suggested Peter buy two of them. The bartering started all over again; after all, selling two is much better for the shop than selling one. We tossed figures around but their price was 950 RMB for two. We were prepared to pay 850RMB for two, but they refused to lower the price, so we walked away.

The shopkeeper followed encouraging us to go back. He agreed to our price, telling us in his woeful voice that as we were his friends he could give us a very special discount even though his profit would be nil. Then the final thrust. We said we'd take a shirt for the same price. So we bought two suits and a shirt for about $150AU. They look very stylish, and after several years are almost as good as new.

China sells the most beautiful curtaining in very unusual fabrics and styles. Lo Wu had lots of curtains, along with some beautiful linen. I splashed out on a fabulous table cloth. Then I found the shops with sewing fabric. I never did see how big this area was, I didn't find the end of it, but there were miles of the most wonderful fabrics.

I swooned over the silks. On asking where they came from they said Shanghai, Hangzhou and Suzhou. Shark was a silk expert, so I waited til I had him with me to buy silk from Hangzhou and Suzhou. This was sewing heaven. I bought several pieces to take back to my dressmaker in Longyan.

仿的，且极其逼真，但假货就是假货。许多商店卖同样的货物，因此货比三家是很有必要的。

不过，我们的确找到了一家男装店。彼得还需添置衣服吗？当然不需要了。嗯，说不定人家想要新衣呢。错了，人家巴望着呢！于是我们进店看了看。衣服料子质量好像不错，很轻，颜色也是彼得喜欢的。彼得试穿了一件夹克，又搭配了一条裤子，非常合身。他决定买一件，问了问价钱。店家出价900元，约150澳元。彼得一听，满脸惶恐，说太贵了，简直是天价！

于是，讨价还价开始了。我们砍到了500元左右，这个价钱太划算了，我叫彼得干脆一口气买两件。新一轮讨价还价又开始了。再怎么说，卖两件总比卖一件合算。我们商量了好一会儿，但对方坚持两件950元。我们想好了，两件850元就买，但他们不肯再降价，于是我们拔腿走了。

店主跟着我们，一直叫我们回去再商量。他妥协了，同意我们的价钱，无比心疼地告诉我们，看在我们是他朋友的份上，才优惠卖给我们，虽然他一分钱都挣不到。接下来，我们进行了最后一轮砍价。我们说，同样的价钱搭一件衬衫，我们才买。就这样，我们花了大约150澳元，买到了两件外套和一件衬衫。衣服很有型，彼得穿了好几年还跟新的一样。

中国的窗帘布非常漂亮，布料和花色都很独特。罗湖商城有许多窗帘布料和漂亮的棉麻织品。我买了一块极美的桌布。后来我找到布店区。我不知道这个地方究竟有多大，只见美丽绝伦的布料一溜一溜地挂着，一眼望不到头。

一看到丝绸我的腿就走不动了。我问店家这些丝绸是什么地方的，他们说是从上海、杭州和苏州进的。沙克是丝绸专家，所以我想等他有空，叫他陪我去买些苏州和杭州的丝绸。这里简直是布料的天堂。我买了好几块布，带回龙岩叫"老板娘"给我裁新衣。

逛了约一小时，我们才离开了这个阿拉丁宝洞。我告诉自己，过几天一定再来一趟。我们回家时又经过了这里，可是卖布区关门了。那天晚上，家家店门紧闭，看不

After an hour or so we left this Aladdin's cave. I promised myself a return trip a couple of days later as we came through this way again on our way home, but the fabric section was closed. All locked up as tight as a barrel. No pieces of material were coming out of there that night. I was most upset. Never mind, more money to spend somewhere else.

I found out later, that under the Lo Wu Mall is a large bus station. From this station you can get buses to the Shenzhen airport for about 20RMB. A taxi to the airport will cost you about 150RMB, but is a little faster, and a private taxi will cost around 350RMB.

Note: If you are approached at the Hong Kong border by official looking men offering taxi rides, be very careful. Don't go with "private taxis". Use cars only if they have the proper signwriting, the legitimate taxi lights on the roof of the car, and correct taxi meters.

http://www.youtube.com/watch?v=IHWhZe5XNBM

http://www.journeywoman.com/shopping_worldwide/china_shopping.html

http://www.orientaltravel.com/tours/HongKong/Shenzhen_shopping_tour.htm

BOOKING TRAIN TICKETS IN ADVANCE | 购票记

到一块布料的影子。我很不开心。不过没关系，省下的钱可以买别的东西。

后来我发现，罗湖商城的下面有一个大汽车站，从这里坐公交车到深圳机场大约20元人民币。打车过去要150元左右，不过速度更快些，要是坐"黑车"，大概要350元钱。

提示：在香港边界，如遇到工作人员模样的人，请你坐他的车，要小心了。千万别上"黑车"。正规的士车身上贴有标识，车顶装了的士车灯，计价器。非此类的士坚决不坐。

http://www.youtube.com/watch?v=IHWhZe5XNBM

http://www.journeywoman.com/shopping_worldwide/china_shopping.html

http://www.orientaltravel.com/tours/HongKong/Shenzhen_shopping_tour.htm

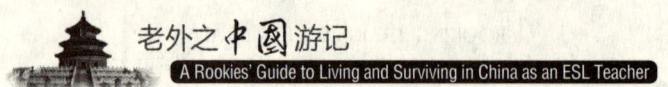

GUT WRENCHING GOODBYES

I knew the last few days would be hard, but I didn't expect it to start so soon. We were due to leave on the 28th June, but on Friday the 9th it started. I was listening to speeches for the final exam in one class, amazed at their improvement, realising I'd played a small part in their progress, and just stood in front of them all wiping away tears. Not a good start to the day. Clark's class, the top class, was still to come and I was a bit of a mess.

I wondered how people who worked as teachers for many years coped with the "end of year" thing. Are all teachers affected like this or was I just more involved than most? If every teacher is so upset at the year's end it's a wonder there are any left at all. In our case, we allowed ourselves to become emotionally involved with many students, and perhaps that was not a good thing. We were friends with many of them, they visited us regularly, and while we were away from our own family, and especially in such a different setting, these became our "Chinese children".

Another matter too, is that while I was in Longyan, I had no hint of depression. I didn't want to go back home. I wanted to go and see my family again, I wanted to be there when Lily had her next baby in September, and I wanted to be there to help out. But I dreaded the thought of going back to the dog-eat-dog materialistic lifestyle and a grumpy mother to look after. I didn't want to go back to the television programs filled with violence, sex and banal stupidity, (of course I could always turn the box off) and I didn't want to go back to working eight hours a day. However, these things weren't

伤离别

我知晓离别的日子肯定不容易，却没料到这么快就到来了。我们定好6月28日离开学校，可是在6月9日周五这一天，我们就迎来了第一场告别。当时，我正在给一个班级进行期末口试，学生们的演讲让我又惊又喜，惊的是这一年他们进步真的不小，喜的是他们的进步也有我的一点点功劳。我站在全班同学面前，不由得热泪盈眶，赶紧抹去眼泪。不妙的开端。接下来要上的是克拉克的班级，学院的尖子班，可我已经心乱如麻了。

我很纳闷，不知从教多年的老师们是如何面对一年一度的学期末？他们都像我这样心情沉重吗，还是我投入太多，无法超脱？要是每个老师，每到年末都如我这般抑郁寡欢，还能坚持教书，肯定是奇事一件。我和彼得与许多学生建立了深厚的感情，或许不是什么好事情。我们成了不少学生的朋友，他们经常到我家做客，因为我俩远离家人来到这个全然陌生的国度，渐渐地把他们当成了自己的"中国孩子"。

另外一个麻烦是，我在龙岩的日子过得非常快乐，本是不想回澳大利亚的。我只是想看看家人，想在女儿莉莉九月生第二个孩子的时候，能陪在她的身边，帮她一把。可我心里是害怕回到那个物欲横流、充满算计的生活之中，害怕一回去又得照顾我那个性情乖戾的老妈妈；我不想回去，不想去看充满暴力、色情，或浅薄、无知的电视节目（当然我可以关掉电视）；我不想回去，不想一天工作八小时。可是，这些

optional. I would just have to carry on as before, smiling and saying, "I am fine thank you how are you?" lying through my teeth. I'd been the breadwinner for the family for a while as Peter's health was not so good. But I loved my life in China and didn't want to go back!

There were things about China that drove me totally crazy, but there were other things that I loved. Apart from the students, it was a very easy lifestyle. I worked less than twenty hours a week. I liked the fact that I lived on campus. To be sure it was 300 steps and several short walks to the classroom, but it was still living on the job. I didn't have to cook, the meals at the canteen were adequate, and eating out was cheap. My housework consisted of general tidying up and some cleaning, but Peter helped out too so that made my life even easier. In Longyan I was respected, I had control over my life, and was pretty much a whole person. In Longyan I felt that I had something to offer the students. There I was known as "me". Also, I just loved the teaching work. Never did I get up in the morning thinking, "I don't want to go to class today". To me it was a "fun" job. Anyway I knew it had to come to an end, so that was that.

On the 10th, at 10am Irene came to our apartment. She left in tears. At 11am Hope and Jolly arrived, and before long Jolly was sobbing her heart out on my shoulder because we were leaving. Later that day, I went to the dressmaker to get the last of my things, said goodbye and left almost in tears. This was just the dressmaker for goodness sake! How things would be at the end of the month I dreaded to think. There was much worse to come.

On June 13th I was shopping when Peter sent me a text message - "One present and lots of tears later I am a mess–I will survive". From this I took it that he'd had a tough time with his first class. They gave him a lovely big woven wall hanging and a card with all the student's signatures. On the front of the card was written, "To our best teacher." All the classes gave us lovely gifts of some sort.

We packed our things into many more bags than the 20kg allowance, tidied up the flat, and said our final farewells to the teachers and students. On the day we left, many students came to help us down with our bags and see us off. The school provided a bus and driver to take us to Xiamen airport. We were surrounded by hundreds of students and many of the teachers as we loaded the van, climbed in and slammed the doors. Faces

事情我不能选择。我只能像以前一样，收拾心情，将不悦压在心头，微笑着说："谢谢，我挺好的，你们呢？"这些年来，因为彼得身体不大好，我已经成了家中的顶梁柱。可是，我如此喜欢中国的生活，真的不愿回去！

的确，中国有些方面让我极其烦恼，但其他一切我都满心喜欢。除了学生，这里的生活极其简单。我一周工作不到20小时。我喜欢住在校园里。虽然到班级需要上下300级台阶、再步行好几小段路，但毕竟离工作地点不远。我不必煮饭，一日三餐到学校食堂吃就行了，况且下馆子费用又不高。家务活不过是整理屋子和拖地洗衣，就这些活儿还有彼得帮忙，所以我的日子过得越发潇洒了。生活在龙岩，我受人尊重，想怎么过日子都行，因此感觉自己是个完整的人。在龙岩，我觉得自己是个有用之人，能有东西教给学生们。在这里，人们知道我"姓甚名谁"。此外，我喜欢教书。从来没有哪一个清晨，我起床的时候会这么想："今天不想上课。"我觉得教书"趣味盎然"。虽然我知道，终有一日我要作别讲台，该来的就让它来吧。

十日早上10点艾琳到我公寓来看我，走的时候梨花带雨。11点荷芙和乔丽结伴过来，两个女孩舍不得我们走，脑袋趴在我肩膀上放声大哭。稍晚，我去"老板娘"的裁缝店取最后几套衣服，顺便与她告别，走的时候，我双眼含泪。老天，我告别的不过是个裁缝师傅而已！六月底情形到底会怎样，我不敢多想。接下来肯定是一天比一天更伤心。

6月13日，我在买东西的时候彼得发了个短信给我："一份礼物，哭声一片，糟透了——不过我能挺过去。"看到他的短信，我知道他这堂课上得很辛苦。学生们送了他一大幅漂亮的针织墙饰和一张全体学生签名的卡片。卡片正面写着："献给我们挚爱的老师！"每个班级都给我们精心准备了可爱的礼物。

我们把东西装进了好多个包，超出了20公斤的限重，再打扫干净屋子，跟同事和学生最后一次告别。我们临走的那一天，来了很多学生为我们送行。学校派了一辆车送我们到厦门机场。几百个学生和一大群老师看着我们把行李放进车子，爬进车厢，关上车门。四面的车窗外都是望着我们的脸庞，一个个抹着眼泪。车子终于驶下

looked in all the windows, tears flowed and finally the van drove down the hill, through the gate, past the floppy fish restaurant, the hairdressers where I got almost shaved bare, the shops we visited almost daily, the fruit carts, through and out of Longyan. It was a sad, sad day.

Deneice was going back to America for six weeks. Mr and Mrs Ngarita, the most wonderful gentle couple who taught Japanese were going home and we were going to meet Jonathan, Katherine and Ashleigh for three weeks travelling all through China.

I was a total mess and couldn't stop crying. We left our spare bags at a friend's place while we were on holiday. We flew to Beijing to meet Jonathan and family and travelled for three wonderful weeks seeing some of the most magnificent things in this amazing country. We visited the Great Wall, the Forbidden City, and many of the sights of Beijing, floated down the Yangtze River on a five star boat cruise and saw the terracotta warriors at Xi'an.

Shark and Twilight met us for three last fabulous days together. Shark was familiar with this area and he took us all round the famous tourist spots. Then came a second round of gut wrenching goodbyes with them. After three busy weeks crammed with countless unforgettable experiences we went back to Xiamen airport to fly home.

Both Peter and I sat in the departure lounge, texting or phoning many of the students, saying one last goodbye with tears rolling down our faces. This year became one of Dr Phil's "Life changing experiences". I wondered how I would ever go back to the old life. I didn't know.

We arrived back in Brisbane. It was wonderful to see the family again. We made our plans to set up house again with Mum, who in her kindly way said, "You needn't have bothered coming back, I can manage fine on my own!"

Too late now, we were back. But not for long. After a few weeks of total misery, after feeling myself succumbing to depression again, I went back to China.

But that is a completely new story.

A picture tells a thousand words so Shakespeare said.

For pictures of our life in China go to www.englishstoriesforfun.com and click on the photo link.

小山，穿过校门，经过"跳跳鱼"餐馆，驶离那间几乎把我剃成光头的理发店，经过那几家我几乎天天购物的商店和那一辆辆水果车，穿过龙岩城区，出了龙岩市。这一天我们真的非常非常难过。

戴妮丝打算回美国呆六周。彬彬有礼的日语老师成田夫妇要回日本，我们要和乔纳森、凯瑟琳和阿诗莱一起呆三周，到中国各地走走看看。

我难过得一塌糊涂，一路上哭个不停。旅行的时候，把行李寄放在一个朋友家。我们飞到北京和乔纳森他们会合，好好玩了三个星期，美丽的中国，江山如此多娇，让我们一家人大饱眼福。在北京，我们看了长城、故宫等许多名胜古迹，而后乘坐一艘五星游轮，顺长江而下，到西安看了兵马俑。

旅游的最后三天，沙克和特莱特加入了我们，我们玩得越发尽兴。沙克熟悉当地，领着我们游遍了每一个著名景点。这三个星期，我们马不停蹄，没有一刻空闲。最后，我们带着数不胜数的难忘经历，返回厦门机场，准备飞往澳大利亚。

我和彼得坐在候机厅内，给学生打电话或发短信告别，泪流满面。这一年的经历的确让我们的人生"大不一样"了，我不知道如何回到原来的生活，我没有主意。

我们回到了布里斯班，又见到了家人确实高兴。我们整理好房子，把老妈妈又接到身边奉养，妈妈非常客气地说："你们没必要回家的，我一个人过得好好的！"

现在说这话为时已晚，我们已经离开了中国，回到了故里。不过，这次回国我们没呆多久。开头几周的日子，我过得非常不顺心，后来觉得自己差点儿要得抑郁症了，于是又回到了中国。

故地重游的感觉自然完全不同了。

莎翁曾说过，一幅画甚过万言书。若您对我们在中国生活的照片感兴趣，请连接该网址：www.englishstoriesforfun.com，点击照片链接即可。

LONGYAN REVISITED

How time flies! It is the year 2012 and I have made a trip back to China. Shark my good friend also known as Alex is getting married in Putian. Roger, Alex's friend who also used to come to English corner is married to his childhood sweetheart and working for an Italian company in Beijing, has an excellent job and travels to Europe often. Twilight, one of our favourite students is now married with a baby and living in Kunshan. Peter 2 is living in Fuzhou, working for an international company and travels overseas for them. Clark is a teacher at the No.1 Middle School in Longyan. Hope is a teacher in Sunming and Jolly is a teacher in Dongshan Island. Jeson came to Brisbane, graduated with his Master's Degree and did some extra study courses in accounting. Many of our students are married, most in good jobs, some have started their own businesses, and are using their English regularly.

During my six weeks in China I planned a week with Deneice. She visited us in Australia a year ago, and she had "the holiday of a lifetime" travelling around our beautiful country. Most of my six weeks was spent in Putian, Alex's hometown, but yesterday I took the fast D train from Putian to Longyan.

China is surprisingly mountainous once you get away from the coast, and to get to Longyan it's a long uphill road, or in this case the tracks climb a long way up. There are also lots of tunnels, after all, why go over a hill when you can go through it? Some of the tunnels are quite long, maybe 5 or 6 kilometres long.

Debbie was there to meet me and we dropped of my suitcase and went into town. I

重访龙岩

光阴荏苒！一晃就到了2012年，我又去了一趟中国。老朋友沙克，又叫亚历克斯，结婚了，要在莆田办喜酒。罗杰，亚历克斯的朋友，以前也常去英语角，娶了儿时伙伴为妻，现在北京的一家意大利公司上班，工作很好，常去欧洲旅游。特莱特，我和彼得最心爱的学生，也结婚了，已经是个准妈妈了，住在江苏昆山。小彼得在福州的一家跨国公司上班，常到国外出差。克拉克在龙岩一中当老师。荷芙在三明教书，而乔丽在东山教书。杰森来布里斯班留学，取得了硕士学历，另外选修了几门会计课程。好多学生都成家了，多数人都找到了一份好工作，有的学生已经有了自己的公司，使用英语已是常事。

我在中国呆了六周，专门安排了一周与戴妮丝呆在一起。一年前，她到澳大利亚看望了我们，走遍了美丽的澳洲，度过了一个"难忘的假日"。这六周我大部分时间呆在莆田，亚历克斯的老家，昨天我才离开莆田，坐动车来到龙岩。

中国的地势很奇怪，一离开海就是山，去龙岩的路都是上坡路，因此动车盘旋而上。沿路还有许多隧道，也是，有办法穿山而过，为什么要绕山而行？有的隧道相当长，可能有五六公里。

黛比（戴妮丝的昵称）在火车站接我们，我们扔下行李箱马上进镇。我想去看看"老板娘"。她店里总有一些漂亮的布料让我心痒痒，但这一次我却一块布料也没看

wanted to go to "my dressmaker". She usually had some lovely fabrics to choose from, but this time there was not even one piece of material I liked. So no clothes will come from her shop this time.

Coming back here after six years has been an interesting experience. It's wonderful to see Deneice again. She has hardly changed at all. She has been at Longyan University now for eight years, and has other foreign teachers for company. Her little flat is nice, but like most Chinese places the floors are ceramic tiles, the walls are tiles or plastered and there is no carpet, so they are quite cold.

I spoke to some of Deneice's classes about Australia. It was wonderful to be in front of a class again, good fun, and the students here are very well behaved. I also think the middle schools are doing a good job. Even the freshmen had pretty good English skills and much of the speaking had the prepositions in the right place, which is one of the hardest things for Chinese students to learn.

This "new" campus is lovely. Well set out with trees and gardens. Peter and I often laugh at our expectations of teaching at the new round building, a place we visited a few times but where we never got to teach. The fifty year old campus we lived on has been turned into a middle school and completely remodelled.

The new Longyan University is in the Dongxiao area, about 20 minutes from the downtown, quiet, surrounded by forested hills and a lovely place for students to concentrate on their learning.

I had the privilege of being taken out for lunch by some of the University leaders. Mr Xu, Paul and Professor Gao were present and it was lovely to catch up with them.

The city of Longyan has also changed dramatically. There is almost a new city built to the south of where we lived, with beautiful new apartment blocks, large shopping malls, and well developed residential areas. The old city is still there, but Longyan, as with most other cities is modernising, and at the same time losing its "Chinese-ness" in the process.

My week in Longyan flew by and it was time to go back to Putian. I had visited Alex's home before, but never for such an extended time, and so I had plenty of time to explore his local area, which was very different from Deneice's quiet area.

Alex's apartment is in a very noisy locality. He is close to a main road, where horns

上，所以没从店里带走任何东西。

时隔六年故地重游，我感觉特别的好。又看到了黛比，让我们欢喜无比。她还是老样子，几乎一点儿也没变。算起来她在龙岩学院已经教了八年书，学校还有其他的外籍教师与她作伴。黛比的小公寓很舒适，但跟中国大多数的地方一样，地板是磁砖铺的，墙壁也贴了砖，或刷了涂料，地板上没铺地毯，因此屋子里冷飕飕的。

我给戴妮丝的部分学生做了一场关于澳大利亚的讲座，再次站在讲台上，让我十分快乐，相当有趣，学生都很有礼貌。我想，这也是中学教育的成功。就连大一新生的英语水平都很不错，许多学生说英语，介词用得恰到好处，介词的用法向来是中国学生学得最吃力的地方。

学校的"新"校区很漂亮，花草树木繁茂葱茏。我和彼特以前常笑话自己的不轨用心，老是巴望着什么时候能到这里上课，这个校区我们来过几回，但从没在这里教过一天书。

新龙岩学院在市东肖镇，从市中心过来要二十来分钟。这里十分安静，群山环绕，是学生专心读书的好地方。

学校的几个领导见我来了，请我吃午饭。许先生、保罗和高教授在场，能跟他们再次重逢，聊聊家常，是件快乐的事儿。

龙岩也变了许多。我们以前住在城南，那里俨然成了一个新城，新公寓楼十分漂亮，大商场遍地开花，住宅小区规划整齐，设施完备。虽然旧城区仍在，但龙岩，像其他大多数城市一样，在现代化的进程中，"中国风"正日渐式微。

转眼我就在龙岩呆了一周，该返回莆田了。我以前去过亚历克斯的老家，但从未像这次一样，呆了这么久，所以我有时间到当地各处走走，这个地方和戴妮丝安静的住处相比，简直就是另一个世界。

亚历克斯的住处非常喧闹，他家紧挨着一条主干道，车水马龙，又长又响的喇叭声整日不断。大货车呼啸而过；公交车每到一个站点，都要"叮咚"两声，宣告自己的来去；摩托车的喇叭震天响，自行车的铃铛也不甘示弱，和人们的谈话声、叫喊

are honked long and loud all the time. Trucks roared along, buses with their "ding dong" announcements at every stop stuttered from bus stop to bus stop, motor bikes honked an octave up, bicycle bells rang out, and people talked, yelled, played the piano and sang with gay abandon. The noise started at about 5am when the Spring Roll Wrap shop started up, and it ended around midnight when everyone went to bed.

His little neighbourhood was fascinating. From his lounge window I spent hours watching them at work, cooking, eating, and living their lives.

On the corner there was a clothing shop. Next to them was the Spring Roll Wrap shop. Surrounded by four 44 gallon drums lined with ceramic and concrete, women from this fascinating family took turns to make Spring Roll Wraps. Using compressed coke cylinders as fuel, they churned out about 400 an hour.

Next to them was a shop where they sorted tea. I didn't see many customers, but I guess they sold it somewhere. Beside them was a sort of fish shop. I spent hours watching this shop. They didn't sell your normal type fish with gills, tails and fins. They gutted tortoises. They sorted live frogs. They skinned and gutted eels. They also skinned and gutted snakes. It wasn't only dead snakes that left their place, but live ones, in tightly tied mesh bags, great whopping things coiled up for transportation and eventually someone's tummy. Certainly not my cup of tea!

Next to him was the dry cleaning man who did a roaring trade. As an iron he used some contraption from the ark. He would get the spent fuel cylinders from the Spring Roll shop and put them into a 44 gallon drum and the heat would increase the pressure in his little grey pressure container until there was enough heat and power to heat his iron. It was the most fascinating thing I have ever seen. His sixteen year old daughter spoke excellent English, mostly self-taught, a very studious girl. He was a fastidious man in his work and he was constantly sweeping his little concrete shop front. It was the cleanest in the street. Another shop was a music shop that gave piano lessons and sometimes the music that floated from there was of recital standard, heart string tugging stuff.

Surrounding Alex's apartment was a "market" type area that sold everything you could ever want. However, for most of the local people I was the first foreigner they had ever seen, and in my whole six weeks there I never saw another foreigner. They would point, stare, and follow me along. I went into practically every shop in his area and

声，以及旁若无人的弹琴声和唱歌声交汇一处，喧嚣之极。凌晨五点，春卷店刚开张的时候，就到处都是声响了，要到午夜时分，人们全部上床安歇了，才会安静下来。

亚历克斯的邻居可有意思了。我常站在阳台上，久久地观察他们，看他们干活、煮饭、吃饭、过日子。

角落有家布店，布店旁边就是春卷店。春卷店周围放了四个大桶，每个大桶装得下差不多200公斤的东西，靠着水泥瓷砖墙，这家的女人们负责摊春卷皮，一个累了另一个马上接手。他家烧的是煤球，一小时能产出400来个春卷。

春卷店旁边是家茶叶店，店员们在里面捡茶。我发现，上店里买茶叶的人并不多，不过我猜，茶叶可能是在别处销售。茶叶店旁像是一家鱼店。我观察了这家店很久，他们卖的不是普通的鱼，都是去了腮、鳍和尾巴的。他们杀乌龟、宰活青蛙，宰杀鳝鱼，把它剥去皮并取出内脏。他们也宰杀蛇，同样剥去蛇皮取出内脏。店里不仅有死蛇，还有活蛇，装在扎着口的网兜里，蜷缩成一大团，被送到这里，最后成为某个人的美食。这东西我肯定不会吃。

这家店旁边就是干洗店了，生意非常红火。老板用作熨斗的东西是一个极其原始的玩意儿。他经常把春卷店用过的煤球拿来，一一放入一个大桶中，煤球的余热能够增强他那个灰扑扑的小压力容器的压力，直到产生足够的热能加热他的熨斗。他的这个装置是我平生见过的最有意思的玩意儿。老板的女儿16岁，英语说得很溜，大都是自学的，非常勤奋。老板这人做事儿毫不含糊，一得空就打扫小水泥店门前的卫生。他家店门外是整条街最干净的地方。另外一家店是家琴行，有教钢琴，有时从里面飘出的音乐，差不多可以达到独奏表演的水平，是那样悦耳动听、扣人心弦。

亚历克斯家周围类似一个"市场"，只要是你见过的东西，这里都有出售。不过，在许多当地人眼里，我是他们见过的第一个老外。他们会指着我看，或者我去哪儿就跟去哪儿。我把他家附近的店几乎全逛了一遍，买了不少零零碎碎的东西。这就是住在一个文化如此不同的地方的有趣之处。太有意思了，真的太有意思了！

这次中国行我见了不少学生。我去了一趟苏州，当时那儿正下着雪，去昆山看了

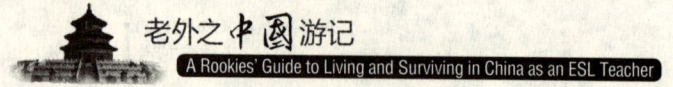

bought quite a few bits and pieces. It's part of the fascination of living in such a different culture. Wonderful, absolutely wonderful!

During this trip I was also able to visit Suzhou where it snowed, visit Twilight and her family in Kunshan, spend some time with Clark in Longyan, Peter 2 in Xiamen, and some other teachers in Suzhou.

Reminiscing, perhaps seeing our students several years down the track, this is one of the best parts of being a teacher. Peter and I only played a small part in their lives, but even now we are remembered fondly by these students, and we can see that our efforts have influenced their adult lives. We tried to broaden their horizons, letting them see the outside world around them, and encouraged them not to allow themselves to be too confined in their thinking or aspirations.

These are the memories we store, memories we cherish, and memories of China that will never be forgotten.

特莱特和她的家人。在龙岩与克拉克见了一会儿面，在厦门见到了小彼得，在苏州还见了其他几个老师。

时隔数年与学生相见，一起回忆过去的时光，或许是身为人师最大的快乐之一。我和彼特在他们的人生中只扮演了小小的角色，但时至今日，他们仍充满感情地记得我们所做的一切，我们能看见，我们当年努力影响着这些业已成年的学生。我们曾努力打开他们的视野，让他们看见外面的世界，鼓励他们不要畏首畏脚，大胆地做个有思想、有抱负的人。

以上点点滴滴就是我们贮藏于心的记忆，我们视如珍宝的记忆，我们终身难忘的记忆。

MY TOP TEN TIPS FOR LIVING IN CHINA

1. Be prepared for culture shock and read up on it before you go.
2. Be reasonably fit physically, there are lots of stairs to climb.
3. Plan carefully, research thoroughly.
4. Forward planning and schedules are not always top priority in China, so don't expect the same level of planning you might be used to.
5. Always carry a couple of packets of pocket tissues with you.
6. Take out travel insurance and take your own medication.
7. Get a working mobile phone as soon as you can.
8. When language problems occur, look for a student, or call your liaison teacher who will translate between you and the Chinese person you need to communicate with.
9. Don't drive.
10. Make sure your visas are correct.

居华十条建议

1. 出国前了解并做好接受文化冲击的心理准备。
2. 保持身体健康，才能有体力攀爬层层楼梯。
3. 计划周全，调查彻底。
4. 在中国，事前规划并非重中之重，因此别再抱着老习惯，以为有了计划，就万事大吉。
5. 随身携带纸巾，以备不时之需。
6. 带上旅游保险和常备药物。
7. 尽快购买工作手机。
8. 遇到语言问题，找学生求助，或打电话给联络老师，他会替你和你必须沟通的中国人传话。
9. 切勿开车。
10. 确保签证无误。

对了，出发时请带上一颗勇于冒险的心和一脸灿烂的微笑。

THINGS WE LEARNED ABOUT LIVING ACCOMMODATION ON OR OFF CAMPUS

If you are going to China to teach, everything is new, including the accommodation. Now, having lived in several cities and private and school apartments I know the ropes, but it takes a while to sort it out. After the first year I made a list of things to check out before I accepted a position. You might find this helpful too.

Many jobs offer you accommodation within the school grounds. This should be free and you will have a fully furnished apartment ready for you to move in with your clothes. Teachers usually have good accommodation, but some have bad experiences with this. The problem is, you usually don't know until you get there. Be prepared for the fact that China is not Australia, USA or England. Some apartments are very nice, but in others it might be compared to glorified camping.

Check out the heating and cooling facilities. You will have a Western toilet, although it is possible there will be no Western toilets in the classroom blocks for you to use during teaching time. Be prepared for some lightning visits home or using the student's toilets if you have a Woolworth's bladder.

If you can get photos of your accommodation before you go that's good. You can check it out. Whatever you get, you can bet your boots it is up stairs, and probably with no elevator. Be prepared to lug bags, groceries, school bags and books up a million stairs over the time you are there. If there are other foreign teachers you will probably all be together in a block of apartments. That's good, you have company. If no others live on

THINGS WE LEARNED ABOUT LIVING ACCOMMODATION ON OR OFF CAMPUS

校内、校外住宿须知

　　如果你打算到中国教书，将面对全新的生活，包括住宿。我们在中国好几个城市生活过，住过私人公寓，也住过学校的公寓，因此略知其中奥秘，但必须亲历其间，方能有所体味。住满一年之后，我把需要注意的事项列了一张清单，供我日后求职使用。不过，这张清单或许也能帮上你的忙。

　　许多教职会给你提供免费的校内住所，里面设施齐全，可以拎包即住。教师大都满意自己的住所，也有个别牢骚满腹的。问题是，只有亲身入住之后，才能知道住所的好坏。但请做好心理准备，这里是中国，不是美国、英国或澳大利亚。有些公寓相当舒适，但另一些差不多就是个像样的露营地。

　　入住之后先检查空调、暖气等设备。里面应该配套的是西式卫生间，但教学楼里可能没有安装，上课期间你得另寻他路。如果你肠胃不好，就得做好准备，火速冲回家中或学生宿舍解决内急问题。

　　离家之前最好能拿到住所的照片，这样可以事先查看。不管你去的是什么地方，毫无疑问你的住所是在楼上，十有八九没装电梯。做好准备，拎着大包小包、教具书本攀登无数的楼梯到达住处。如果学校聘有其他外教，很可能与你同住一座楼房。这样是最好不过的了，你们可以作伴。要是校园内没有其他外教，每逢周末、夜晚、长假、短假或任何学校停课的时候，你都得孤身一人。这时，你就把此行当作改变

site, you will be on your own for weekends, holidays, days off, nights and any other "out of school" time. Treat the whole thing as a life changing experience and you'll be fine.

Explore Your Local Area

As soon as you can, get out and explore your local area. Find the shops, bus stops, public toilets, supermarkets, wet markets and restaurants you might want to try. Make a drawing if you need to, so you can find places next time.

Most universities and schools are little communities with many small shops surrounding the gates. It's probably a very different concept to what you are used to.

Most people find it beneficial to make themselves known locally. Go into every shop, potter around, find out where you can buy your sugar, milk, fruit, toilet rolls, phone cards etc. Buy as much as you can in the local shops, the prices are similar to supermarkets. If language is a problem just giggle, throw your hands in the air, and give them a handful of change for them to take what you owe them. You'll soon figure out if you are being cheated and not return, but the shop keepers are generally honest and very helpful.

One of the great advantages of shopping locally is that you will feel as if you become "their" foreigner. They'll all know who you are and that will give you a sense of security. Another huge advantage is that the shops are usually open from about 8am to about 11pm, so you can get things after being out late.

Your local area will not just sell food. Often housing estates will have a hotel, small hospital, doctor available all day, hairdressers, drycleaners, fruit shops, public phone booths where you can top up your mobile phone or even buy a mobile phone, bus stop, printing and photocopy shops, drug store, a set of public toilets, a security office, snack bars, many different restaurants and more. These places are little cities within cities and worth knowing your way around.

Eeeeekk! Which is My Apartment?

This might sound basic, but remember if you are living off campus, your neighbours probably don't speak English and won't be any help to you.

On school campuses and in city housing estates, the buildings often look the same.

THINGS WE LEARNED ABOUT LIVING ACCOMMODATION ON OR OFF CAMPUS
校内、校外住宿须知

人生的经历，心里就会好受得多。

尽快熟悉当地环境

尽快走到外面熟悉周边环境。查找商店、车站、公厕、超市、市场和你想尝试的餐馆。必要之时画上地图，这样下次就能按图索骥。

多数大学和学校都是小型社区，校门附近小商店林立，可能与你以前的想法大不一样。

许多人都由此感受：尽快融入当地社区，大有益处。逢店就进，到处瞧瞧，看看在哪家商店能买到糖、牛奶、水果、手纸以及电话卡等生活必需品。尽可能在当地商店购买，因为这里的价格跟超市的差不多。如果语言不通，就以笑声代之，张开双手，取出一把零钱，让店主自取你的商品价钱。对方要是不诚实，你稍后便知，下次就别再光顾此店了。但店主一般都很诚实，乐于助人。

就近购物有一大好处，就是你会觉得自己成了"他们的"老外。他们都知道你是谁，这样你会觉得很有安全感。另一大好处是周边的商店一般是从早上八点开门营业到晚上十一点歇业打烊，即使很晚出去都能买到东西。

你家附近的商铺不只出售食物，通常你居住的片区会有酒店和小医院，二十四小时都有医生值班，还有理发店、干洗店、水果店，以及公用电话亭，你可以在那儿给手机充值甚至购买手机；此外，还有汽车站、复印打印店、杂货店、公厕、保安室、零食店和许多不同风味的餐馆，应有尽有，简直就是一个城中城。花点儿时间熟悉自己的生活环境，是完全值得的。

妈呀！我的住所在哪里呢？

或许这个问题有点儿简单，可是别忘了，如果你住在校外，周围的邻居又都不会讲英语，帮不上你的忙，该如何呢？

不管是学校里还是城中的楼盘，楼房的模样常常大同小异。有一个老师，她住

One teacher, who lived in a community of twenty six identical buildings, went there alone to move in and got completely lost. She knew her building was up the back, knew the apartment was on the third floor, but there were four entrances all the same, every stairwell was identical, every landing and every doorway was identical. The apartments are often numbered in some way, but the problem is that numbers can be missing in part or entirely.

If you are living independently from your school and you get your own apartment, almost every building will have a number on one end. Write that down in your notebook. If there is more than one entrance, make a note of which one to use.

If there is a hand rail or something similar, tie something to it, maybe wrap a small piece of ribbon or string round it. When you reach your landing, on the outside doorknob, tie something distinctive. It doesn't have to be big, some cotton wound round the knob, a Chinese knot, a piece of ribbon or string will do fine.

Remember you will often be going home in the dark. Most stairwells have lighting but sometimes they don't work. In larger or newer buildings there will be elevators but in buildings up to six floors there are often no elevators, so make this easy on yourself to start with.

Not only will you know you have got the right place, but saying, "the knob with the green ribbon", is a failsafe method for others to find you when delivering parcels or water bottles.

Think ahead. Be prepared

My Method for Never Getting Seriously Lost

I was now living in a land where I couldn't read or speak the language, and often taxi and bus drivers can't speak English. You might like to use these ideas too.

Take with you a small pocket notebook, preferably with alphabet sections. This is your lifeline for directions. Before you leave home make sure your school emails you their address in English and Chinese. Print this out and put a copy in all your bags. You can put these in your luggage labels too.

Make several photocopies of your address in English and Chinese. Staple a 100RMB

THINGS WE LEARNED ABOUT LIVING ACCOMMODATION ON OR OFF CAMPUS
校内、校外住宿须知

的小区里有 26 栋一模一样的楼房，搬家的时候她一个人只身前往，根本找不着北。她知道自己住的那栋楼房在后面，也知道公寓在三楼，可是小区有四个一模一样的大门，而且里面的楼道、平台、门口都完全一样。每套公寓都有门牌号码，问题是有的数字或整个号码都可能丢落不见了。

倘若你是独自一人住在校外自己的公寓里，会发现几乎在每幢大楼的一侧都标了楼号。将楼号记在你的笔记本中。如果你所住的小区不止一个大门，选择好自己平日进出的大门。

要是大门口有栏杆之类的东西，或许可在上面系上一段丝带或绳子当做记号。在自家大楼门外，一样系上东西方便识别。无需大件的东西，只需拿一小片棉布裹在门把手上，或者系个中国结、一条丝带或绳子即可。

要记住，如果你常常是天黑了才到家，大多数楼道里安装了照明灯，但灯有时坏了不亮。比较新的大厦里一般安装了电梯，但六层楼以下的楼房通常没有电梯，因此刚入住的时候这样做，可以省去许多麻烦。

一来你可以知道自己来对了地方，二来只要告诉对方"我家的大楼门把上系了一根绿丝带"，那些送水、送包裹的工人肯定不会走错地方。

还是那句话：有备无患。

避免彻底迷路的秘诀

如今，我居住在一个语言不通的国度，这里的语言我既看不懂也说不来，而的士司机和公交车司机往往不会讲英语。或许，你也会觉得我的招数管用。

随身带一本小笔记本，最好是按照字母排序的那种本子。它将是你识别方向的救生索。离家之前，务必请学校写邮件把学校地址的中文和英语告诉你，然后把地址打印出来，放一份在包里。也可以把地址写在行李标签上。

多复印几份写有中英两种语言的地址。每张纸张上用订书机订上一张百元人民币，往可能会背的每个包里各塞一张。平时遇到事情，掏出记事本就行，但是即使

note to each copy and keep one copy tucked away in a pocket of every bag you use. You will use your little notebook frequently, but even if you lose it you will have your address with enough money for a taxi ride home in every bag you use. It's quite common at first to get lost, but with your note and enough money for a taxi ride home you will never be lost for long.

Set out your first page thus.

Lana — your name

Xia Yuan Xin Cun — name of your housing estate

Shar You-en Shin Choon — phonetic pronunciation

Zhong Shan Lu — the street address

Jong Shan Loo — phonetic address

Building 3 — your building number

夏园新村— Written in large Chinese characters

Do a page for the following places:
1. Your local train station
2. Your local bus station
3. The large supermarket you use mots
4. Your nearest hospital
5. Your school address-
6. If you are travelling, staple the hotel address printed in Chinese
7. If you are travelling, your intended train station name
8. The closest airport address in Chinese

Almost all housing estates have a name. Once you learn the name in Chinese, just giving the name of your apartment area to taxi drivers is enough, they know them all. However sometimes there are two apartment areas with almost the same name so pronunciation is very important.

You should get all names written in Chinese characters in large print. Many a time foreigners get into a taxi at night, and in the dim light the driver struggles to read the

THINGS WE LEARNED ABOUT LIVING ACCOMMODATION ON OR OFF CAMPUS
校内、校外住宿须知

本子丢了，包里还有一页地址，外加足够打的回家的费用。刚到一个地方，迷路是常事，但是有了地址和打的回家的费用，很快就能顺利到家。

记事本的第一页可写上这样的信息：

Lana——你的名字

Xia Yuan Xin Cun——居住的小区名字

Shar You-en Shin Choon——该小区英语读音

Zhong Shan Lu——街道名

Jong Shan Loo——该街道英语读音

Building 3——住所楼号

夏园新村——用中文大号字体

另起一页写明下列信息：

1. 当地火车站名

2. 当地汽车站名

3. 经常光顾的大超市

4. 最近的医院

5. 学校地址

6. 旅行时将酒店中文名字装订于记事本上

7. 旅行中准备乘车的火车站名

8. 最近机场中文名字

几乎每个小区都有名字。知道用中文说小区名字后，只要告诉的士司机小区名便可找到地方。不过，有时两座楼名字相仿，念准读音便至关重要了。

应当把所有的名字用大号中文字体写在本子上，我们外国人经常晚上打的士，昏暗的灯光下司机看不清楚你写的东西，只能向你借眼镜一用，可有时即使带上眼镜也

characters, borrows your glasses to try and make it clearer, and sometimes even then couldn't read it. In the early weeks when you are learning how to pronounce your home address you will sometimes say it incorrectly, so having it written is really important.

There will be times when you may be able to get into a taxi and just point your way round the streets. It is also a good idea to learn how to say, "turn left' and "turn right". You can often manage quite well if you know your way.

Maps

The other thing you will need is a map of your city. When you are ready to go, Google your school or apartment area and print that off. When you arrive, get a full map of the city. You may have to hunt around to find one with English street names. Xinhua book shops may have them. Buy at least two of them.

Your little pocket notebook will be your lifeline, but your map will be your safety harness. On your map, mark with an X or O places you want to go to. The number of X's will increase over time. The things you want to put on your map are:

1. Restaurants you want to revisit
2. Shops you want to revisit
3. Dentist, doctor, drug store
4. Your local fruit and vegie market
5. Friends places etc.

The reason your little notebook doesn't work for this is because you will probably never know the names of these places. You will eat at restaurants many times and never known their name. Everything is in Chinese, and you will start making up your own codes for these places.

On the map put your X, then a line out to a spare spot on the map and write in English what it is - shoe shop, vegetarian restaurant, good video shop etc. Then when you are in that shop, ask them to write the name of the shop in large Chinese characters. They may give you their business card, but you end up with a bag of business cards to sort through. Carry your map at all times. You will find it a godsend for taxi drivers, or on a bus to show another passenger if you need help.

THINGS WE LEARNED ABOUT LIVING ACCOMMODATION ON OR OFF CAMPUS

校内、校外住宿须知

看不清楚。头几个星期，你才刚开始学说公寓地址的中文，可能经常说错，所以清清楚楚地写上地址，非常重要。

有时坐在的士里，光用手比划便能指路。此外，学会说"左转"和"右转"也很有用。这样，在认得路的情况下便能顺利到家。

地图

你需要的另一样宝贝是本市地图。准备出发前，到谷歌上搜索你的学校和楼盘名字，将它们打印下来。抵达目的地后，买一张全城地图。可能得到处淘，你才能找到标着英文街道名的地图。新华书店可能会出售。至少要买上两张备用。

小记事本是救生索，而地图则是安全带。在地图上把你要去的地方标上大写字母X或O。随着时间的流逝，标着X的地方会越来越多。你想在地图上做标记的地方有：

1. 想再次光顾的餐馆

2. 想再次光顾的商店

3. 牙科诊所、医院和药店

4. 附近的水果店和菜市场

5. 朋友家地址等等

把这些地方记在小本上不管用，因为很可能你一直学不会用中文说出它们的名字。可能你会多次光顾同一家餐馆，但你就是不知道餐馆叫什么名字。到处写的都是中文，你得开始给这些地方自编代码。

在地图上标上字母X后，再用过渡线引至一空白处，上面用英语写上这是什么地方，比如鞋店、素菜馆、音响店等等。如果你人刚好在商店里，可以请人写上该店的中文名字。他们可能会送给你名片，可是要在成堆的名片中翻找，很不方便。走到哪儿都要随身携带地图。你会发现的士司机看见它时是多么高兴，或者坐公车的时候，可以拿出来向同车乘客求助。

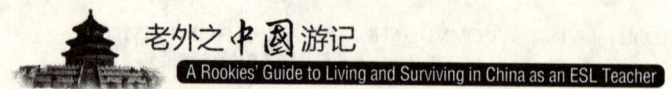

Water Bottles

Everyone drinks bottled water in China. It is generally not considered safe to drink from the tap. You will find that every building, your school, your school office and every home has a water dispenser. Large plastic containers of about 5 gallons are used. In schools, a school janitor will keep the supply constant. In your apartment you will have to ask for it to be delivered when you need a refill.

It will be easy enough if you are living on campus. Find out from your liaison teacher what to do. If you live independently you will need to buy these bottles. It's inexpensive and easy to do, but you need the phone number. There are different systems in place for delivery, and you will usually have it at your door within an hour or two of phoning the company. Get your liaison teacher to help with this.

Landlines and Mobile Phones

Our apartment had a fixed land line, but hardly anyone used it. Everyone used their mobiles and now with ipads and more comprehensive technology, we seem to use our mobile phones for all forms of communication.

Your apartment will probably have a land line, and often this is basically used for its internet connection. Many places now have wifi, so wireless laptops and mobiles are workable without landlines. If you are looking at an apartment with a view to renting it, check this out first.

If you have a mobile phone at home that you love, take it but make sure it's unlocked and usable in China. Mobile phone shops are everywhere in China but the prices are probably on a par with your home country.

On your first or second day, get a Chinese teacher to go with you to buy a SIM card. There are several large telecom companies and lots of smaller ones. China Mobile was good because there were shops everywhere and topping up was easy and convenient at their ATM type machines. Some machines are only in Chinese but the staff will help, even if they don't speak much English they know what you want.

Buy a SIM card that has international calling capabilities, and make sure they activate it while you are in the shop. It may take 24 hours before you can call overseas.

THINGS WE LEARNED ABOUT LIVING ACCOMMODATION ON OR OFF CAMPUS
校内、校外住宿须知

桶装水

在中国，大家都爱喝桶装水。他们认为直接从水龙头喝水不卫生。你会发现，每栋楼房、学校、学校办公室以及家家户户都备有饮水机。大大的塑料桶能装五加仑的水。在学校里，保洁员看见没水了会及时更换。但在自己的公寓里，如果水用完了想添加，就得叫人送水。

住在学校这不成问题，只要向联络教师请教就行了。但若是独自住在外面，你就得自己买桶装水。水不贵，也容易买，但你得知道电话号码。此地送水有好几种方法：一般打电话到公司后的一或两小时，就会有人把水送到你家门口。可以叫联络老师帮你联系商家。

座机和手机

我们的住处装了一台固定电话，但大家都很少打固话，平时都爱用手机或现在的 ipad 等更高端的通信工具。我和彼得也都是用手机跟人联系。

你的住所很可能安装了固定电话，主要用来上网。我住的地方现在已经有了 WiFi，因此无需电话线，手提电脑和手机都能上网。要是你在找房子住，应该事先了解清楚房内是否安装了无线宽带。

如果你在国内已经有了心爱的手机，可以带到中国，但一定要确保手机已经解锁，在中国能够使用。这里到处都是手机专卖店，但价格并不比国内的便宜。

抵达学校的第一或第二天，请一个中国老师陪你去买一张 SIM 卡。这里有几家大的电信公司和许多小电信公司。中国电信相当不错，因为公司门店多，可以在 ATM 一样的自动缴费机上充值，简单又省事。有些机子只设了中文，但工作人员会帮助你，虽然他们不大会说英语，但能明白你的意思。

用手机打国际长途非常贵，但发短信就便宜多了。你还可以买张国际长途 IP 卡，通话时间长的时候用。平时聊天最好用 Skype。要是你的 Skype 账户中有钱，通

Then, in case of emergency, you can contact home and they can contact you instantly, which will give you great peace of mind.

Making phone calls overseas on your mobile can be quite expensive, but texting is cheap. You can also buy IP cards, which are international calling cards for longer phone calls. Skype is best for general chatting. If you put some credit on your Skype account you can use if to call any mobile or landline in the world at a minimal cost. This is especially useful if you need to call home on business matters, where you might have a long time on hold.

Practically every Chinese person owns at least one mobile phone. Phoning and texting are very cheap, making communication easy. Some teachers use the reminder facility to keep track of their lesson schedule. You will soon find that it becomes a necessity in your daily life.

过它给世界各地的手机或座机，费用都最便宜。尤其是当你因为公务需要往国内打电话时，用它好处更多，因为一般公务电话都得打很长时间。

几乎每个中国人至少拥有一台手机。打电话和发短信费用都不高，因此相互联系非常方便。有些老师会用手机上的提醒功能，提醒自己的课程进度。很快你便会发现，手机是你日常生活中不可或缺的伙伴。

DRIVING YOURSELF IN CHINA

In a word,
Don't!

A couple more words. The public transport is fabulous. It is very expensive to own a car in China. You might consider an e-bike after living there a while. It is quite difficult for foreigners to get driver's licences.

在华自驾

两个字,"切勿!"

容我再多说两句。中国的公共交通非常好。但在中国购车费和养车费却是极其之高。等你在华居住一段时间后,可以买辆电动自行车。再说,外国人要想拿到中国驾照,相当困难。

SHOPPING

Shopping in China was always great fun. There are shops galore with shoes, clothes and handbags. You can browse to your heart's content in any part of town. Some large department stores have brand clothes, much more expensive but often better quality. You normally can't bargain there.

In many shops you can barter, so ease yourself into it and learn the skill. In the cheaper shops remember, that just because it has a brand name, doesn't mean it's genuine.

Shopping for household items is a bit more complicated, although supermarkets generally have a good variety. Some cities have large shops with extensive kitchen gear. You just need to find them. Write these on your map so you can go back anytime. Most electrical appliances are available and cheap, but you will probably never find an electric frypan in China. Consider taking your own. There is a huge selection of kitchen utensils, but potato mashers are like hens teeth. Take one with you.

Most cooking is done on gas. Your apartment will have a wok and probably a rice cooker. If you are not used to gas, or if you are scared of it, you can buy excellent hot plates that plug into the electricity. Have a look round the larger supermarkets. They are easy to use and clean. (Electricity is 240 volt not 110)

Shops are set out differently in China. If you want to buy shoes, you will find somewhere a whole area set aside with just shoe shops. If you want to buy curtains, and they sell some fabulously beautiful curtains, there will be a curtain city somewhere. If you need hardware, it will be the same. It seems to defeat the purpose of competition to

在华购物

在中国购物其乐无穷。商铺遍地开花，鞋子、时装和箱包，琳琅满目、款式齐全，城里的任何一个地方，都能让你流连忘返。一些百货大楼里，有许多品牌服饰专柜，虽然价格更贵，但质量更好，一般不能讨价还价。

但许多商铺是可以讲价的，所以先学会砍价技巧再上街购物。在一些便宜的商店里，不要以为货物上标的是名牌，就当成正品行货。

购买家庭用品要稍微复杂一些，虽然各大超市大都各色物品一应俱全。有些城市有大商场，里面厨房用具品种繁多，但你必须找得到这些商场。把商场的名字写在地图上，以便你随时查看。大多数家电这里都买得到，价格也不贵，不过可能买不到电平锅。可以考虑从国内自带。这里各种各样的炊具都有，但土豆压泥机却难得一见，你自己带一个过来吧。

煮饭烧菜多用煤气。公寓里会有一个炒锅，很可能还有一个电饭煲。要是你用不来煤气，或者害怕使用煤气，可以用电磁炉。大超市里都有卖，使用、清洁都很方便。(功率是240伏不是110伏)。

中国商店的布局很不一样。如果你想买鞋，得找到卖鞋区，那里有许多卖鞋的商铺。买窗帘，得到某个窗帘城去，那里的一些窗帘极其漂亮。买五金也是一样。把卖同一类货物的商店聚集一处，似乎颠覆了同行相斥的竞争原则，可这里都是这么规

have all the same shops together, but that's how it works.

For fruit and vegetables, don't be afraid of the wet markets. There will be one near you, but maybe hidden away. Go in and check it out. Smile to everyone, talk to them in English, find the stall that you prefer and stick with that one. You can also buy meat, eggs, rice, noodles, cakes, fish, live chickens, spices etc. Once you know your way around you will frequent these places for fresh food. They are fascinating to wander around and often cheaper than supermarkets. You may not want to buy fish there. Some now have freezers and frozen products.

Supermarkets abound, and you will discover some very big ones. One of the larger ones had 104 checkouts! The trouble is they are often hidden away one level underground. Some like Walmart, are within the Walmart buildings, but again one level below ground, accessible by stairs or escalator. Carrefour is another large supermarket, and their food section might be on level three or four. Once you have found them you will be amazed at what they stock.

Not only is there food, they contain a bread department, butchery, fish department, fast food areas, clothing, shoes, home appliances, bedding, everything from the kitchen sink to the toilet seat. Unfortunately all the labels are in Chinese. However, there is often an "imported goods" area where you will find lots of stuff you recognise, and even if the labels are in Chinese you will know what it is. Milo looks like Milo in any country, it's just the labels that have different language on them. In the supermarkets in smaller cities you may have to find someone who speaks some English. Allow yourself plenty of time and have a good browse around. The prices are very cheap compared to the West.

They sell the cloth type shopping bags that have become so popular now. One major problem you will face, especially for your first few visits, is that you have quite a few heavy bags to take home. You can get around this by taking your carry-on luggage suitcases on wheels, fill them up after you have been through the checkout, and wheel them home, or out to a taxi. There are usually lines of taxis outside large supermarkets. You can take your shopping home on the bus, but it's hard work if you have a heavy load, whereas a taxi will take you right to your door most times.

Some larger cities have "Metro" shops. Ask about these. They have a wider range of Western foods, but can be more expensive and often not so conveniently located. You

划的。

想买果蔬就别害怕上菜市场。学校附近就会有菜市场，不过可能地点比较隐蔽。找到地点后可以进去看看。逢人便微笑，用英语给他们说话，发现喜欢的摊位，就别朝三暮四。也可以在菜市场上买肉、蛋、面条、蛋糕、鱼、活鸡、调味品等等。一旦摸清了门道，你就会经常到这样的地方买新鲜的食物。在里面到处逛逛，特别有意思，东西往往也比超市的便宜。你可能不爱上那儿买鱼。现在，有些货摊上有冷藏柜，卖冷冻食品。

超市到处都有，你还会看到几家大型超市。其中一家大超市有 104 个收银台！麻烦的是，这些大超市总是藏身于地下一楼。比如沃尔玛，在沃尔玛商场里，可以走楼梯或坐扶梯下去。家乐福是另一家大超市，食品区可能是在三楼或四楼。如果你能找到地方，里面的货物肯定会令你惊喜。

不仅有食物，还有面包坊、生鲜处理区、海鲜区、快餐区、衣服、鞋子、日用品、床上用品，从洗碗槽到马桶无所不用。遗憾的是，货物标签都是用中文写的。不过，商场里大都有"进口商品区"，你可以在那里看到许多眼熟的东西，即使标签上写的是中文，你也知道它们的用途。譬如，米罗酒在哪个国家都是一样的，只是标签上的文字不一样罢了。去小城市中的超市购物，可能得找个会说英语的人陪同。时间留充裕一点，这样可以看个仔细。跟西方国家的超市相比，中国的商品相当实惠。

商场有卖布购物袋，如今中国百姓都爱拿着布袋购物了。伤脑筋的是，可能你得拎好几个沉甸甸的袋子回家，尤其是最初几次购物，更是如此。可以带上有轮子的便携行李箱，买完单之后把东西全部装进箱子里，拉着回家或到外面打的。大超市外面通常排着一长溜的士。你也可以坐公车回家，不过提着这么重的货物，坐公车很辛苦，坐的士就方便多了，大多数时候的士可以送你到家门口。

有的大城市有麦德龙，可以打听一下它们的位置，因为那里的西方商品更齐全，不过价格也更贵，而且通常地点比较偏远。记得带上护照办会员卡。

另一规模略小的本地超市是精嘉。无需大宗采购的时候上精嘉不错，不过那儿的

must take your passport to join them.

Another group of smaller local supermarkets are Vanguard. They are good when you want a few things, but don't always have such a good selection. There will be several convenience stores within a minute or two of wherever you live.

EFTPOS is used widely with Chinese cards, but trying to use overseas credit cards is not so easy.

It is cheap to post things home. When you leave you will probably have far more than your baggage allowance, so post home your excess baggage a week or so before you leave. You can take large suitcases full of gear to the post office and pack everything into boxes they provide. They will tape it up and make it secure and send it on its way. For about 20kg you will pay around $45.00AU. It takes a few weeks by sea and is internet traceable. It is rare for a box go missing.

Online shopping is huge in China, but you need someone who can read Chinese to help you. You can buy online with a Chinese credit card, but a Western one may not be accepted. This is a very convenient way to shop. They will fill your order that day, and it will be on your desk in a couple of days. You can return what you don't want to keep. If you do any online shopping, have it sent to your school address, one of the teachers will help you with the enclosed invoices and if you decide to return something they can help you.

In smaller cities in the past it has been hard to buy some of the Western food we rely on like butter, bacon or yoghurt, but today there is a proliferation of shops stocking Western type foods. There will be things you will never find in China, such as Marmite or Vegemite, so if you can't live without them get your family to post you a food parcel from time to time.

商品种类不多，选择范围不广。不管你住哪儿，走一两分钟路，都能找到好几家便利店。

若有中国银行卡，刷卡购物非常普遍，但外国卡不予受理。

从中国邮寄东西回国费用不高。离开中国时，你的行李可能会超重，可以提前一周把超出的部分邮寄回家。可以把行李装进一个大箱子拉到邮局，再用邮局提供的箱子打包。他们会用胶带把箱子捆牢，这样运输途中不会散架。45公斤左右的货物大约45澳元，海运一般要几周之后才能到货。可以在网上跟踪物流进度，货物丢失的情况鲜少发生。

在中国，网上购物非常火爆，但得找个懂中文的人帮你才行。可以用信用卡付款，但国外的信用卡不能使用。网购真的非常方便，当天就能下单，两三天后货物便送到了你桌上。不满意的话可以退货。网购的送货地址写学校地址，可以找同事帮忙查看货物发票，如果想退货，他们会帮你处理。

以前在小城市里，很难买到我们常吃的西方食品，比如黄油、培根和酸奶，但是今天，许多商店里都有进口食品。不过，还是有些东西在这里找不到，比如Marmite(马麦酱)和Vegemite(中国人戏称它为澳洲臭豆腐)。要是少了这些东西，你便食不下咽，叫家人不时给你买一些邮寄过来吧。

TRAVELLING — BUSES, TRAINS AND HOTELS IN CHINA

For the first few weeks the long distance public transport gave us nightmares. It seemed so complicated and so huge that we felt overwhelmed by it all. In fact, it is easy once you know what to do. At first we got students to help us all the time, but we soon got confident enough to tackle most things on our own, and we soon had our own little systems in place. Our little systems might help you too.

Buses

Using City Buses

Public transport is everywhere, all the time, and cheap. You may want to invest in an E-bike once you know your way around, but you don't need a car.

Buses go in a set route, either round and round or there and back. In either case, you will eventually end up where you got on. The buses charge 1 or 2RMB for most trips. They are often stuffed to the gills with people, but that's part of the fun. The bus drivers know we are foreigners, know we often don't know where we are going and they rarely speak English. If you are stuck, call out and see if anyone on board speaks English or look for a student.

The bus stops usually have the stop names written in Pinyin, (English letters) and the drivers all know the names of the stops. If you write this down in your little notebook and show the driver they will make sure you get off at the right place.

在华旅游——巴士、火车和酒店

最初的几周里,长距离的公共交通使我们梦魇不断,复杂而庞大的公交系统令我们晕头转向,事实上,当我们搞清楚其如何运行,一切都轻而易举了!刚开始我们总是向学生寻求帮助,但很快我们就可以自信满满应对自如了,我们也很快组建了一套自己的乘车攻略,希望对您有所帮助。

巴士

乘坐市内公交车

中国的公共交通四通八达,24小时运营,而且票价低廉。或许等你熟悉了自己居住的环境,可以买一辆电动自行车,但无需买车。

公交车定线运营,或一辆车反复运行,或开至一地即返场,不管哪种形式,你最终都能回到你上车的地点。大多数路程票价为一或二元。车内人多,所以又挤又闷,不过这也是乘车的乐趣之一。司机知道我们是外国人,常常不知该在哪里下车,而司机几乎全都不懂英语。要是你迷了方向,大声求救,看看车上有没有会说英语的人士,或者找学生帮忙。

车站通常写有站名的汉语拼音(英语字母),司机熟悉各个站点。如果你在小笔记本上写下站名,拿给司机看,到站了他们肯定会提醒你下车。

China is gradually introducing buses which are less pollutant but some of them are real old rattly smoky things. In the big cities they are much cleaner.

There are timetables, always written in Chinese, and almost impossible to follow. In many cities now they have LED screens at each bus stop with the bus numbers and how many stops away they are. This is a great system which is updated by GPS in real time. In any event, the buses just keep coming, and rarely is there more than a ten minute wait.

Once you work out which bus numbers you need to get to different places you will be fine. Make sure you wait on the right side of the road, depending on the direction of travel.

This applies to taxis too, if you want to go west, stand on the appropriate side of the road. Taxi drivers are averse to doing U-turns in heavy traffic. Any time you want a taxi you stand on the side of the road and wave them down. They roam the streets constantly day and night and are very cheap in comparison to Western prices. Most places have rickshaw taxis and motor bike taxis, which are great fun.

Depending on which city you are in, the buses may not go between about 11pm and 6am. Check this out in your area.

You must get on the bus at the front and off at the back. You pay as you get on. Using a bus card is a simple way to get around, it saves carrying change. Your school will help you buy a card and tell you how to top it up.

Using Long Distance Buses

Long distance buses also go everywhere all the time. Local students will use these buses all the time so they will be a wonderful source of information for you. Some have toilets on board, but sometimes they are locked and the driver will not unlock them. They stop at every town anyway and there are always restrooms there.

In the smaller cities and country areas, buses are often faster than trains. Check with your Foreign Liaison Officer or teacher about the local arrangements. Some of the country buses are small and uncomfortable.

For long distance bus travel you can get overnight buses. They have sort of sleeping areas, mattresses where you sleep during the journey. They are cramped, and there are stories of them not being so secure for your personal belongings. For long distance travel take trains or planes.

Many cities within an hour or two of an airport have regular buses to the airports and

TRAVELLING - BUSES, TRAINS AND HOTELS IN CHINA
在华旅游——巴士、火车和酒店

中国正在逐步换用污染较小的公交车，但有些车辆的确破旧，尾气如滚滚浓烟。大城市的公交车比小城市的干净许多。

站台有时刻表，写的是中文，因此我们看不懂。现在许多城市，在每个公交站点都安装了液晶显示屏，上面会出现各路汽车号和差几站会到该站点。后来，这套了不起的系统又增加了 GPS 实时客运信息，更为便民。总之，公交车一辆接着一辆驶来，候车时间很少长于 10 分钟。

一旦弄清楚了到什么地方应坐哪路车，一切便好办了。一定要根据目的地，站在道路正确的一侧候车。

等的士也一样。如果你要往西走，应站在路的西侧等车。司机讨厌在繁忙的路上掉头。需要打的的时候，只要站在正确的一侧，伸手拦车即可。从早到晚的士都在路上跑，与西方的士费用相比，价格非常便宜。许多地方有三轮车和摩的，乘坐这样的交通工具特别有趣。

有些城市晚上 11 点至次日早上 6 点，公交车停运，请自行核对自己所在城市的信息。

你应该前门上车后门下车，上车时付费。使用 e 通卡能让出行方便许多，省去带零钱的麻烦。学校会替你办理 e 通卡，并告诉你如何充值。

乘坐长途巴士

同样，随时都有长途巴士发往各地。当地学生经常乘坐，向他们咨询是极佳的途径。有些大巴上安装了厕所，有时厕所被锁上，司机也不愿把门打开。他们每到一个小镇都会停车，那些地方都有厕所。

在小城市或村镇里，坐巴士往往比坐火车更快。请跟联络老师或其他老师核对当地的巴士状况，因为有些乡村巴士很小，非常舒服。

坐长途巴士外出旅游，可坐夜间巴士。这些巴士提供睡觉的地方，有供你在途中睡觉的卧铺。地方比较逼仄，分上下两层，私人物品不好保管。长途旅行首选火车或飞机。

sometimes have check-in facilities available. If you are able to check in for a flight at the bus depot, do so. Even if there is a delay on the road, you are already checked in and can go straight to the boarding gate.

Buying Bus Tickets

There are offices spread all round your city where you can buy bus tickets. You sometimes cannot buy more than ten to fourteen days in advance, sometimes only about five days in advance. You may not get an English speaking salesperson, so make sure you get your information written down in Chinese or take someone with you. If you have time constraints, for example if you are taking a bus to a city to catch a flight then buy your ticket a few days in advance. If you have plenty of time you don't even need to book. Intercity buses may go as often as every ten to thirty minutes.

Making Your Trip

Once you are ready to travel, go to the bus station. Remember, there may be more than one bus station in your city depending on where you are going so make sure you know which one to go to.

You will find lots of waiting rooms in a big city bus station, maybe only a few in a smaller city. There will be LED signs showing all the departure information. The information is often in Chinese only, so if you can learn to read the name of your city in Chinese that's a help. When boarding time comes, your destination will be called out over a loudspeaker in Chinese and occasionally in English too. Everyone will queue, (Chinese queuing) and someone will check your ticket and let you through. You will often be given a bottle of water once on board. Feel free to take along lots of snacks, it's the done thing.

At first, before you get to know the system, go to the boarding gate, show the staff your ticket and they will point for you to wait close by. When boarding time comes they will make sure you get on.

The bus system is cheap, very efficient and runs on time.

Using the Train System in China

Your first experience will make your head spin, but, after you have used the train system a few times, you will realize the whole thing is a well-oiled machine.

在许多城市，如果去机场路途较远，都有开往机场的班车，有时配套了设备，能够换登机牌。要是在大巴站能够换登机牌，一定要换，因为换好了登机牌，即使迟到了，你也可以直奔登机口。

购买大巴车票

在你居住的城市里，到处都有大巴售票点。有时，只能提前购买10至14天的车票。也许售票员不会说英语，一定要把购票信息用中文写下，或者找人与你同去买票。如果你有时间限制，比如你是坐车到一个城市赶飞机，那么需要提前几天购票。如果时间充裕，甚至无需提前购票，因为城际大巴通常每隔十至三十分钟便发一班车。

制定旅游计划

出行准备妥当后就可去车站候车。记住，你的城市可能不止一个汽车站，去不同的地方需到不同的车站上车，因此，一定要弄清楚自己该去哪个车站候车。

大汽车站里有许多候车室，小城市的候车室可能比较少，只有几间。车站有液晶显示屏，显示各辆汽车的发车时间，但通常是用中文写的，因此要是你能够学会认读自己的城市名，对你的出行大有助益。到了上车时间，广播会用中文念出发车的目的地，偶尔也会用英语通知。大家都会排队（中国式的排队），检票后即可上车。车上通常会发一瓶水。多带点零食上车，没关系，车上允许吃东西。

大巴票价便宜，而且迅捷准时。

乘坐火车

第一次坐火车会让你昏头转向，但多坐几次，就会发现中国的铁路系统如同上好油的机器，运行良好。

Buying Train Tickets

The obvious place to buy your ticket is at the train station. But you will find that there are little offices around town where you can also buy tickets. The problem is they are often in obscure corners and easy to miss. Sometimes they are in hotel foyers and an extra charge of a few RMB may be required, a small fee to pay for the convenience of buying your tickets locally.

In the large stations there may be an English counter. Otherwise you will have to deal with Chinese speakers only, in which case, get someone to write in English and Chinese your destination and take that note with you. Travel is not expensive and trains go from everywhere to everywhere.

If you are planning a trip and need to be somewhere at a certain time it is advisable to book in advance. If time is not so important, and you have an idea of the timetables, just go to the station and buy your ticket for the next available train. You will not have to wait long.

Trains from the major cities, Beijing, Shanghai, Guangzhou, Shenzhen etc to stations within 100 kilometres or so, will go every twenty or thirty minutes.

If you are planning a long trip, say from Beijing to Shanghai, buy your ticket in advance, as sometimes these trains are full.

Luggage

Using the train system with hand luggage only is easy. If you want to take large baggage it can be done, but it is not quite so convenient. If you have just come off a flight, you will have to get a 20kg bag, a 7kg carry-on bag, your handbag and maybe a laptop up and down lots of steps to get to the platform. There are sometimes escalators but not many elevators. It can be done, and others will offer to help you but by the time you are on the train you will be exhausted. You can check baggage through, but finding it at the other end if you can't speak any Chinese is not so easy either. You will soon learn that the Chinese all travel light. It's something you will do too. Get yourself a light carry-on bag and use it for trains and planes.

TRAVELLING - BUSES, TRAINS AND HOTELS IN CHINA
在华旅游——巴士、火车和酒店

购买火车票

毋庸置疑，买火车票就去火车站。不过，城里有许多小售票点，你也可以上那购票。问题是这些售票点通常设在不显眼的角落，不大好找。有时，酒店大堂也有售票点，但需加收几元人民币的手续费，花一点儿钱能够就近买票，挺划算的。

大火车站可能有英语售票窗口。如果没有，就得跟只会说中文的售票员打交道了，要是这样，请人把你的目的地用中英文双语写好，把纸条带在身上。旅游花费不多，火车来来往往，四通八达。

如果打算外出旅游，需要在某个地方住上一阵子，最好提前预定火车票。如果时间不紧急，对火车的始发与到站时间心中有数，就可以到火车站直接买下一列火车票，只需稍后片刻就可上车。

像北京、上海、广州、深圳等大城市，开往一百公里左右之内的站点，每隔20到30分钟便有一列火车。

若是长途旅游，比如从北京到上海，事先买好车票，因为有时火车票可能已经售罄。

购买火车票时必须出示护照，购买汽车票大抵也是如此。一定要随身携带护照，或把护照交给替你买票的人。

行李

坐火车外出，若是只带了手提行李，自然轻松。如果你想携带大件行李，没问题，但会比较辛苦。要是你刚下飞机，得手提20公斤重的行李袋，肩背7公斤重的大包和一个拎包，兴许还有一台手提电脑，上上下下许多台阶到站台等车。有时火车站有电动扶梯，但电梯不多。这也可以搞定，有人会主动帮助你的，但是等你上了火车，人早已累趴下了。你可以托运行李，但行李到后，要是你不会说中文，提货也够呛。很快，你就会发现，中国人坐火车大都轻装上阵，你也应该效仿。找个轻便的手提包，提着它坐火车、乘飞机。

Using the Train Stations

Train stations are communities within themselves and always very busy places. There are plenty of places selling food and drinks, some restaurants and often KFC or MacDonald's. They are also the main bus stops for the city.

There is now a new online booking system for train tickets. There have been a few teething troubles with their computer systems so be aware of that.

Your ticket will show the train number you are on. They use different letters to identify different services. In the entrance of the station you will see large electronic boards listing all the trains leaving in the next few hours. They list the train name, for example, G123, the destination, time of departure and which waiting lounge you need to go to. These will be listed in Chinese, but you will soon learn to read the Chinese characters for your home town, and it will also be on your ticket.

Go to the prescribed waiting lounge. There will probably be hundreds of others waiting too. Along one end of the waiting room you will see more electronic signs, giving the destination, time of departure and platform you leave from. These will usually be in red or green. If they are flashing red, it means the train is now boarding.

Find your train number, get a seat close by, watch the other passengers and follow them. Everyone surges at the same time, so get in the mass and go with the flow. If you are unsure, ask the staff or look for a student, they are very helpful and know that foreigners don't always know the ropes.

Your ticket will be punched and checked as you exit the waiting room. Follow the group to the platform, often up or down stairs. You are herded onto the platform five to ten minutes before the train arrives. The carriage numbers are painted on the platform. Find the right number for your carriage which is on your ticket. There is always staff on the platform to ask.

Once the train pulls in, allow the others off before embarking. This is a very quick process as the train only stops for a minute or two.

You will find your seat number on your ticket, or if you are doing a long trip with a sleeper, you will need to find your cabin.

Don't be surprised if there is someone in your seat. Sometimes they sell standing room only tickets, and these people will take any vacant seat until someone comes along with a ticket. They will vacate for you.

火车站

火车站本身就是一个社区，通常人来人往，相当繁忙。有许多卖小吃和饮料的店铺，餐馆也不少，肯德基和麦当劳通常就在附近。一般火车站附近还有一个大公交站。

如今新增一套网上订票系统，不过电脑系统经常出现一些小问题，挺让人讨厌的，还是小心为妙。

车票上有你的火车车号。他们使用不同的字母指代不同的火车。车站入口处，有几个大电子牌，显示近期发车的火车车号。他们会打出火车车名，比如 G123，终点站、发车时间、以及相应的候车厅。这些信息都是用中文显示的，但你很快就能认识自己城市的中文名，这个也会写在车票上。

去规定的候车厅等车。里面十有八九已有几百个旅客在候车。在候车厅的一端，还有许多电子标牌，显示终点站、发车时间和上车的站台。通常用红绿两色显示。如果是红色，说明本列火车已经开始检票。

找到自己的车次，找个离检票口近的位子坐下，注意其他旅客的动静，跟着他们走。时间一到，大家全都往检票口涌去，所以跟着人群走。要是心中仍没底，可以问工作人员或找个学生咨询，他们非常乐于助人，知道我们外国人不熟悉中国的情况。

离开候车厅的时候，把车票交给列车员检查并打孔，然后跟着人流到站台，通常要爬楼梯或下台阶。火车进站前5至10分钟到达站台。站台上用涂料写着各车厢号，依照车票上的车厢号，找到正确的位置。站台上一直都有工作人员，可以询问他们。

火车一进站，等车上的乘客下车完毕再上车。大家动作都很利索，因为火车只停一两分钟。

车票上有座位号，如果是长途旅行，买的是卧铺，得找到自己的卧铺车厢。看到座位上另有他人，不必惊讶，因为有些人买的是站票，看到空位就先坐下，等到座位的主人来了就会让开。他们会把位子还给你的。

火车到达终点站时，下车跟着人群出站。出站的时候可能需要出示火车票。

Once you arrive at your destination, get off and follow the crowd to the exit. You may have to show your ticket as you exit the station.

Every train station has a very busy taxi system attached to it.

If you are new to the city a taxi is the easiest way to get around. Book your hotel online before you go, print off the receipt and show this to the taxi driver.

Once you become familiar with a city you can use the buses and underground systems with ease.

All the modern trains are clean and if not luxurious at least nice to travel in. They should have a Western toilet at one end of the carriage and a Chinese toilet at the other end. Long distance soft sleepers (a misnomer, they are pretty hard to sleep on) often provide a large thermos of boiling water for drinks, and these are refillable at one end of the carriage. There are often dining cars too.

If you are a woman travelling alone it is unlikely you will ever have any trouble being in a soft sleeper compartment with three other strangers, often men. Carry your passport and money in a body bag on your person.

Even the hard sleepers which have six to a cabin in layers of three, which are not so flash, are still safe ways of travelling. Most foreigners, men and women, have travelled alone extensively all over China. Be aware of pick pockets. They are likely to be your only problem.

The large cities have several train stations. Shanghai has a north and south station and you need to know which one you want. You can go from one to the other by bus or underground if you have lots of time, but taxi is the best way to do it.

There are now train links from Shanghai Hongqiao Airport to Pudong International airport. Allow about two hours for this trip. There is also a number 5 bus from Shanghai North train station to Pudong airport. This is a good service and you can take large bags with you. Allow an hour for this bus trip.

Beijing has five major train stations. See the link below. They are huge stations. Your ticket will tell you which station you will leave from.

The first few times you use the trains, allow yourself plenty of time to find your way around. After a while you will feel quite at home and use them constantly. It's a great way to see the country.

TRAVELLING - BUSES, TRAINS AND HOTELS IN CHINA
在华旅游——巴士、火车和酒店

每个火车站都有很多的士进进出出。如果你是初来乍到的陌生客，坐的士最为方便。旅游之前在网站上订好酒店，将收据打印出来交给的士司机。

等你熟悉了这个城市，就可以从容地坐公交车或地铁了。

所有新式火车都很干净，即使称不上豪华，但坐在里面至少是舒服的。火车上应该在车厢一头安装一个西式卫生间，另一头安装蹲式卫生间。长途软卧（其实名不副实，床铺硬梆梆的，相当不好睡）车厢里，通常提供一个大热水壶，里面装了热水，可供饮用，水用完毕，可到车厢一头装水。火车上也有餐车。

如果你是女性，单独出行，软卧车厢中的另外三个旅客全是男性，你与他们共处一室，遇到麻烦的可能性微乎其微。把钱和护照放在贴身的口袋里以防万一。

即使是乘坐硬卧，车厢里有6个位置，一边三层，条件比不上软卧，但也是安全的。大多数外国人，无论男女，常在中国各地游玩。谨防扒手！可能他们是你旅途上唯一的麻烦。

大城市有好几个火车站。上海分南站和北站，你得知道自己要去的火车站是哪个。如果时间充裕，可以坐公交车或地铁从一个火车站到另一个火车站，不过还是打的最为方便。

现在，从上海虹桥机场到普通国际机场可坐磁悬浮列车。车程约两小时。从火车北站到浦东机场，还可乘坐5路公交。这趟车服务很好，可以带上大件行李。车程约一小时。

北京有5个火车站，个个都很大，车票上会注明你下车的火车站。详情可查看最后的链接。

最初几次乘坐火车，时间安排要宽松，应该预留出认路的时间。过一阵子，等你比较熟悉火车站的情况了，就可以经常乘坐火车了，这是欣赏中国美景的极佳途径。

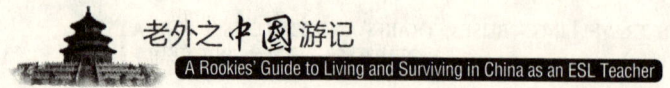

Suburban Underground Systems

There are vending machines for tickets or you can buy go-cards. There are also manned offices where you can talk to staff. Trains go everywhere every couple of minutes. There are good train maps of every main station on the internet. The underground is fast. They move millions of people a day. In Shanghai it is a little expensive but Beijing is very cheap. In most cities the trains are very full, so be prepared for a squash. Don't use the underground at peak times if you have large luggage. If you can't deal with crowds, use buses. They will be crowded too, but you get to see outside in a bus. Try

Check these websites.

http://www.travelchinaguide.com/china-trains/tickets.htm

http://www.beijingtrip.com/transport/train/

郊区地铁

可以使用自动售票机买票或者购买 e 通卡。地铁站内也有售票窗口，你可以向工作人员问询。去哪儿的地铁都有，每隔两三分钟一趟。网络上可以找到每个大车站的详细地图。地铁很快，一天可运输几百万人。上海的地铁票价稍贵些，但北京地铁非常便宜。多数城市的地铁均人满为患，你得做好人挤人的准备。如果提了大件行李，不要在高峰期乘坐地铁。如果不习惯人多的场景，可以乘坐公交车。虽然车上也很拥挤，但坐在公交车里，可以欣赏外面的景色。

具体请查阅下列网址：

www.travelchinaguide.com/china-trains/tickets.htm

www.beijingtrip.com/transport/train/

STAYING IN HOTELS IN CHINA

In the west, staying in hotels is often seen as an expensive business. In China it is cheap. It took us a while to get our heads around this, because we travelled often during our weekends and holidays, and being used to motels, a completely different concept from the Chinese hotel, it took some adjustments.

If you are going to China on holiday through a travel agent, your itinerary is probably all set out for you. Chances to venture out on your own may not be available. If you are planning your own holiday you will have the opportunity to choose your own hotels. If you know no Chinese, then maybe use the four and five star hotels where you will get English speaking staff.

By all means, if you are an adventurous soul and want to go to the smaller cheaper hotels, go, but be aware that language could be a problem. There are also quite a few back-packers hostels. These are much cheaper of course, and there will almost certainly be English speaking guests there. Many young people from all over the world stay at these hostels.

In Hong Kong many of the hostels are hidden away in huge buildings and are a real maze. One to check out is Alisan Guest House, alisangh@hkstar.com, in Causeway Bay on Hong Kong Island. They may also be able to help you with getting a visa to enter China. Email them and check this.

In Beijing, consider staying in a Hutong, just for the experience. If you go to Inner Mongolia, you may have to use the five star hotels. A few days in Hohhot will give you

入住酒店须知

在西方国家，住酒店一般花费甚高，而在中国，住酒店其实所费不多。这个区别是我们在华居住了一段时间才弄明白的。因为我们以前在周末或假期外出旅游的时候，一般都是住在汽车旅馆里，而这种旅馆跟中国的酒店差异迥然。这个也是我们后来慢慢琢磨出来的。

如果你打算通过旅行社到中国度假，行程大抵已经安排妥当，不大可能自由行动。如果你自助游，就得自己选择酒店。要是你完全不懂中文，或许可以选择四星以上的酒店，因为这类酒店都有懂英语的员工。

如果你爱冒险，又想尝试一些便宜的小酒店，尽管去住，只是得做好心里准备：语言会是一大问题。还有一些背包客爱住的小旅馆，价格自然更便宜了，里面很可能还有其他讲英语的住客。这些旅馆里，住着许多来自世界各地的年轻人。

在香港，这样的旅馆常藏身于高楼大厦之后，弯来拐去，非常难找。可以试试港岛铜锣湾的阿里山宾馆，网址是 alisangh@hkstar.com。这家宾馆还能替你办理中国签证，写封邮件一问便知。

到北京旅游，可以住在胡同里，体验老北京人的生活。去内蒙古，就得找五星级酒店落脚。可以在呼和浩特小住几日，看看大草原，到沙漠骑骑骆驼。

如果你是来华教书的老师，会有很多旅游的机会。中国的每个城市，无论大小，

the opportunity to get out to the grasslands and ride a camel in a desert.

If you are living in China as a teacher you will have many opportunities to travel. China has hotels everywhere in every town and city. The choice is mind boggling. If you want to splash out, go for four or five star hotels. It is also possible to find no star hotels, and these are often well equipped and clean. Don't be scared of the little ones, they can be cheap and just as good as the more expensive ones. Ask to see the rooms first, and if possible take a Chinese speaker with you on your first few forays out and about. You will probably visit your nearest large city often, so once you have found a good hotel stick with it, they will get to know you.

As a foreigner you must have your passport when you travel outside your home city. The hotel will take a photocopy of it. No passport, no room. You will also have to pay a deposit in advance in case you damage anything. You get this deposit back when you leave. They will give you a receipt that you must produce as you leave, so take good care of this receipt. Occasionally you may find a hotel will flatly refuse to have you stay there. This may be due to their star rating, and foreigners sometimes can't stay in the poorer quality places.

Book your hotel online before you go. If you can, get a Chinese person to help you, there are Chinese websites with a much greater selection of cheaper places to stay.

Most hotels provide breakfast, but many of the cheaper ones only have a Chinese breakfast, so ask about this when you check in. There will probably be a KFC or MacDonald's close by.

The higher the rating the more likely it is they will have English speaking staff. If you get stuck anywhere at all, look for a five star hotel. They will help in any way they can.

These cheaper chain hotels are all fine to stay at.

Home Inns. Almost always bright yellow buildings.

http://english.homeinns.com/phoenix.zhtml?c=203641&p=irol-homeProfile

Jinjiang Hotels.

http://www.jinjianghotels.com/portal/en/ji_ji_ho_ca.asp?fid=206

Hanting Hotels.

http://www.sinohotelguide.com/beijing/hanting.php

皆有酒店。选择酒店的确相当麻烦。要想图省事，就得选择四星级或五星级的大酒店入住。也可以住在没有星的旅馆里，这些旅馆大都设施齐全，干净整洁。不要畏惧小旅馆，其实它们价格实惠，条件不亚于那些费用更高的酒店。先查看一下旅馆房间的设施。最初几次外出旅游，可以的话，邀请一个中国人作陪。也许，你会经常到自己居住的周边城市走动，只要找到一家满意的酒店就别更换，这样一来，多住几次，酒店的员工就都能认识你了。

离开居住地外出游玩，作为外国人，你一定要带上护照。酒店会影印一份存档。没有护照，开不了房间。另需交一定数额的押金，以防你损坏东西。退房时押金会如数退还。他们会给你一张收据，退房时需提交，因此要好好保管。偶尔，你会遭到某些酒店的拒绝，可能是因为该酒店的星级不够，不能接待外宾。

离开之前在网上订好酒店。可能的话，请一个中国人帮忙，用中文网址搜索，可选酒店更多，价格也更实惠。

多数酒店提供早餐，但是许多便宜的旅馆只供应中餐，因此预定住处之时，一定要询问清楚。酒店附近大都有肯德基和麦当劳。

下面几家连锁酒店舒适而价廉。

如家酒店。几乎每个地方的如家酒店外观都是明黄色的。

English.homeinns.com/phoenix.zhtml?c=203641&p=irol-homeProfile

锦江之星

http://www.jinjianghotels.com/portal/en/ji_ji_ho_ca.asp?fid=206

汉庭酒店

http://www.sinohotelguide.com/beijing/hanting.php

外国人常入住这些酒店，没有问题。

如果你想图省心，就选择比较高档的地方下榻，譬如瑞颐国际大酒店。这家酒店是五星级，价格不菲，但床铺舒适，不硬不软，西餐美味，早餐丰盛，酒店位置极好，员工个个都能说一口漂亮的英语。下面是俯瞰厦门港的厦门瑞颐大酒店的网

Foreigners use these hotels and have no problems at all..

If you do decide to splash out and stay at something rather posh, consider the Swiss International Hotels. Five star, and a bit more expensive, but with comfortable beds that are not too hard, they have excellent western food, a huge breakfast selection, good locations and the staff all speak very good English. This is the link for the Xiamen hotel that overlooks the harbor.

http://www.swissinternationalxiamen.com.cn/en

One of the main problems I found when booking hotels is that when you Google a hotel, you get heaps of different sites that will do the booking for you, such as Agoda, Ctrip etc. I found comparing them to be time consuming, but sometimes I got good deals this way. There are several sorts of travel "clubs" like Ctrip that are pretty good to deal with.

站链接：

http://www.swissinternationalxiamen.com.cn/en

我在预订酒店时经常遇到一个问题，就是在用谷歌搜索酒店的时候，一下子会跳出许多网站，比如雅高达网和携程网，能够帮你预订客房。虽然对比这些网站非常耗时，但有时通过它们能够拿到价格相当优惠的房间。有好几家旅行"俱乐部"，像携程，都值得一试。

HEALTH CARE, DOCTORS AND HOSPITALS

If you are going to go to China to teach, you should have a thorough medical check-up and see if any vaccinations are recommended. Once you are at your school, you will have a full medical check-up as part of your visa requirements. No matter what tests you've had in your home country, you will have to do this check-up in China. They screen everyone for things such as AIDS, STD's and serious illnesses. It takes about an hour and the school should pay for this.

Your school can arrange a health and life insurance policy for you. It will cover some health matters and not others. If the school insists on taking it out for you do so. But take your own comprehensive health insurance and sort it all out at home before you leave. Get it for as long as you know you will be there, and ask if it is possible to extend the policy online if you stay longer.

If you have pre-existing conditions, make sure you are covered for those too. Health care in China can be cheap. One teacher had five days in hospital and it cost about $450.00 AU. But if you get really sick it can be very expensive, and you may opt to return home for serious matters.

When you arrive in your city, find your nearest good hospital. Hospitals, like schools are numbered. So a number one hospital is considered the best, number two second best etc. You will find some doctors speak English, as many of them travel overseas for training. You will also find in your neighbourhood small local hospitals or doctors rooms. You can use them often for blood pressure check-ups or other small matters and

HEALTH CARE, DOCTORS AND HOSPITALS

中国的医保、医生和医院

如果你即将成行，到中国教书，应该在国内做一次全面体检，看看还有什么疫苗应该注射。一到学校，就得按照签证要求去体验。不管你在国内做了什么检查，到了中国都得重新体检。他们会对每个外籍教师做艾滋病、性病及重大疾病排查。体检大概要花去一个小时的时间，费用由校方承担。

学校会替你投保健康险和人寿险，能够提供某些与健康有关的保障，但其他项目概不在内。若学校坚持不替你购买该保险，随他们的便。但是出国前，须带上自己的各项保险，把每种保险分门别类整理清楚。保险期须包括你居华的所有日子，并打听清楚，如果推迟回国，保单是否可以在线展期。

过往病史也一定要包含在保险中。中国的医保费用较低。有一个老师住院治疗了五天，花费了大约450澳元。但如果得了大病，医疗费用就会很高，因此遇上大麻烦，宁可回国就医。

到达工作的城市之后，应马上找到一家离你最近的好医院。医院和学校一样，用数字命名。因此，第一医院就是最好的医院，第二医院略次一等，以此类推。你会发现，有些医生会说英语，因为许多医生都曾在国外学习或进修过。在住家附近，或许你也能看见一些小医院或小诊所。可以上那里检查血压，或者看些小毛病，他们一般不会向你收费。他们会知道你就住在附近，而你也会发现他们能帮你不少忙。

they often won't charge you. They will get to know you are around and find them very useful. Language doesn't matter, miming having your blood pressure taken works every time.

You will also find some large chemists or drug stores in your area. You can buy medications over the counter in China that are prescription only in the West. They sell night and day flu preparations and Imodium for diarrhoea and vomiting. Take a few with you, and buy more there, they are cheap to buy.

When you have found a medication you want to buy again, keep the packet to show the shop attendant. I've resembled a performing monkey, using sign language in a crowded drug store trying to tell them I wanted pills for diarrhoea.

Sometimes foreigners have stomach problems at first. The food is quite different, so keep a few Imodium tablets with you all the time. If your stomach is seriously in trouble you can buy a type of antibiotic that will kill the bugs. Always research these products before you take them, to make sure are okay for you.

The main problem with bugs and insects are mosquitos. There seems to be plenty of the little blighters in many cities. Take some insect repellent with you.

If you are over sixty years old, then insurance is a different matter. Investigate this carefully with your school.

Many Western medications are freely available, but if you are on prescribed medications for any reason, take enough with you to last you several months. Try and get your doctors email address so you can ask him or her questions if necessary and if you want to take medication bought in China to replace your prescriptions pass it by your GP first. Because the Chinese people are petite their medications are made in smaller doses. Check this on the packet.

If you live on campus there are often doctors and nurses available all day at the school or university. If you get sick at other times, your liaison teacher will help you. If necessary, doctors may come and visit you at your apartment.

Doctors and Hospitals

Your first impressions when visiting a doctor at a hospital may leave you breathless. However, this, like the transport system, is pretty much a well-oiled machine that cares

语言不通没有关系，我每次都是打手势告诉他们，我想量血压，次次成功。

在住处附近，你也能看见几家大药房或小药店。你可以在那里上买到我们西方国家的处方药。药店有卖白天、晚上均能用的感冒药和治疗腹泻与呕吐的易蒙停。出国时带一些药物在身边，用完后可在中国购买，药价不贵。

如果找到下次还想购买的药品，留住药盒，到时拿给卖药的店员看，他就明白。我曾经像只杂耍团的猴子，当着一大群顾客的面，用手比划着告诉柜台店员，我要买止泻药。

初到中国，有时候外国人会肚子不舒服，这是因为饮食不同的缘故，所以要随身携带几片止泻药。要是腹泻严重，就要买抗生素消炎。服用这类药物之前，须仔细研究药物性质，确保对症下药。

在中国，虫子骚扰主要来自蚊子。好像许多地方都有蚊子，这些小东西成群结队，相当可恶。因此出国前要带上驱蚊药。

如果你已经年过60，保险的内容会有所不同，这一点要向学校打听清楚。

许多西药可在药店随意购买，但如果你因某个毛病正在服用处方药，就要带足能够维持几个月的药量。向自己的医生要邮箱地址，必要的话好向他咨询。如果想用在中国买的药替换医生开的药方，需先征得自己的医生同意。因为中国人身量较小，因此服用的药物剂量更少，所以务必仔细查阅说明书。

若住校内，学校一般24小时都有医生值班。若在其他时候生病，联络老师帮忙。必要的话，医生会上门给你看病。

医生和医院

初次走进中国的医院，眼前的景象肯定令你诧异万分。虽然里面人来人往，宛如一个交通枢纽般热闹，其实这里的医院是台上好油的机器，运转良好，每日照料着数百万人的身体。

中国的医疗体系和中国人对待生病的态度，都与西方人截然不同。医院中的治疗

for the health of millions of people daily.

The entire medical system and the cultural mindset of Chinese when they are sick is completely different from the West. There are few if any medical centres or doctors rooms as you know them. If you have a cold, you go to the hospital. Doctors often prescribe medication that is administered through a drip, so you will see people of all ages, including young children, sitting or wandering around the hospital with a drip inserted. This is normal for Chinese. The doctors generally know it is not the Western way and will prescribe normal Western medication.

Hospitals seem to come in two sizes, big and small. There are many small clinics spread all through the towns and cities with one or two nurses and doctors on duty. You just walk in and if necessary wait. You will be seen as soon as the doctor is free and possibly will be seen in an open area, so if you are suffering from something personal like haemorrhoids, this is probably not the place to go. This is a good place though to get your blood pressure checked, and if you have a really bad cold or flu they may be able to help. In many cases they will prescribe Western medicine or traditional Chinese medicine, herbs etc. There is little English spoken in these small clinics.

The large hospitals will rival any large hospital in the West for size and frantic activity. At first you will need an interpreter with you, and depending on the city, after a while you may get to know your way around quite well.

When you first go into the hospital you will see large, noisy waiting rooms, lots of people and somewhere a desk where you go and register. You have to fill in forms and pay some money, usually 100RMB. This is a type of deposit. You will also be given a small record book and maybe a type of ID card with your own number on it for future visits. Once you have been receipted for your money you will be sent to whichever department you need, radiology, blood testing, ear/nose/throat specialist, etc. Often you will be sent to a general practitioner first. All these doctors will probably have their own small consultation rooms off a long corridor on one of the upper floors.

Most of these doctors speak no or little English, so you need a translator. The fact that there is already someone in the consultation room being attended to is no reason to wait. Your translator will probably barge in and start talking to the doctor, explaining your problem. It is possible the existing patient will have friends or family too, so the

HEALTH CARE, DOCTORS AND HOSPITALS
中国的医保、医生和医院

区或医生诊室屈指可数。要是你感冒了，到医院看病，医生常常叫你挂瓶，你会看见不同年龄的病人，包括小孩在内，挂着吊瓶，有的坐在椅子上，有的在医院走动。打吊瓶在中国是常事。医生通常都知道，西方人不爱挂瓶，因此会给你开普通的西药。

医院好像分为大小两类。每个城市都有许多小门诊，只有一两个护士和值班医生。只要走进门诊等候即可。只要医生手头没病人，就会立刻给你看病，通常看病的地方都无遮无挡，要是你得了痔疮这类病，最好就别上小门诊治了。但检查血压到这样的地方就对了，或者是得了重感冒或流感什么的，小门诊兴许也很管用。他们经常开的是西药或中草药。小诊所里很少有人会说英语。

中国大医院的规模和紧张程度跟西方国家的相比，毫不逊色。首次上大医院看病需带上翻译随行，看你落脚于哪个城市，一般生活了一段时候之后，大概都能摸清医院的情况。

第一次走进医院，首先看到的是喧闹的大候诊厅，里面熙来人往，厅里摆了一张桌子，你就到那里挂号。先填表格、再交预付款，通常100元就行，当作押金。你会拿到一份病例，或许还有一张 ID 卡，上面有你的卡号，方便下次看病。拿到押金收据后，就到各个有关科室看病，比如拍片、血检、耳鼻喉科等等。一般他们会叫你先去看医生。医院大楼二楼以上沿着长走廊两侧，有许多小诊室，所有医生都有自己的小诊室。

多数医生不懂或只懂几句英语，因此看病时需要翻译陪同。即使诊室里已有其他病人正在看病，也无需等待，翻译经常会径直走到里面，跟医生解释你的病况。那个病人或许也有家人或朋友陪同，因此诊室里会相当拥挤。医生问你情况的时候，允许其他人在一边倾听、旁观，这些人要等看完病后才会走。除非你清楚地告诉翻译，做检查的时候无需陪伴，否则翻译也会守在里面。

像其他从业人员一样，医生也可以一心二用。一边听翻译解释你的病情，一边给手头的病人看病。等病人离开座位，医生才会把注意力集中到你身上，但病人和家属不会马上离开诊室，他们会等在一边，听医生说你生了什么病。医生给你看病的时

room can get quite crowded, and it is quite permissible for all and sundry to watch as you get assessed, listen to what the doctor has to say about you, and move out when they are ready. Your translator will also be there unless you expressly ask him or her to leave while you are examined.

Like many Chinese people in the workforce, doctors multitask, listening to your translator while dealing with the existing patient. You will get your own personal attention once the existing patient has left, although they may not leave the room until they have watched what happens with you. Then, while you are being attended to, others will probably wander in and ask questions of the doctor or stand by the doctor's desk waiting for their turn.

The doctor will make his diagnosis and write in the record book you were given when registering. He will also give you a slip of paper with an amount of money on it. When you have finished you go to the dispensary to get the medication, then back to the registration desk where they deduct the costs involved from your 100RMB. Normally, the balance would be left on the card for your next visit, but sometimes you are refunded the balance.

You keep your own record book and take it every time you go back to that hospital. There is no guarantee you will see the same doctor, it seems to be pot luck as to who you see.

There are many Western medications available, and you can ask for these. The costs of visiting a hospital doctor and getting medication is ridiculously cheap compared with the West. If you have some sort of health insurance you can probably claim it back. Even buying over the counter medication is very cheap in comparison.

Your medication will probably come in a tiny plastic bag, enough for what you need. So if you need four pills, you will get four pills. This obviously cuts down on the wastage we have in the West.

One of the best phrases to learn when you arrive in China is, "can you speak English?" Here it is in Pinyin:

Ni hui shuo yingwen ma?

Phonetically it is, "knee whey shwore ingwen ma?"

Literally translated it means "you know how to speak English" and the "ma" is the

HEALTH CARE, DOCTORS AND HOSPITALS
中国的医保、医生和医院

候,其他病人也会走进来咨询,或站在医生的桌边等候。

医生会在你的病例上写下诊断,同时交给你一张治疗费账单。看完病后,需到药房取药,再回到挂号处结算,从一百元中扣除医药费。通常余款留在卡内,下次可用,但有时医院会结清余款。

病例自己保管,每次上这家医院的时候都要记得带上病例。无法保证给你复诊的是同一位医生,遇到哪位医生似乎全凭运气。

医院有许多西药,可以请医生开给你。与西方国家相比,这里的医药费会便宜许多。如果你投保了健康险,费用大都可以报销。甚至去药店买药,费用都比西方国家的便宜。

到中国后,最应该学的一句中文就是:"你会说英文吗?"用拼音写就是下面这句:

Ni hui shuo ying wen ma?

英语读音就是: knee whey shwore ingwen ma?

按字面翻译就是,"你知道怎么说英文",那个"吗"放在问话的最后,表示疑问。

外加一句"ting bu dong",念成"ting boo dong",意思是"我听见但我不明白。这两句话就是外国人成天挂在嘴边的话。

如果医生和护士都不会说英文,他们会想方设法找个懂英文的人来帮你。在大医院里,许多医生都在国外留学或工作过,英语说得都挺好的。

医院也都有急诊中心,但是如果得了重病,还是叫救护车好。或许救护车的条件不如国内,但救护车就是救护车,在去往医院的途中就可施救。

大医院进行了许多医学研究,外科医生的技术大都与国内的不相上下。

上医院的时候联络老师会陪你前往。有时会预约好看病时间,但这种情况不常发生。有些老师发现,身为外国人,尤其在小城市,可享受特殊待遇。有时遇上懂英语的医生,医生会把自己的名片留给你,告诉你有事儿可以随时找他。

spoken question mark, which is said at the end of every question you ask anyone.

Add that to "ting bu dong", spoken phonetically as ting boo dong, meaning, "I hear you but don't understand you", and you have the two sentences foreigners use all the time.

If the nurse or doctor can't speak English, they will often go out of their way to get you to someone who can. In the larger hospitals, many of the doctors travel overseas for study and experience, so they will have good English.

Some of the larger hospitals have a department for foreigners. It is more expensive but you get better facilities and usually don't have to wait long at all. Most of the staff will have some English abilities, and some will be very good.

Hospitals do have emergency centres too, but if you have suffered something serious, call an ambulance. They are not always as well equipped as you might be used to, but they are there and will get you immediate attention on arrival at the hospital.

A great deal of medical research is carried out in the large hospitals and the skill of the surgeons is probably equal to what you would have at home.

Your liaison teacher will go with you to the hospital. Sometimes appointments are made, but not often. Some teachers have found that being a foreigner, especially in a smaller city, they got preferential treatment. At times, when they have made contact with an English speaking doctor, they were given the doctor's business card with the offer to contact them any time.

If you are admitted into a ward, most of the staff will not speak English. Some wards are very big and others can be one or two beds with an en-suite, air conditioning and television. If you are admitted you must pay a deposit, maybe 1,000RMB or more and you have to pay for everything. An itemised account will be given to you and you may have to pay more once your 1,000RMB is used up. You will pay for every pill, injection, doctor's visit and a daily cost for your room. Again, in comparison with Western costs the amount you will pay is minimal. One teacher spent five days in hospital, did not have surgery, but needed extensive antibiotic treatment, pills and drips, and it cost about $450.00AU in total.

One other thing you need to know. Generally there are no meals provided for the patients. Family or friends must bring in meals for you. There are often restaurant type

如果住院了，住院部的医护人员大都不会说英语。有些病房很大，有些很小，只有一两张病床，浴室一个，空调和电视各一台。

住院要交 1000 元以上的押金，各项费用自理。医院会提供医药费清单给你，费用也许高于 1000 元的押金。费用包括药费、注射费、医生查房费以及病床费。与西方国家相比，住院费依旧不足挂齿。比如，有个老师住了五天院，没有动手术，但一直在做消炎治疗，既服药又挂瓶，总共费用也就差不多 450 澳元。

另一件应该注意的事情是，中国的医院大多不负责病人的一日三餐。得靠家人、朋友送餐给你。医院大门附近有许多类似餐馆的小店，如果你能走路，可上那些地方吃饭，不然就得请人送饭。他们还得替你送衣服和洗衣服。

最后，说点儿轻松的话题。住院时一定要带上睡衣，或者叫人送睡衣给你。前面提到的那个老师需要照 X 光，医生立刻安排他去拍片，护士过来帮他起床。护士脱去他的衣服，放到一处，他以为自己是坐轮椅到附近的拍片室。结果呢，他就穿条难看的内裤，走出病房，坐拥挤的电梯下楼，穿过几条人来人往的走廊，经过大楼外的一个院子，来到另一座大楼，乘坐另一拥挤的电梯上楼，再走过一条人来人往的走廊，到拍片室拍片。他感到无比尴尬。他觉得自己一个白人老外，走在一群小个子中国人中间，特别醒目。最糟糕的是什么？是他明白，待会儿还得走回自己的病房，再丢人现眼一回。

凡事均需未雨绸缪！如果可能，提早准备，方为上策。

places around the hospital gates and if you can walk you may be able to go and get food yourself, otherwise people must bring it to you. They will also need to take your washing and do that for you.

To finish on a lighter note, make sure you take, or someone brings you, a nightgown or dressing gown. The teacher mentioned above needed an x-ray. The doctor arranged it immediately and the nurse came and got him out of bed. His clothes had been taken away and stored. He expected he was going to be wheeled to an x-ray room nearby. In only his rather grotty underpants he walked out of his room, went down several floors in a crowded lift, walked through several busy corridors out into an open quadrangle, walked over the quadrangle into another building, up a few floors in another crowded lift, along a busy corridor and into the x-ray area. He was embarrassed beyond belief. He felt terribly conspicuous, especially as he was a larger white man walking amongst many smaller Chinese. And the worst part? He knew he had to do it all over again to get back to his room.

Think ahead! Be prepared if possible.

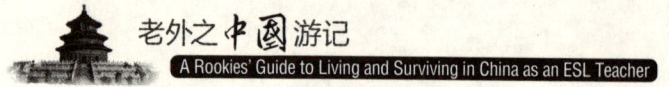

ABOUT THE AUTHOR

Lana Kerr (Ke Lan —— 柯兰) grew up in a small country town in New Zealand, and was educated at Te Awamutu College. After marrying Peter and raising five children, the author and her husband moved to Australia. They later moved to China for some years, working as ESL Teachers. Lana taught at several universities including Xiamen University, several private and public schools, and a Hotel Management School affiliated to a Sydney University. Belatedly realising teaching was in her blood, this became a life changing experience for her.

Apart from living in New Zealand and Australia, her time living in China has given her a great deal of experience dealing with Chinese people and learning how to manage in a country where she couldn't speak the language and most people couldn't speak English.

Lana has a TESOL International Teaching Licence, Certificate in Editing and Proof Reading, Bachelor of Arts in English Literature and Writing through Griffith University, Queensland, and Master of Arts in Writing through Swinburne University, Melbourne.

Lana lives on the Gold Coast, Australia

作者小传

柯兰（Lana Kerr）自幼生长于新西兰一小镇，后在蒂阿瓦穆图大学（Te Awamutu College）读书。与彼得结婚后育有五子。儿女长大成人后，作者与丈夫迁居澳大利亚，后至中国任教数年。曾任教于中国的多所学校，包括厦门大学、苏州的悉尼大学附属酒店管理学院和其他几所公办或民办大学。柯兰发现，教书乃其生来所爱之事，因此中国之行为她的人生带来重大改变。

除却新西兰和澳大利亚，柯兰在华生活的经历，令她学会了如何在一个语言不通的陌生国度生活，获得众多与中国人交往的经验。

柯兰是个素质优秀的教师，拥有 TESOL 资格证书和编辑校对证书，获得昆士兰格里菲斯大学英语文学和创作文学学士学位（Griffith University）和墨尔本斯威本大学创作文学硕士学位（Swinburne University）。

作者现居住于澳大利亚昆士兰州的黄金海岸市（Gold Coast）。

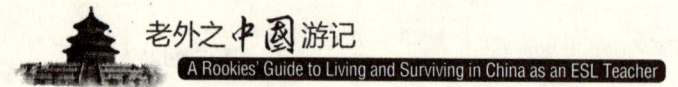

APPENDIX: TRAINING AND CONTRACTS

The TESOL training was good fun. TESOL stands for "Teachers of English to Speakers of Other Languages", in other words teaching people whose second language is English. Classes were from 6pm to 10pm on a Wednesday, Thursday and Friday evening, and all day Saturday and Sunday. The tutor did a fabulous job. We were in a smallish class of about fifteen.

We received our teaching manuals a couple of weeks before the training started, and apart from some of the deep theoretical stuff I managed to read all six hundred pages before we started our training. Peter and I passed our assessments, were presented with our Certificates, official photos were taken, and we went home well satisfied with ourselves.

The next few months were taken up with studying extra modules on-line. By the time we applied for work we held our International TESOL Teaching Licenses plus other certificates including Teaching Business English, Teaching Tourism English, Teaching Adults and Teaching Children. With these credentials also came extensive manuals that proved to be invaluable resources in the classroom.

Peter was quite nervous about the prospect of teaching. During his career he'd been involved in training and teaching, but not in a classroom setting, so was unsure about how he would cope. I was full of confidence and I was certain Peter would have no problems either. He had great teaching skills and excellent interpersonal skills.

The next hurdle was to find and secure a job. I searched the internet and found Daveseslcafe.com, a terrific site with thousands of jobs advertised from all over Asia. There was a special job board for China and I soon started emailing some schools for information. There were TESOL jobs available in many parts of the world including Europe, but China was the place that appealed to us.

附录：培训与签约

TESOL 培训相当有趣。TESOL 是指对外英语教师，也就是学习对象是把英语当成第二语言的群体。课程安排是：每周三、四、五晚上 6 点到 10 点；周六、周日全天。老师课上得非常棒。班级为 15 人左右的小班。

培训前几周，我们就收到了《教学手册》，除了一些理论性太强的东西，厚厚 600 页的资料都被我在开课前读完了。彼得和我成功通过了考核，提交完各种证书，留下证件照，春风得意地回家了。

接下来的几个月时间我们又上了一些网络课程。等我们着手申请工作的时候，我们已经拿到 TESOL 教师资格证，外加其他几种证书，包括商务英语教师资格证、旅游英语教师资格证，以及成人英语和儿童英语教师资格证。跟证书一同抵达我们手上的，还有五花八门的指南，这些材料对我后来的教学大有裨益。

彼得一想到自己将为人师便忐忑不安。他虽然做过培训，也上过课，但没有在正儿八经的教室里教学的经验，所以心中非常没底。我倒是充满自信，也确信彼得没问题，因为他懂得很多教学技巧，也深谙与人交往的门道。

第二个障碍就是找工作。我上网查到 Daveeseslcafe.com 这个网址，这个网址超赞，里面有亚洲各国好几千个岗位的招聘信息，还有中国专版。我迅速给几所大学写邮件要资料。世界上有许多地方都需要 TESOL 教师，包括欧洲在内，但我一心向往的地方是中国。

不久我便意识到，必须想办法简化应聘流程。我老是把地方和学校名称搞混，因为我知道的中国城市屈指可数，所以单单比较各校信息就够我折腾的了。我写了一封求职信样本，里面清楚地列出我们所取得的各个证书，并请对方寄份合同供我们

I soon realized that I would have to streamline the entire process. It was so easy to get the places and schools confused, especially as I didn't know where many of the cities were, so comparing all this information got rather complicated. I composed a basic covering letter outlining our credentials and asking for a copy of their contract. The schools would reply, asking us to go there.

By comparing the contracts we could then see what was available at each school or university. There was a standard contract for many schools outlining the hours to be worked, the accommodation provided and a few clauses about obeying the laws of the land etc. I soon learned how to weed out the contracts that didn't suit us.

We decided to try for work in a university. Although we had our new qualifications, we did not have university degrees. The classes in the junior schools often had sixty or more students, and this didn't appeal to us. I received a contract from Paul at Longyan University. His first email appealed to us. "We will talk and negotiate until we come to an agreement that suits us both," he said. This sounded reasonable. Paul emailed and spoke to us by phone several times explaining what the work entailed.

Because everything was so new we were rather flying in the dark, so took our time choosing which university to accept. We made a list of basic requirements, including the weather, size of the city, proximity to larger cities, and the language levels of the students we would teach.

In China, a "small" city is from about half a million people to several million. Coming from Australia our biggest city was four million. We were conscious of the fact that we spoke no Chinese and might get lost, an experience that could be somewhat frightening, so a small place was our first choice.

The weather was also an important factor. Cities in the north, including Beijing, were very hot in summer, but fell to 20° or 30° below freezing in winter, whereas cities in the south were warmer in winter but very hot in summer. Longyan seemed to fit our criteria. Paul said our TESOL qualifications were sufficient, and they would be delighted to accept us. For them, having a married couple was an advantage. Not only would they get two teachers, but it meant that the husband and wife would act as mutual support, easing homesickness and culture shock. It also meant good role models for the students, and as our year progressed we became surrogate parents or grandparents to many of the

参考。学校会回信邀请我们前往任教。

对比不同学校的合同有一大好处，就是能够清楚了解每所学校或大学开出的条件。许多学校使用的都是合同范本，标明工作时长、提供的住所以及几条应聘人应该遵守当地法律法规的条款。很快我就找到了窍门，知道如何筛选出不符合我们要求的合同。

我们决定到大学教书。虽然如今我们增添了新的资历，但我们没有大学学历。中学的班级通常有60多个学生，这么多学生让我们望而却步。我收到龙岩学院的保罗寄来的合同。保罗的第一封邮件便正中下怀，他写道："有问题我们可以商量，直到结果令双方满意为止。"这话说得很在理。保罗给我们写过几封邮件，还打过几通电话解释工作要求。

因为这是我们头一遭到外国求职，的确只能摸着石头过河了。我们慢慢挑选着学校，列出基本要求，譬如天气、城市规模、是否紧挨大城市及学生的英语水平等等。

在中国，人口在五十万至几百万的城市都算是"小"城市，而澳大利亚最大的城市人口也只有400万。我们很清楚，我们不会说汉语，容易迷路——每每想到这一点，心里就不寒而栗，于是小城市成了我们的不二之选。

天气也是一个重要因素。北方城市，包括北京在内，冬冷夏热，有时温度低至零下二三十度；南方城市虽然冬天气温略高，但夏天却热浪滚滚。似乎龙岩这个城市符合我们的要求。保罗说，我们持有TESOL证书就够任教资格了，他们学校很高兴聘用我们。在校方看来，我们夫妻同行有一大好处。他们既可以一举聘用两个教师，而且夫妻两人可以在日后的教学上相互帮助，还可以缓解思乡之苦，减轻文化碰撞的影响；同时还能给学生树立一个好榜样。果然，我们后来成了许多学生心中的父母或祖父母。

保罗寄来的龙岩学院的图片相当漂亮，学校很新、很大，但是工作生活都在一幢设计精美的大楼内，大楼呈一个巨大的半圆形。我们最终与这所学院签了约。之

students.

The picture of Longyan University Paul sent us was very appealing. It was a new university, large, but all in one well designed building, shaped like a huge semicircle. We finally agreed to go there. We booked our flights, took out travel insurance, got Mum organized, packed up the house, survived Mum's tantrums and aftermath thereof, and were ready to start an exciting new chapter in our lives.

APPENDIX: TRAINING AND CONTRACTS
附录：培训与签约

后就开始忙着订机票，投保旅行险，安顿母亲，整理房子，听母亲怨忿的唠叨并处理她老人家因生气而带来的种种后果，总算万事已妥，可以开始书写我们人生中最激动人心的新篇章了。

图书在版编目(CIP)数据

老外之中国游记:汉英对照/(澳)柯兰著;邱益鸿译. —厦门:厦门大学出版社,2014.3
ISBN 978-7-5615-4914-8

Ⅰ.①老…　Ⅱ.①柯…②邱…　Ⅲ.①英语-汉语-对照读物②游记-中国
Ⅳ.①H319.4:K

中国版本图书馆 CIP 数据核字(2014)第 037952 号

厦门大学出版社出版发行

(地址:厦门市软件园二期望海路 39 号　邮编:361008)
http://www.xmupress.com
xmup@xmupress.com

厦门集大印刷厂印刷

2014 年 3 月第 1 版　2014 年 3 月第 1 次印刷
开本:787×1092　1/16　印张:20.25　插页:2
字数:336 千字　印数:1～3 000 册
定价:39.00 元

本书如有印装质量问题请直接寄承印厂调换